The Politics of Urban Potentiality

The Politics of Urban Potentiality

Spatial Patterns of Emancipatory Commoning

Stavros Stavrides

BLOOMSBURY ACADEMIC
LONDON • NEW YORK • OXFORD • NEW DELHI • SYDNEY

BLOOMSBURY ACADEMIC
Bloomsbury Publishing Plc
50 Bedford Square, London, WC1B 3DP, UK
1385 Broadway, New York, NY 10018, USA
29 Earlsfort Terrace, Dublin 2, Ireland

BLOOMSBURY, BLOOMSBURY ACADEMIC and the Diana logo are trademarks of Bloomsbury Publishing Plc

First published in Great Britain 2024

Copyright © Stavros Stavrides, 2024

Stavros Stavrides has asserted his right under the Copyright, Designs and Patents Act, 1988, to be identified as Author of this work.

For legal purposes the Acknowledgments on pp. x–xii constitute an extension of this copyright page.

Cover design by Adriana Brioso

All rights reserved. No part of this publication may be reproduced or transmitted in any form or by any means, electronic or mechanical, including photocopying, recording, or any information storage or retrieval system, without prior permission in writing from the publishers.

Bloomsbury Publishing Plc does not have any control over, or responsibility for, any third-party websites referred to or in this book. All internet addresses given in this book were correct at the time of going to press. The author and publisher regret any inconvenience caused if addresses have changed or sites have ceased to exist, but can accept no responsibility for any such changes.

A catalogue record for this book is available from the British Library.

Library of Congress Cataloging-in-Publication Data

ISBN: HB: 978-1-3504-1395-5
PB: 978-1-3504-1394-8
ePDF: 978-1-3504-1397-9
eBook: 978-1-3504-1396-2

Series: In Common

Typeset by Newgen KnowledgeWorks Pvt. Ltd., Chennai, India
Printed and bound in Great Britain

To find out more about our authors and books visit www.bloomsbury.com and sign up for our newsletters.

To Evgenia, to Zoe, and to all those who struggle for an emancipatory future

Contents

List of Figures   ix

Acknowledgments   x

1. **In Search of Emancipatory Potentialities**   1
   - Potentiality as Performance   1
   - G. Agamben and the "Potential-Not-To"   6
   - A. Badiou: The Event as Surprise   9
   - H. Lefebvre: Mimesis and Rhythmicality   12
   - Patterns of Repeating   15

2. **Metropolitan Urbanity and the Project of Urban Order**   21
   - Urban Domestication   22
   - Urban Normalization   27

3. **Spatial Practices of Repeatability**   33
   - Habits in Place   35
     - The Potentialities of Habits   35
     - Habits as Place-Making Practices   42
   - Rituals and the "Magic Circle"   44
     - Ritual as Performance   44
     - Rituals in Change   47
   - Tracing Trajectories   56
     - Following and Leaving Traces   56
     - Pervasive Connectivity: Instant Tracing?   59

4. **Challenging Urban Order**   63
   - Collective Inventiveness   63
   - Beyond Ordering Polarities   67

5. **Reinventing Urban Communities**   71
   - Autonomy as Community *Autopoiesis*   71
   - Autonomy as Collective Creativity   74
   - Beyond Tradition and Modernity?   78

	A Politics of Being-in-Common?	83
	Collective Habits Invented	85
	Community Building by Inventing Rituals	94
	Traces that Support the Reinvention of Community	104
6	Cooperation as Commoning	115
	Cooperation Captured, Cooperation Liberated	115
	The Potentialities of Cooperation Habits	119
	Rituals of Cooperation	126
	Cooperation and Tracing	135
7	Contested Imaginaries of Potentiality	147
	Shared Patterns of Imagination	147
	The Imaginary of Affect	152
	Affective Solidarities	154
	The Imaginary of Flexibility	156
	Flexibility as Solidarity	159
8	Conclusion	163
9	Opening: Geometries of the Future	167
References		169
Index		181

Figures

1. *Mística* ritual during the 6th Congresso Nacional do MST, in 2014 at Brasília (DF) — 96
2. *Mística* ritual during the celebration of thirty years of MST in 2014 — 97
3. Poster announcing the Exarchia Carnival celebration: "Against Gentrification and Touristifcation. Let's Keep Exarchia as a Neighborhood." 2022 — 101
4. A collective meal during the days of Ramadan between the ruins of a neighborhood in Diyarbakir. 2017 — 104
5. Refugee camp in Skaramangas, near Athens. 2019 — 108
6. City Plaza occupied hotel: a refugee self-managed shelter. 2017 — 109
7. City Plaza occupied hotel poster — 110
8. F. Traverso placing his stencil bicycle at a wall of the Alexandras Prosfygica social housing complex. 2009 — 112
9. A CECOSESOLA assembly. Barquisimeto, Venezuela. 2023 — 121
10. The CECOSESOLA hospital. Barquisimeto, Venezuela. 2023 — 122
11. Nordeste vernacular Art Deco facades. Penedo, Brazil. 2018 — 125
12. Graffiti in support of People's Guelaguetza. Oaxaca. 2007 — 131
13. A *minga* meeting at the *Estrela Roja* settlement of Popayan, Colombia. 2023 — 134
14. December 2008 uprising in Athens: an invented trace. 2008 — 141
15. Monumento de Resistencia in Cali, Colombia. 2023 — 145

Acknowledgments

This book is the result of many encounters. Encounters with people in struggle, with students in search of knowledges open to different cultures, with scholars questioning the limits of academic research, with activists dreaming of a just society, with men and women who in their everydayness develop latent resistances and admirable thoughts about the future, and with many of those who refuse to fit in the identities imposed on them (be they gender identities, national identities, or cultural identities).

I feel grateful to all those people for giving me the opportunity to learn from their ideas, actions, and aspirations. I may refer to certain of those by name, but my thanks are to all of them. Colleagues in universities and independent scholars, especially from Latin American cities, have on many occasions supported my research and generously shared thoughts and suggestions. Among them, Carlos Vainer and Lucia Capanema Alvarez in Rio de Janeiro, Suly María Quinchía Roldán, Análida Rincón Patiño, and Ivan Ricardo Castro Diaz in Medellin, Manuel Rozental and Vilma Almendra in Popayan, Maria Kavoura and Luis Carlos Valencia Sarría in Cali, Carlos Torres Tovar in Bogota, Humberto Gonzalez Silva, and Óscar Coraspe in Caracas, Raul Zibechi and Pola Ferrari in Montevideo, and Andrés Ruggeri in Buenos Aires.

I am also grateful to the people of CECOSESOLA, who hosted me during my research focused on their marvelous organization; to the people of MTST in São Paulo, who helped me become acquainted with their struggle and visit their encampments; to the people of SESC, also in São Paulo, who revealed to me a world of rich possibilities; to those activists of urban movements in Athens, with whom I often shared the streets of struggle; to the common activists in Napoli *Beni comuni* network who generously shared with me their stories, questions, and experiences; to the *Primera Linea* militants, who welcomed me at their Monument of Resistances at Cali and who impressed me with their determination and their enduring collective aspirations; to the struggling inhabitants of the *Estrella Roja* settlement of displaced people in Popayan and especially to Andres Maiz, for hosting me in their *Minga* and for proving to me how powerful commoning can be in efforts to build communities of solidarity; and to the Zapatista comrades to whom we owe the certainty that another world is possible: a world of solidarity, equality, and freedom.

In Athens, many friends have contributed with their enthusiasm, their criticism, or with their caring support to the intellectual adventures that have created this book. Among them, my beloved PhD students who have created their own working group called Stubborn Spaces, the members of the Critical Interdisciplinarity Group in which I participate, the people of the Lampidona Squat open cultural initiative, and the art activists and scholars with whom we cofounded the Laboratory for the Urban Commons.

I would also like to extend my thanks to Penny Koutrolikou, Socratis Stratis, Mel Jordan, Andrew Hewitt, Raquel Rolnik, Ioanni Delsante, Gilberto Cuhna Franca, Massimo de Angelis, and Giorgos Tsarbopoulos for the fruitful and collaborative encounters I had with them.

Thanking Evgenia Michalopoulou in public can in no way adequately express my gratitude, my love, and my admiration for her inspiring and supportive presence in the life we share. Zoe Stavridi Michalopoulou proves to me how inspiring can be a form of criticism grounded in love and developed through the creativity of everydayness. Both she and Evgenia make it possible for me to experience invaluable moments of happiness in a world often dominated by hate and aggressive individualism.

Some previously published texts have been partially or totally reworked to be used for this book. More specifically:

In Chapter 1, a reworked version of the text "Repetir o citar" was used (published in Spanish in the web journal *Desinformemonos* at https://desinformemonos.org/repetir-o-citar/).

In Chapter 3, small reworked parts of the text "The Space–Time Relation in Collective Memory" were used (published in Greek in the collection of papers, *Memory and the Experience of Space*, S. Stavrides [ed.], Athens: Alexandreia, 2006).

In Chapter 3, a reworked version of the text "Conectividad" was used (published in Spanish in the web journal *Desinformemonos* at https://desinformemonos.org/conectividad/).

In Chapter 5, a reworked version of the text "La armonía como práctica artisanal" was used (published in Spanish in the web journal *Desinformemonos* at https://desinformemonos.org/la-armonia-como-practica-artesanal/).

Chapter 5 forms a slightly reworked version of the text "Reinventing Community through Commoning" (published in L. Volont, T. Lijster, and P. Gielen [eds.] *The Rise of the Common City*, Brussels: Academic and Scientific Publishers, 2022).

In Chapter 6, a reworked version of the text "Recuperar la ornamentación" was used (published in Spanish in the web journal *Desinformemonos* at https://desinformemonos.org/recuperar-la-ornamentacion/).

In Chapter 6, a reworked part of the text "The December 2008 Uprising's Stencil Images in Athens: Writing or Inventing Traces of the Future?" was used. (In K. Avramidis and M. Tsilimpounidi [eds.], *Graffiti and Street Art. Reading, Writing and Representing the City*. London: Routledge, 2017).

In Chapter 7, a reworked version of the text "Solidaridades afectivas" was used (published in Spanish in the web journal *Desinformemonos* at https://desinformemonos.org/solidaridades-afectivas/).

In Chapter 7, a reworked version of the text "Flexibilidad" was used (published in Spanish in the web journal *Desinformemonos* at https://desinformemonos.org/flexibilidad/).

Chapter 9 is a reworked version of the text "Geometrías del futuro" (published in Spanish in the web journal *Desinformemonos* at https://desinformemonos.org/?s=Geometr%C3%ADas+del+futuro).

1

In Search of Emancipatory Potentialities

Potentiality as Performance

In the days of a corrupt president in a Latin American country, activists used to wash the country's flag every week in the central squares of the country's cities. A collective gesture of protest, an invented ritual based on cooperation?

Refugees forced to live in one of the camps of a European country used to repeatedly decorate their identical house-containers with symbols of a shared feeling of belonging to an uprooted community. In such traces of escape from an imposed reality, do they reinvent their community even when this community is characterized by imaginary as well as actual bonds between its members?

In a city in which they were given the opportunity to express their aspirations for equality, insurgent indigenous women demanded not the right to be equal with men but the establishment of a collective habit: to be, act, and feel as equal.

In all those cases, an important question emerges: Are practices and imaginaries that we usually connect with stability and continuity merely the necessary pillars of regulated social reproduction, and thus markers of conservatism? Do repetitive behaviors and imposed collective representations unavoidably establish and reproduce social taxonomies? Or can we reinvent forms of repeatability that support relations of sharing and solidarity while remaining open to changes that the collectivities that institute them may decide? If the word commoning may describe both the production and the institution of what a community considers as important for its well-being, then could we explore commoning habits, commoning rituals, and commoning tracing acts? Related to diverse traditions of community sharing that under different names indicates a world that explicitly differs from capitalist ethos, commoning may encompass the emancipatory potentialities of egalitarian and cooperative development of the common. But can commoning, a process, a series of practices and shared views, flourish without enacted forms of repeatability? Indeed it can't, provided it will remain open to the differences (including variations, complementarities, and deviations) that constitute the motivating force of sharing. Commoning, thus, will always be a process of establishing and developing common ground between those who orient themselves toward this collective task.

This is an effort to understand contemporary big cities, metropolises, not only by trying to penetrate the layers of spatial and temporal complexity that characterize them but, predominantly, by locating in city life indications of a different urban future. Understanding metropolitan urban order would in such a context mean understanding the emerging dynamics of urban acts and experiences that implicitly or explicitly defy this kind of order, challenge it or provide an escape from it. "Contemporary metropolis" stands for a model of today's big cities that at first glance seems to ignore particularities, or worse, forces singularities to an abstract uniformity. However, metropolis in this context rather stands for a form of social organization that is especially shaped through certain spatial arrangements: Metropolis is considered here not as a type of city but, rather, as a historically definable arrangement of power relations performed in and through an arrangement of spatial relations. Metropolis then may be considered as a concrete paradigm (the term used in the way Thomas Kuhn does) of social organization.

The question can therefore be formulated thus: What forces may possibly challenge this paradigm from within? In other words, is this form of social organization maintained through the metropolis city-form, or are there experiences, acts, practices, imaginaries, and relationships that create problems, to say the least, in the reproduction of this social organization?

This book will explore the ground on which such phenomena grow. Is it that metropolis is an inherently contradictory project, the latter being considered more like a projected utopia than as an established reality? Is it that metropolis, in all its complexity, merely gives the impression of a certain prevailing urban order to only those who want to see it (or profit from it or conveniently describe a clear enemy)? Is it that metropolis is by its nature an always contested terrain, because it has to sustain itself in conditions of social antagonism?

One could, for a start, try to categorize the views: It is mainly those who consider that metropolis inherently develops what opposes or challenges it and those who believe that challenges come from outside—from what is not metropolitan, in terms of space but also in terms of values, habits, or "forms of life."

As the exploration of the metropolis's potentialities for a different urban future will develop in this book, it will become clear that this preliminary distinction between two sets of views does not stand. The question of what is external to metropolis is closely connected to the problematization of potentiality as it is ascertained in concrete urban practices. Some of them, as we will see, base their activation of potentialities on the effort to establish a certain externality. Others seem to claim a deeper essence of metropolitan existence allegedly lost or alienated in the historical spatiality of contemporary metropolis. Given, as I will try to show, that potentialities may only be deduced from practices and from expressed imaginaries that activate them, we may only trace the field of potentialities bearing in mind that the defining attribute "inherent" has only relative value. In other words, potentialities are not one of the characteristics of metropolis but actually shape metropolis itself as a historically dynamic phenomenon, sometimes integrating to metropolis what used to be external to it and sometimes expelling from metropolis elements that used to be part of it during a certain period.

Potentialities do not simply exist, they do not simply belong to the concrete reality of a certain historical period and to a certain social setting. Potentialities are being performed. They come into being, or, rather, they become discernible when and while being performed. This means that they are neither creations of the minds of different actors (or thinkers) nor objectively determinable by distanced researchers. It is important to locate the place from which someone detects potentialities and thus gets involved in performing them (including ways of performing them, as we will see, that may be linked to shared imaginaries). For example, an organized struggle for decent housing may refer to the potentialities for the satisfaction of relevant collective demands but at the same time it may create, by the force of its presence, potentialities that did not "exist" before. In other words, people are motivated and sometimes determined to fight by becoming convinced that what they ask for or fight for is possible to be accomplished, gained. So, potentialities are literally made visible and developed while being diagnosed by those who need them, hope for them, dream of them.

It is not only a problem of rearranging the limits of the sensible, as Jacques Rancière seems to suggest (2010), although a great part of the potentiality performing process has to do with challenging the imposed order of the sensible. Acting or imagining in the context of defining potentialities means becoming able to extend the limits of the possible by actually creating new possibilities. As Arturo Escobar proposes, "another possible is possible" (Escobar 2020)

Rancière seems to be specifically interested in clarifying the results of challenging dominant patterns of sense and perception as they are individually experienced. Performances, however, are, as we will see, sets of practices that can be oriented toward specific goals (individual, or mostly collective), practices that are often repeatable and transferable to different contexts, that can be expressive and productive at the same time, that combine meaning production and symbolization, and that involve differently hierarchized participation of the senses, mental activities, and psychological mechanisms (depending on the social context).

Potentialities are performed and performative. They come into being in the process of being performed and, at the same time, when performed they acquire the power of shaping the present. This is not equal to saying that potentialities may be only substantially documented after their actualization. The gap between a potentiality and its actualization presupposed by such an approach is meant to completely distinguish potentialities from action. Potentialities are considered as preexisting action, whereas in a performative approach potentialities emerge, develop, and take shape through action.

Walter Benjamin used a quasi-theological term to describe the act of reclaiming the potentialities of the past: redemption. Through redemption, unrealized potentialities are given mew momentum in the present of "total actuality." The past is not considered as finished and gone but acquires a new meaning (a new life?) at the moment a certain present understands itself in relation to it: "For every image of the past that is not recognized by the present as one of its own concerns threatens to disappear irretrievably" (1992: 247). In such an approach, the past is pending: the present, especially in a "moment of danger" (in a period in which questions about the future are pressing and full of uncertainty), looks at the past for the means to understand itself. As in a constellation of stars in which the "meaning" of the overall impression is constructed through the relation of stars, and not by adding separate "meanings" describing each star, so in a constellation of moments past and present, both past and present acquire new meaning by being related (Benjamin, 1992).

Redemption, thus, importantly, directs one's attention to the active search of potentialities buried in the past. In such an approach, a total break with the idea of progress and the related approach to history considered as taking place in "homogeneous, empty time" (1992: 252) is emphatically suggested.

Benjamin relates his theory on the redemption of the past through the unearthing buried potentialities with his problematization of tradition. Acts that may be taken to repeat the past (commemorating it or elevating it to the status of a canon for the future) are acts that shape the present and are shaped by it. Actuality and actualization are the most important Benjaminean terms to describe this process. What is at the root of actualization is a montage-like gesture: bringing elements of the past to a surprising proximity with elements of the present (1992). Such a constellation does not use the past to explain the present but, we may say, potentializes the present by potentializing the past. Actualization, then, is an act of interruption, an act of challenging the mythology of time's homogeneity and the belief in time's continuity—an act of extracting fragments of the past in order to compare them in a new, revelatory interpretation.

There is a clear connection of this exemplary act with what Benjamin describes as the "citability of gestures" (Benjamin, 2006: 305). The term was used to single out the defining characteristic of B. Brecht's Epic theater (Benjamin, 1998). "'Making gestures quotable' is one of the signal achievements of the epic theater. An actor must be able to space his gestures the way a typesetter spaces type" (2006: 305).

Gestures on stage must become citable, according to this approach. Citability is a kind of introduced characteristic to repeatable gestures (therefore recognizable gestures) that makes them tremble over the abyss of homogenization. As Samuel Weber suggests in his study on Benjamin, this is "not repetition as the confirmation of an original identity, but rather as its transformation. It is this that endows the gesture with its singular *citability*" (2008: 10). Gestures repeated, therefore understood as copies of previous gestures, and, at the same time, abruptly separated from their usual context, are therefore surprisingly different. Brecht was hoping that such gestures would trigger reflection rather than benign identification.

Citability is transforming gestures to more than phrases of meaning available to be transported to unusual contexts. Citability could be a way of integrating to familiar gestures the potentiality to differ. The potentiality to hint toward difference. Just before they become merely emblematic signs and while they still tremble between the reproducible and the unique, such gestures may be acts of interruption. Acts of sudden stop in the flow of reproducibility, acts that introduce gaps in the appreciation and welcomed proliferation of the "same."

Citability is in this case the substratum of inventive interpretation, and, thus, of the inventive appropriation of the reproducible in gestures. Take a scene depicting a devastated bombed city and print it in soft tones with colors meant to depict a cozy and safe home environment. Paint a tear gas mask on an image of the Virgin (a Virgin of Barricades as it was called during the Oaxaca rebellion, an example we will discuss in a following chapter). Obsessively repeat a gesture of cleaning a chair left out of use in an abandoned airport. These are examples of gestures which are distanced from the sequence they normally take part in (a media war reportage, a religious ceremony, a mundane cleaning effort). In this way gestures are cited: they are both recognizable and strange in their new context. Such gestures of citing escape or may have escaped from a theater stage only to infect the theater of urban everydayness. They thus introduce the potentiality of a dissident interpretation.

The aspiration to support and create uncontaminated uniqueness as a way to fight the predominant culture of the reproducible and the copy is a self-defeating aspiration. Exactly for the same reason that the struggle against dominant mythologies cannot proceed without accepting that myths actually shape reality rather than being external to it (and therefore easy to become separated from it). Let us employ then the power of citability: Could we embark on guerilla-like performances of repetition that possibly explore difference through a creative destabilization of dominant forms of reproducibility? And could these acts contribute to the collective invention of emancipatory habits crafted in ways that encompass change without reducing it to heroic acts of allegedly continuous innovation?

The approach to potentiality introduced so far has the merit of delinking relevant diagnoses from a positivist, essentialist reading of the present as well as from a reading of history that is called upon as the present's interpretation. Actions and performances shape not only "reality" but also possibilities that develop within it and often against reality's dominant interpretations.

G. Agamben and the "Potential-Not-To"

For Giorgio Agamben, a rethinking of the concept of potentiality passes from the effort to construct a theory on human acting. The first step is an acknowledgment of Aristotle's contribution in the shaping of Western philosophy regarding the relation between an act and the conditions that made it possible (1999, 2016). As Agamben suggests, Aristotle distinguishes between a potential to act (*dynamis*) and the action itself (*energeia*—being-at-work). The link between the two is habit (*hexis*), "the form in which potential exists and is given reality as such" (2016: 59).

Agamben attributes to Aristotle a thesis that offers him the opportunity to develop his own theory of human acting: "potential is essentially defined by the possibility of its non-exercise" (2019: 17). In Agamben's interpretation, "Adynamia, 'impotential' does not mean here the absence of any potential, but the potential-not-to (pass to the act) dynamis mé energein" (ibid.).

By using this concept of potential, Agamben develops his own theory of "inoperativity" considered as the core characteristic of human life. In order to establish this view, he completely rejects the division between act and potential. It is not enough to prove, as Aristotle does, against the Megarians in his *Metaphysics* that potential is not consumed in the act that "actualizes" it (Agamben, 1999). One has to close the gap between potential and acting. And this is not made possible by establishing a relation between them (a relation of coexistence in place of a relation of succession) but by fusing them both in the process of "use." Use is for Agamben the way in which human beings constitute themselves not as identity bearers but as living selves: "The self, which is constituted in the relation of use, is not a subject, is nothing other than this relation" (2016: 60). Use primarily refers to the use of oneself and living is essentially constituted by the unfolding of such use. Human life should be reduced to the deployment of socially inculcated habits that shape action.

In such a view, the uses of oneself are not contextualized in specific historico-political settings. Since Agamben described his work as an archeology of (Western) politics (2016: 263), his only references to a historical context are in his dubious generalizations that address Western thought and modernity. The originary split between *zoe* and *bios*, pure biological life and life bearing social meaning, is, according to his approach, at the root of Western politics which effectively produced a biopolitics (2014: 65), a politics based on the control of "bare life" (of life reduced to its biological status). To go beyond this split and the politics of control that sustain it, it is necessary to reclaim "a life that can never be separated from its form, a life in which it is never possible to isolate and keep distinct something like a bare life" (2016: 207). Agamben describes this by the term "form-of-life" (2000).

To use oneself in the prospect of living a "form-of-life" means actually to pursue inoperativity, to suspend action while contemplating action's own potentiality (2019: 27). Here is where use replaces both *destiny*, considered as the *vocation* of the human animal (based on either theological or cultural assumptions), and *duty*, explicitly introduced to Western ethical philosophy by the Christian thinkers. Use of oneself, then, includes the distinctive modes of being that constitute a self well beyond the polarity existence—essence (2016: 56). A self is not a subject but a mode, a manner, a form of life as it unfolds in living. This kind of self may enter through his or her acts and contemplation (on those acts) into the areas of politics and art. Both those areas are not related to the production of a work. "Liberating living human beings from every biological and social destiny and every predetermined task" will "render them available for the peculiar absence of work that we are accustomed to calling 'politics' and 'art'" (2016: 278).

Clearly, as Agamben insists, this is not simply a call for not doing anything at all, a call for laziness (although in some cases he is not really able to offer a distinguishable description of how his approach differs from a lack of action), but a call for liberating action by opening it to other possible uses. Although the escape from state control and capitalist Western politics is implicitly or explicitly suggested as the way to reclaim life as form of life, no specific indications on how to connect this with real existing struggles are given (Negri, 2008).

There is however a rather more explicit reference to the role artistic creation has in promoting a living that contemplates its own potentialities (including its potential-not-to). In an effort to comment upon "the act of creation," Agamben introduces the idea of a "poetics of inoperativity" (2019: 27). According to this idea, creation already includes a force that prevents it from being reduced to a finished work. This force is equated to the potential-not-to. In a way, the artist is caught in this struggle between the potential to do (a capacity) and an inherent resistance that "prevents potential from being resolved and fully exhausted in the act" (2019: 19).

The work, thus, is characterized by the dialectic between the capacity to create and the resistance to it that makes the hand of the artist "tremble." It is this very same dialectic that is being expressed in the contradiction between habit (the impersonal element, the potential-to) and the inspiration (which "de-activates habit," "the reticence that the individual opposes to the impersonal" (2019: 21), the potential-not-to). The result of creation, thus, is at the same time "a suspension and exposition of the potential" (2019: 23). "A potential that does not precede the work, but accompanies it, makes it live, and opens it to possibilities" (2019: 27).

While artistic creation is caught in this dialectics that opens it to the potentiality which is characteristic of the human, politics may be constituted by this potentiality as long as it deactivates the dominant apparatus of governance. Inoperativity becomes the attitude that will make this possible. Opening human works to other possible uses will be the result of such an operation. To illustrate this view, Agamben refers to the power the feast has to suspend existing social relations (as in carnival feasts) or to make different uses of established habits (to walk differently, to eat differently, to speak differently, etc.). In every feast, then, there are "destitutive elements" that render "inoperative the works of men" (2014: 70). Thus, "the feast [can] furnish a paradigm for thinking inoperativity as a model of politics" (ibid.).

To rescue the inherent potentiality of the human from its appropriation by Western politics that entraps it in the finitude of the work (and, in ethical terms, in the closure of the duty) we need, Agamben seems to suggest, to release human action from any predetermined finality. However, the resulting proliferation of singular modes of being, of beings that are their manners, their mode of being, cannot easily be equated to an emancipated humanity. If emancipation is a process that has to confront and "use" specific historical opportunities, inoperativity without the collective choice of emancipatory scopes (i.e., gender equality, anti-colonial cultural exchanges, and so on) will remain an empty call for "living a life" (2014: 74). The coming politics that Agamben talks about will need to learn from the power art has to suggest a beyond of exploitation (of nature as well as of humans) and the power of rituals to prefigure alternative social relations. As we will see in this book, deactivating dominant habits is not enough. To create new habits as forms of life, which show that a society of equality and mutual care is possible, is urgently needed. To deactivate the biopolitical governing machine, we need the power of a dissident *hexis* as well as the creativity of resistance. This is how the potentiality of human emancipation will be collectively crafted in performances that give it life—in performances that are already instances of life liberated from capitalist command and from hierarchical forms of governance.

A. Badiou: The Event as Surprise

As it will become apparent, the argument that supports the adventure of this book distances itself from ideas of absolute and non-reducible novelty. However, attributing emancipatory power to recurrent practices (as are the habitual practices based on deviant habits) does not amount to accepting conservatism as the essential status of social behavior. Quite the opposite: recurrent practices may be the only way to transcend established patterns of action that sustain and reproduce dominant hierarchies and the exploitation modes that characterize non-egalitarian societies (capitalism obviously included).

In such an approach, to confront Alain Badiou's view about the source and political meaning of potentiality might prove fruitful. As we know, one of Badiou's highly commented upon concepts is the concept of "event." Revealingly, "an event is the creation of new possibilities. It is located not merely at the level of objective possibilities but at the level of the possibility of possibilities" (Badiou, 2010: 6). Furthermore, "[an] event is the occurrence of the real as its own future possibility" (ibid.: 7).

The concept of the event is, then, directly linked to the question of change. Badiou's ontology is primarily oriented toward the exploration of change not as a process of becoming—this distinguishes his approach from vitalist theories (Constantinou and Madarasz, 2009: 788; Badiou, 2009: 381–7)— but a process of rupture, a process of radical contingency. And this kind of change becomes possible as long as the "inconsistent multiplicity" of a situation is unpredictably disrupted.

Subjects of action, according to Badiou, do not preexist in the form of an established identity. Subjects emerge in actions that orient them toward an event: it is the fidelity to an event that makes certain humans subjects (Badiou, 2001 and 2005: 392–4). We should thus understand subjectivation as a problem of agency rather than as a problem of identity. However, if humans become subjects, and only remain ones as long as they decide to remain faithful to the event that made it possible for them to emerge, the question is what makes certain humans actually take such decisions. Badiou insists on the contingency of the event. Events come to us in the form of a surprise. And this is not the kind of surprise that is the result of lack of knowledge or awareness. It is a surprise that cannot be predicted.

There is a suggestion that in a way faces the problem of surprise in a possible theory of praxis based on Badiou's ontology. We may become prepared while waiting for the event. And this preparation includes the awareness that our fidelity to prior events has actually changed the conditions of our world. Our actions have contributed to the formation of new situations, to use Badiou's terminology. In terms of politics however, the crucial issue is: Do those new situations depart from or confront the "state of the situation," "the system of constraints that limit the possibility of possibilities" (Badiou, 2010: 7)?

"Inconsistent multiplicity" characterizes the being-qua-being, according to Badiou. There is however, within any situation that includes elements which are inconsistently different, we might say, a certain area to which the possibility of change may arise: the evental site (Badiou, 2005: 173–7). In another Badiou's term, this may be equated with the "void" (Badiou 2001: 68), the element belonging to the set of elements included in the situation which cannot be counted, cannot acquire a specific value and thus be represented in a knowledge of the situation that presents it in the form of structure. There is a certain similarity here with Rancière's understanding of the "distribution of the sensible" which can be disrupted when those who are not counted for introduce a rupture to the sensible's structure by acting and speaking in ways that were considered as unthinkable (2006 and 2010).

The "evental site" is where an event may explode. There is then a kind of understanding of potentiality in Badiou's thought that is different from both historical determinism and vitalist becoming. The "evental site [is] an entirely abnormal multiple; that is a multiple such that none of its elements are presented in the situation" (Badiou, 2005: 175). However, as opposed to natural multiplicity which is always normal, a multiple may be singular in one situation (and thus become an evental site) while being normal in another one. For Badiou, this is the constitutive difference between History and Nature. Historical situations are those "in which at least one evental site occurs (2005: 177), therefore these are the ones that are open to the occurrence of an event.

The relative status of a certain multiplicity in relation to its being an evental site somehow sketches an area of potentiality. However, as it seems, there are no characteristics inherent to a multiple that make it prone to, available for, or even suited to occurring as an evental site. "Historicity is a local criterion" (ibid.) which is another way of saying that contingency and chance make history. Events, as the necessary "supplement" (another Badiou's term) to an evental site, will trigger transformation and radical change. An additional problem, however, arises in this absolutely indeterminable potentiality: if an event acquires its transformative power as long as subjects constituted by it recognize it and develop a fidelity to it, then which will be the possible criterion for distinguishing a true event from simulacrums of events? It is here that Badiou steps in to judge (or perhaps to instruct): This or that is not a true event because all it does is a renewed way of establishing a state of a situation (2004a: 128–9; also Badiou, 2004b: 236–7).

It seems that at least in the case of the political event, what distinguishes it from a mere reproduction of the state of a situation is its emancipatory orientation. The transformation of a situation by an event is defined by the "egalitarian" (Hewlett, 2007: 48). "A political process is a chance fidelity, militant and only partially shared, to a singular event, which is legitimized only by itself" (ibid.: 54). No matter how specifically oriented toward egalitarian scopes, such fidelity, then, is only based on the contingency of a happening. Subjects, by definition emerging after the event, appear not to be in a position to produce the event. Potentiality, thus, becomes not the ground which connects acts with the results of their action but the outcome of a decision of fidelity that from then on gives subjects the opportunity (the power?) to become part of the transformation process.

The question then becomes: If subjects are really constituted after the event, what kinds of actions make the event possible (and surely not inevitable) in the first place? What this book will try to explore is almost the opposite: What kind of actions will produce the potentiality of change? And, furthermore, what kinds of actions will develop emancipatory processes that will result in an emancipatory society (or community)? Could it be that such actions will not be simply singular (and local in Badiou's terminology) but recurrent and, possibly, exemplary? Perhaps, as we will see, this is the way to trace potentialities of emancipation that may develop in different parts of the world which, nevertheless, are comparable and mutually translatable rather than universal.

Both Agamben and Badiou try to understand potentiality by connecting it to action. Both, however, depart from the idea that actions actualize preexisting potentialities. A theory of social praxis that distances itself from the idea that transformative events are necessarily contingent—as well as from the view that recurrent actions only reproduce a certain social order—will eventually have to deal with the question of human creativity. And this question will inadvertently have to face the constitutive dilemmas concerning human history. If people make their own history, as Marx suggests, how do they actually manage to do it? Do they use what is available, becoming thus guided by the heavy limitations inherited from the past, or do they invent freely because radical contingency opens history to unpredictable ruptures? Do people manage to trespass the limits of the past because of social order's inherent contradictions that make this possible, or to they create such potentialities by acting, implicitly or explicitly, against a social, temporal, and spatial order that prevents them from living in ways they desire and need?

H. Lefebvre: Mimesis and Rhythmicality

Any attempt to understand the transformative power of human acts—whether transformation refers to the relations with nature and nonhumans or to the relations between humans—needs to problematize the conditions of possibility of social praxis. Praxis may be understood as the capacity to act, which humans employ not simply to satisfy needs but also to attribute value and meaning to the expected or experienced results of their actions. Social praxis, then, engenders socially meaningful acts that address human relations directly or indirectly.

Henri Lefebvre's work is a possible source of a theory of social praxis that focuses on the conditions of collective creativity. His most important contribution seems to be located in disentangling creativity from genius or talent and connecting it to patterns of action inherent in everyday life. A thinker who has spent a lot of time and energy on reclaiming the potentialities of everydayness will help us recuperate the transformative power of the repetitive, recurrent acts in the context of human history.

Henri Lefebvre saves mimesis from the anathema of banality and submission. Finding elements of collective creativity and resistance to capitalist ethos in everyday life was one of his major contributions to the rethinking of social emancipation (1971, 1987). And it is in the effort to disentangle everydayness from servile social reproduction that he found it necessary to trace a kind of history of mimesis.

According to his suggestion, mimesis "is a modality of praxis" (2016: 229). Therefore one should distinguish the grounding characteristics of mimetic acts from those that were developed in different historical periods. There was a time when "mimesis was not yet distinguishable from poiesis" (2016: 205). In Lefebvre's approach, poiesis encompasses all those acts that transform man's relation with nature, including human nature itself. This transformative process is creative, which means that it generates both new material realities as well as new meanings.

Referring to the ancient times, he suggests that the poetic praxis was being expressed in the making of the cities: the city was the poetic work par excellence, the work of works (1996). In an explicit confrontation with structuralist and analytic approaches that prioritize rational thinking and abstract taxonomies in the development of human societies, Lefebvre insists that poetic praxis provides the common ground on which shared significations, patterns of action, and, finally, abstract thinking and knowledge may grow.

"Man is poetic. He is born from poiesis, with it" (2016: 243). It is this inherent capacity to transform that makes it possible for men to produce and create, to change themselves by creating. Out of this capacity, mimesis is developed. Initially there was no clear distinction between mimesis and poiesis. What we usually connect with mimetic behavior, as in games, rituals, religious beliefs, and manners (etiquette) was, at a certain period, part of a process of constructing the world in which humans used to live. Mimetic acts were neither separated from this world by being reduced to the following of behavior codes (and rules of conduct) nor considered as an area of significations distinct from the flow of life. What was repeated in human acts, then, was not yet simply reproduction, a redundancy without differentiation. Repetition was not imitation, if by imitation we mean a passive repeating of recognizable acts with fixed meaning. Repetition was still transformative, it produced changes.

According to Lefebvre, the separation of mimesis from poiesis can be compared with the separation of the poetic from language and with the separation of the ludic from behavior. In all those cases "formalisms" (2016: 216) have developed that have reduced repetitions to the following of established rules, therefore to the reproduction of established systems of meaning. Mimesis loses its power to transform, the power to transgress all sectors of social life and thus to support a "style of life" characteristic of a certain epoch. A growing uniformity reduces mimesis to the imitation of rules, replaces style with culture (2016: 217), and ends up in the segmentation of social life, which is divided in sectors with their own autonomous structure and functioning. A homogenization of behavior within each of those sectors results from this segmentation. Oppositely, a "style of life" encompasses all social life as a totality that corresponds to the unsegmented totality of the human.

"Mimesis is active. It decomposes and recomposes the real" (2016: 229). Imitation is passive. It copies. And, as Lefebvre suggests, it is mostly linked to "the sensory and perceptual level" (ibid.). Imitation becomes a dominant mode of behavior in a society that deprives individuals of the transformative creativity that is only attributed to the gifted and exemplary individual. Repetition and reproducibility are "effectively hidden by semblances of creativity" (1991: 354) in capitalist industrial society. However, active mimesis may keep its bond with poesis. It may generate changes within the realm of the everyday, within the everyday repetitive performances.

What Lefebvre describes as the "infinite at the heart of the finite" (2016: 323) or the "residue," which will always escape any systematization of knowledge or behavior, is the *possible* that arises within the socially established closure of the real. In search of the possible, the possibility to transcend existing capitalist society, mimesis should be restored along poesis as the power to discover while repeating, as the power to exceed the necessary formalism of social relations (of the rules that govern them) toward a creative recuperation of life in its totality. Will this be through the liberation of desire "that starts from need, supersedes it and yet returns to the original?" (2016: 322). Will this signal the identification of philosophy with life, the dissolution of philosophy into life? Or will it lead to the recuperation of a relation to nature that was destroyed by instrumental reason along with capitalist extractivist ethos? A lot can be said about the actuality of Lefebvre's suggestions as well as about their limitations arising from the historical contingency that made them possible. What is, however, important in his claims is the fact that repetition may be a source of discovery and change, as long as it reconnects to poiesis. Poetical repetitions may indicate an emancipatory effort to establish habits and rituals of emancipation. And this effort should always be considered as a *work in progress*—as a form of collective creativity that emerges in new ways of living in common.

Lefebvre's approach to everydayness and to everyday life offers an additional theoretical link to the problematization of repetition in social praxis. Departing from a view that considers the everyday as merely banal, endlessly repetitive, and, thus, simply a normalizing process, Lefebvre traced a history of everydayness that unearths the potentialities of collective creativity. Before "the advent of competitive capitalism … the quotidian as such did not exist" (1971: 38). Social life was characterized in its totality, according to Lefebvre, by a certain *style* which "gives significance to the slightest object" (ibid.). Style is to be distinguished from culture; the latter being characterized by fragmentariness rather than by unity. Style is taken to permeate life and the works of every distinct society. Let us not however think that by style Lefebvre attempts to present precapitalist societies as beautiful or endlessly creative. "There was a style of cruelty, a style of power, a style of wisdom; cruelty and power (the Arts, Rome) produced great styles and great civilizations, but so did the aristocratic wisdom of Egypt or of India" (ibid.).

What modern capitalist society lacks is this kind of unity that did not set apart the rhythmicality of everydayness and the rhythmicality of the feasts, the rhythmicality of rituals and the recurrent practices that reproduced each society's predominant worldviews. Style was the kind of poetic mimesis that capitalist society lacks, since it has replaced the unity of social life with the fragmentariness of a culture based on the rationality of exchange value, a shallow rationality accompanied by the irrationality of make-believe advertising spectacles. Repetition, in this context, is reduced to the linear rhythmicality of a machine (Lefebvre, 2004), to recurrent practices that characterize both the production as well as the reproduction of society.

Interestingly, at the root of the problem of the everydayness and the quotidian is the problem of repetition. Repetition may trap social praxis to the recurrence of identical acts or provide it with the necessary canvas on which the works of creative variations will develop. The festival, being expelled from capitalist boring everydayness (or being domesticated in the advertising fantasies of a society of organized consumption) will return in an emancipated society "rediscovered and magnified by overcoming the conflict between everyday life and festivity" (1971: 206).

Opposed to the "programmed change," which is simply the result of the "planned obsolescence" that is necessary for the workings of endless consumption, emerges the recuperation of the cyclical rhythms of the festival, the game, and the ritual (Lefebvre, 1987). In his criticism of modernist functionalism, which reduces everyday life to the functions necessary for social reproduction, Lefebvre did not abandon the essentially modernist aspiration of a totally innovative rupture of history that will open the road to social emancipation. Everyday life and, more specifically, urban everyday life was, however, for him both the place from which "urban revolution" would have to start and the place in which it will have to reach its successful end. "The revolutionary process begins by shaking up the condition of everyday life and ends by restarting it" (1969: 88). To move away from "the generalized terrorism of the quantifiable" (2003: 185) meant for him to defy instrumentalized rationality as well as the illusionary spectacle of controlled consumption.

Patterns of Repeating

Potentialities arise in action. They cannot be separated from action; neither can action be explained. Potentialities are performed. Potentialities should not be reduced to the workings of chance and contingency. They are crafted by people in the process of their efforts to transcend the limitations of their present. Potentialities, thus, are not there waiting to be fulfilled, to be accomplished, to become actualized. They are openings created by action, openings to future action.

Potentialities are the scaffolds erected in order to support a future being built with materials collected from the past and the present. However, no plan of the future building preexists. Potentialities are being created in the process and the process itself is the unfolding of those potentialities.

Recurrent acts establish potentialities by clearly distinguishing them from opportunities arising from chance. Performed potentialities, thus, are generating collective capacities. They are opening collective action to the future through the development of new patterns of acting, new skills and habits, new gestures and symbolizations. As able and inventive craftsmen people make their history not by following predetermined paths but by developing new capacities. By expanding themselves. By transforming themselves.

That is why potentialities are also performative: they make things happen. They transform experienced reality by opening paths to different experiences. And this leads to an understanding of human action considered both as generator of potentialities and the receiver of potentialities that were generated in the past. Redeeming potentialities that are considered as pending means actually regenerating them in the present. And, to follow Benjamin's reasoning, this means giving them new meaning in the present. In this context, actualization is a process of transformation.

If potentialities are performed and performative, from which position is this study supposed to look at the potentialities of urban metropolitan life? Trying to learn from the ways metropolitan inhabitants perform potentialities of urban forms of life that transcend urban order, this study actually takes sides: It explicitly tries to support such performances by examining the links between spatial conditions and action within the historical context of contemporary metropolis in the prospect of an urban emancipated society.

In such an approach, emancipation, understood as a process rather than as a describable Arcadian "beyond," is at the bottom line, a chain of potentiality performances. Emancipation is not the end of a series of efforts but the emerging dynamics of a different society, based on solidarity and equality, which develops through collective action.

It remains to be demonstrated that such collective actions are at least of three distinct kinds:

- Actions focused on collective survival through the **reinvention of urban communities** (in the metropolitan life context of populations excluded from the right to the city, as we will see).
- Actions focused on **cooperation and collaboration experiences** (related to labor under capitalist command but also escaping from it through mutual aid practices).
- Actions related to **new imaginaries of change** (actions that shape visions, dreams, and aspirations which should not be considered as mere passive contemplations but as a shaping factor of action itself).

These actions create opportunities of escape from capitalist command if they develop in and through **commoning practices**. Thus, survival actions based on sharing are completely distinguishable from individual (and individualist) survival tactics that will very well fit in the dominant capitalist logic. This logic in its neoliberal moment is based on the idea of "individual responsibility," a determinant "cultural glue" that, according to Loic Wacquant, "pastes the various components of [neoliberal] state together" (2012: 72). Individuals are deemed responsible for their fate (so poor people are responsible for their poverty). The "entrepreneur of the self" (Lazzarato, 2012) is measured for its successes and failures through its responses to individual responsibility. Each and every one is responsible for his or her fate.

On the contrary, in practices of urban commoning, survival (and success in pursuing a decent life) is measured by the efficiency of relations of solidarity within the group of commoners. Survival in this case means surviving together—not the one surviving in spite of the other's demise, destruction, or failure to survive. Urban commoning, as we will see, is not a choice made necessarily due to convictions held or values preferred. Sometimes urban commoning emerges as the only path to survival, especially for the urban poor and the marginalized.

In the same way, practices of cooperation and collaboration can escape capitalist command and be developed as forces of a more just society when they promote mutual engagement in collectively planned tasks. Equality may become a true collective experience in such a context, and those who collaborate will become able to appropriate collectively the product of their cooperation. Mutual aid practices and their corresponding ethics as well as the subjectivation potentialities they inaugurate are instances of urban commoning.

New imaginaries of change may indeed be captured by capitalist ideologies (for example by the ideology of progress, by developmentalist ideologies, by environmental awareness projects channeled to green capitalism, etc.). Actually, there is no predetermined Archimedean point from which anti-capitalist, on noncapitalist imaginaries can establish their externality. However, imaginaries of change constructed through the commoning of knowledges, aspirations, and affects may possibly be able to disentangle themselves from dominant perceptions of the future. At the same time, such imaginaries will be more close to the capacity of conceiving, dreaming, and feeling life as commons.

In search of the spatial embeddedness of potentiality, a central hypothesis is suggested and explored in this book: What if potentiality is performed in practices that punctuate lived space in distinct recognizable ways? What if those performances, necessarily recurrent, as it will be shown, are space formative in ways that may be described through the specific qualitative characteristics that categorize them—the specific spatialities that constitute them?

This set of hypotheses has led to a research that seems to support the suggestion that lived space becomes socially meaningful, and thus inhabitable, by being divided and ordered. Depending on the society that inhabits it, space is divided and ordered in different ways. It is beyond the ambitions of this book to offer an all-encompassing anthropological theory that may include all such possible different ways. What will be attempted, however, is to locate the specific ways through which urban capitalist societies impose their culture-specific forms of urban ordering, as well as, importantly, the ways resistances to such ordering create antagonistic performances of spatial divisions (and thus alternative forms of spatial ordering in the making).

Three modalities of space emerge from the performances of urban potentiality in such societies: the spatiality of **place** as performed by collective habits, the spatiality of the **magic circle** as performed in rituals, and the spatiality of **trajectory** as performed in practices of tracing. Those three modes that simultaneously shape lived, represented, and imagined spaces are connected to performances of potentiality: They actually emerge in those performances and support them by their repeatability. If what characterizes performance acts is their recurrence in time (which as we will see is inherently inscribed in their repeatability) their actualization depends on their power to reinstitute specific ways of space, specific spatialities every time. Exactly as recurrence punctuates time flow by introducing discontinuity as a means to differentiate and compare instances ("events," "moments," "instants," etc.), recurrence also punctuates space by introducing discontinuity as a means to differentiate and to compare locations. This book's suggestion is that locations take the form of places of habit, of magic circles of ritual, and of trajectories of tracing.

Comparing different societies by using this categorization of performed spatialities might seem promising. At the core of this categorization seems to emerge a potential anthropology of spatial performances. However, this book will only try to show that those distinct types of spatiality help us understand the way potentiality is being performed in contemporary urban societies. Openly accepting that the scope of this endeavor is to find ways to sustain acts and hopes for a more just future, the findings and questions that follow will emerge in support of all those who unearth in today's metropolises the promise of an emancipated and emancipatory society.

Following my previous efforts to theorize space as potential (2019: 5–27), this book develops a line of arguing and a research trajectory that tries to profit from an important ongoing discussion: The discussion about potentiality as an issue implicitly or explicitly connected to the questions of building a different, just, and emancipatory urban future. Some of the contributors to this discussion have attempted to ground their thoughts on a general view about human nature. Paolo Virno (2008) starts from the assumption that it is the openness of the human animal to the world (the lack of instincts that direct toward prescribed choices for a distinctly human habitat) that establishes the role of potentiality in human existence.

Some contemporary thinkers, including Derrida, Deleuze, Guattari, Foucault, and Agamben explored language (and the formation of concepts) in order to locate the ways meaning is constructed and expressed through the development of the potentialities of a structured system with distinct components. Although their approaches differ as well as the terms they use, they seem to share an interest in the ways the possibility of meaning emerges by being skeptical toward any kind of historical or naturalistic determinism.

What is being suggested in this book is that potentialities are being performed and that they transform reality in the process of being performed. Space and time, socially experienced space and time, are not simply the parameters of experience (inculcated through culture or biologically innate) but are the means through which experience may be transcended. This means that space and time do not host and express potentialities but rather develop as explicitly historic capacities (therefore culture bound) through which humans create, invent, actually performed as well as imagined potentialities. If there is a distinctly human capacity for the human animal, it seems that it lies in the capacity to "other," to "other space" and to "other time." But this capacity, as it will be suggested, stems from the capacity to socially organize patterns of repeatedness. Because "othering" the power to create a present different from the established one (and from the past which is always recalled in a certain present) can only become transformative as long as it invents new patterns of repeatedness that confront the established ones. Otherwise, difference becomes the setting of the hopeless wandering of a disoriented "animal open to the world" (Virno, 2008).

2

Metropolitan Urbanity and the Project of Urban Order

We are witnessing a period in which two processes of urban ordering converge. Both processes, as we will see, present the city as threatened by its other. But the way they describe this other is different. Also, both processes have concrete effects on the form and life of contemporary cities but their power depends upon the way they are legitimized through representations of the city and its other. Being, at the same time, concrete and abstract, those processes generate practices, both at the level of dominant policies as well as at the level of everyday actions of compliance or dissent.

A few words about the urban order to begin with—the term does not imply that a group of masterminds decides and implements plans that shape cities according to explicit targets. Although there are of course planners and policymakers who join forces to control the city and its layout, the city is a force field in which a constant confrontation between different interests and aspirations takes place. Confrontations cannot simply be reduced to describable asymmetries of power: they are grounded on what may be described as the material conditions of the city as well as on the differing flows of meaning attributed by different urban actors to these material conditions. Urban order, thus, is the result of processes that unfold in the city, some of them being explicitly focused on maintaining this order, others on implicitly contributing to it, and still others on escaping from it or disputing it. As long as this highly complex order does not block (or clash with) the defining imperatives of capitalist reproduction of the corresponding urban society, we can talk about an urban order that in the last instance serves capitalism.

It is more appropriate to refer to an ongoing process of urban ordering than to an established urban order. We need to keep in mind that ordering takes place within the limits of a specific historical contingency and according to a specific configuration of the urban force field.

Let us now see which are the two processes that seek to maintain urban ordering within the main imperatives of contemporary capitalism. One is the process of **urban domestication** and the other is the process of **urban normalization**. Their crucial difference lies in the way they define the threatening "other" of urban order. The first one needs to describe this other as wild while the second one needs to describe it as abnormal (or divergent, etc.). This difference generates different strategies for establishing and maintaining urban order as well as different imaginaries that legitimize those strategies.

Urban Domestication

The project of domestication of plants and animals has a long history. For many, it marks the first world-shaping revolution humanity has experienced. The neolithic revolution, a term coined by Gordon Childe (1936), is considered as a period of major changes in human history. Crucial among them are the advent of agriculture and the breeding of animals, both related to practices of domestication.

Domestication, however, has been a very ambiguous phenomenon and may still be studied by comparing different societies and their approach to such phenomenon, once considered universal. We in the West may take for granted that domestication necessarily defines an area outside of society, distinct from it and hostile to it: the wilderness. Depending on each society's understanding of territory, wilderness is supposedly an outside, or another territory. For urban societies, this reasoning will easily conclude that domestication faces a world outside the city with the aim of taming it, and thus putting it into the service of the city.

We have enough indications to question the presuppositions of this reasoning. As Philippe Descola (2013) shows us, in some societies the domestication of plants and animals is a selective process that is not only dependent on subsistence needs but also on shared worldviews. Commenting upon the fact that Ameridians are not willing to domesticate autochthonous animals although they did easily accept European domestic animals, Descola notes: "The trouble was that the adoption of such domestication would have necessitated a serious reorientation in the modes of relating to nonhumans and would have entailed modification to their ontological status" (2013: 385).

Domestication also does not necessarily need to be based on a division of the world to two clearly demarcated parts: social territory and wilderness. What Descola describes as the Great Divide is an understanding of the world that has become predominant in the so-called Western societies and which distinguishes between society and its outer, nature.

Marshall Sahlins explores what he calls "the western illusion of human nature" (2008) by locating the founding prejudices that shaped a demonizing view toward nature. Ancient Greek philosophers and historians as well as early Christian founding thinkers seem to agree that nature (especially the part of nature that we carry within us as human animals), only directs behavior toward the egoistic fulfillment of individual desires. A potential war of all against all (in its Hobbesian explicit formulation) will allegedly result from this condition unless society intervenes to suppress individual aggression and to establish order. As Sahlins shows, this approach was used (and is still used) either to justify a strong sovereign rule (despotic or oligarchic) or a republican rule (based on the balancing of opposing interests). Interestingly, Sahlins suggests that even democracy in Western culture is based on the suppression of an allegedly malign human nature and on the "realist" acceptance that opposing needs and desires necessarily push toward "the law of the jungle."

The taming of nature proves to be a crucial project for the so-called Western culture. It amounts to nothing less than the project of social order. What makes this project difficult to execute, and thus all the more urgent, is the fact that this kind of "outside," nature, cannot easily be expelled from society and culture because it is also an inside, an inside carried by each and every one of the society's members. If urban order is meant to be the concrete form this project of social order takes, we need to trace the ways the taming of inner and outer nature develops through practices that shape city space. It is those practices that sustain the imaginary of a hostile nature, which does not simply exist outside the city but has to also be included in the city by constantly suppressing its alleged hostility.

To the well-targeted critique of the current *extractivist* culture (Acosta, 2013; Gudynas, 2013), which only sees nature as a reservoir of resources to be exploited, we need to add a critique that targets the imaginary of nature-as-threat. It is on this popular as well as scientific imaginary that practices of taming are based. And the taming of a nature presented as essentially and always hostile is, in the end, aimed at controlling forms of action and behavior that challenge an imposed unjust social order.

Sometimes it is the extreme case that reveals the mechanisms at play in conditions considered as normal: The urban engineering of racism in South Africa's apartheid settlements was explicitly targeted at clearly demarcating housing areas for the separated categories of inhabitants—"whites," "Indian," "colored," and "Blacks." Separating the areas for the whites from those of all the "other," green belts, huge highways, or even empty land were used as buffer zones. "In moving to and from work no race group was permitted to cross the residential area of another" (Bremner, 2005: 124).

As Lindsay Bremner suggests, apartheid planners were drawing upon models introduced by the nineteenth-century English reformers Robert Owen and Ebenezer Howard to shape the country's urbanization through the construction of urban villages (ibid.: 123). In this approach, the model of the Garden City and the idea of developing urban self-sufficient communities with a lot of green spaces between them were used to maintain segregation rather than support the development of societies of equality and cooperation.

In the Garden City utopias, nature was meant to be the common ground, the connecting canvas for the different communities living in harmony with each other (Howard, 1902). Natural landscape was the connecting tissue of such a projected network of collaborating communities. Quite contrarily, the apartheid engineers used green belts to separate. Such green spaces were meant to emphatically describe the outside—a barrier that indicates the existence of others. Natural buffer zones were especially meant to keep all the others away from the privileged "white" areas.

And, of course, it was the villages of the Black people, the *Bantu*, which had to be planned according to this reversed Garden City ethos: ideally they would consist of minimal houses surrounded by gardens. "It was here and in its parallel landscape, the *Bantustan*, that the category of 'native' would be constructed, simultaneously, as dehistoricized, primitive, tribal savage and as modern, docile urban subject" (Bremner, 2005: 126).

The apartheid urbanism is perhaps the clearest example of a process of domestication in support of urban ordering. Obviously, this kind of ordering has been of the most harsh, violent, and discriminatory kind. The way it was manufactured and sustained though becomes indicative of the urban domestication mechanism: some (predominantly the native Black people in this case) have to be considered as "wild," as belonging to an out-of-the-urban world. And nature can become the carefully developed out-of-the-city world, a metonymy of wilderness that separates the true urbanites from the "others" and their "otherness."

Domestication of nature, which is being considered as an externality to society, has taken different forms that relate to the envisioned, sought for, or implemented urban order. One of them relates to the development of areas for holidays, such as holiday villages, seaside hotel complexes, summer or winter sport paradises, exotic thematic resorts, and so on (Gosseye and Heynen, 2013). We may actually trace two distinct strategies related to such spaces. One puts an emphasis on hygiene and the therapeutic results of being immersed, so to speak, into a kind of tamed nature. The other puts an emphasis on pleasure and consumption, usually presenting the tamed natural surrounding as a source of recreation and rest.

Both approaches were developed through policies that were referring especially to the population of great cities and industrial centers and not to the chosen few, the elites who could spend time for leisure at will. From the *Front Populaire* in mid-war France to the Nazi German Labor Front and the

Italian fascist *Dopolavoro*, from the paid holiday policies in East and West after the war to the market-oriented mass tourism rising in most parts of the globe, vacations in "nature" were a model to be pursued.

In the East, what may be called the "socialist resort" has developed as an area of necessary recreation for all those who worked in the corresponding countries within the planned production economy (Mrduljaš, 2018; Tanović and Mraović, 2018; Maxim, 2015). Rest was not only considered a necessary break from all year's work but also an opportunity to extend and develop the values connected to a new society under construction. Thus, physical education and leisure based on an organized collective everydayness were meant to connect vacations with the ethic of collective work and measured productivity. Following the essentially modernist logic of using nature as a resource, a logic that prevailed in centrally planned production, organized vacation areas were using natural settings and "goods" (the sun, the seawater, the tree shade, etc.) as resources to be exploited in order to shape the bodies and mentalities of "the socialist worker-citizen." As Juliana Maxim suggests, "resorts in socialist Romania, at least in the early years, were in continuity with life in the new socialist city, and their architecture was seen as anticipatory of an ideal social and spatial condition rather than a realm of exception" (2015: 77).

This idealized contact with nature, which was meant to become a pedagogic exercise in socialist values, characterized the policies of the state in its effort to identify a model for the socialist city. Productivist logic, functional rationality, and hygienic ideology were all mobilized in the grandiose project of domesticating nature. It was coal and oil extraction or planned cultivation that represented this domestication process in production. And it was seaside sports and body exercise in sunny, clean-air settings that represented this process in recreation activities.

In the West, priorities were different (Avermaete, 2013). Already in the 1950s, the Club Méd type of vacation village came into existence, epitomizing the ideology of leisure time as an opportunity to escape from everyday burdens. Club Méd villages were advertised as "antidotes to civilization" as Łukasz Stanek suggests (Stanek, 2011: 177, compare also Maxim, 2015: 23). This approach, quite distinct from the Eastern "sober" recreation policies, favored a hedonistic use of leisure time and introduced simulated exotic settings to support relevant fantasies of escape. In many cases, a mythologized-as-pure local culture becomes the setting and the staged narrative for exotic vacations. Whether the thematic trigger is Tahitian tropics or Greek islands, holiday areas in the West perform a distinct type of domestication. Nature is reduced to an activator of sensual experiences, many of which became almost impossible in the growing industrial cities. Thus, the sun, the clean air, the sea, or the snow are converted to controlled stimulators of senses in a secure and sanitized quasi natural setting. Far from providing stimulating antidotes to civilization, various types of vacation areas are actually controlled environments in which people may taste a simulated and staged civilization's "outside." And as mass tourism has already showed us in a very explicit way, this outside is in reality a powerful inside of consumption culture.

Whereas in the West a rupture, a temporary liberation from the dull or harsh everydayness, was advertised to be the core of vacations experience, in the East continuity with everydayness was at the core of recreation-as-(socialist) pedagogy. Of course, in the Western world, holiday experiences were equally pedagogic: To learn to see holiday time and space as merchandises to be bought and sold (or provided under certain conditions for a certain period by the welfare state) is to learn that everything that you may experience or long for is mediated by the market. Domesticated nature is thus reduced to an array of products packaged in different ways in order to be consumed.

We may therefore conclude that both in East and West, the taming of nature is really a way of domesticating human behavior.

In terms of territory arrangements, the two paradigms of domestication have quite distinct characteristics. In the East, resorts were often designed and usually functioned as areas not completely separated from actual cities. Their "outsideness" was in many cases a matter of emphasis rather than of complete separation. And as some scholars attest, the shape of new housing areas in "socialist cities" was greatly influenced by the design of resort areas. Modernist planning axioms (including the idea of integrated "new cities" as satellite urban organizations) as well as the prefabrication production logic were in many cases tested in recreation complexes before they were implemented on a larger scale in the corresponding developing cities.

In the West, the idea of total immersion in fantasy places has become popular especially in the so-called exclusive holiday packages. Of course, always depending on the price of the offered package, places were designed to offer within a clearly marked perimeter everything that will support the specific escape fantasy (seaport facilities, casinos, massage lounges, bars and restaurants, shops of various kinds, etc.). Epitomized in the member's bracelet that authenticates authorized participants is the logic of the tourist enclave that includes the domesticated part of nature.

A swimming pool just by the seaside can indeed convey the image of a tamed natural element (water-sea) to replace the unpredictable, or even hostile, sea nearby. Not that any swimming pool is simply an ersatz sea: The kind of swimming pool arrangement just mentioned is especially appropriate to enjoy a natural element in a safe, predictable, and repeatable way. It is not by chance that such swimming pools may include bar installations, safe play areas for the kids, and, of course, the necessary *passerelle*: One has to show oneself as somebody worthy of jealous remarks or of being a protagonist in erotic fantasies (his, hers, or of the onlookers).

It is just one step away to create gated communities influenced by the fantasy enclave resorts. Characteristically, in Istanbul a new gated community is advertised as being the glorious transposition of Bosporus seaside villas. Located in a newly designed residential complex, the villas (as well as the tower apartments for the less affluent) are on the artificial waterfront of a canal constructed for this purpose. In Cairo, a new residential area advertises itself as the "Greek village." Arranged as an almost labyrinthine Greek island village, with individual houses stylistically referring to the forms of the corresponding vernacular architecture, this place imitates, albeit not very convincingly, the natural setting of its model. Terraces full of flowers, small courtyards, unadorned construction materials, and, of course, the ubiquitous sun: a domesticated nature imported, as in the case of the Istanbul complex, from a defined and mythological elsewhere.

Urban Normalization

As we know from Michel Foucault (1983), the project of normalization has its own distinct history, or, rather, genealogy. And it is especially connected to the shape cities have taken since urban order has been a major contributing factor in the development of this project.

Foucault, let us remember, distinguishes between three types of power that correspond to three forms the normalization project takes. Sovereign power excludes and applies techniques of segregation to those stigmatized as deviant, that is, not normal. Disciplinary power "concentrates, focuses and encloses" (2009: 44). Its role is to observe and control in order to avoid the deviant behavior. Whereas sovereign power prohibits and punishes, disciplinary power classifies and distinguishes the normal from the non-normal. Disciplinary power directs and prescribes (ibid.: 47). Finally, security tries to establish and sustain the normalization process by studying and predicting the behavior of the population. The term governmentality (ibid.: 108) was introduced by Foucault to describe this process of enacting a kind of power that "has population as its target, political economy as its major form of knowledge, and apparatuses of security as its essential technical instrument" (ibid.: 109).

Foucault is quite clear that those modalities of power may coexist or work together (ibid.: 107). Distinguishing between techniques and technologies of power, he assigns to the second term the role of condensing "the dominant feature" of power as it is practiced at a given period in a specific society (ibid.: 8). Thus, the technology of security comes to characterize contemporary times in Western societies and actually establishes a distinct form of governmental reason. With the risk of simplifying a view that has preoccupied many commentators of Foucault's work and terminology, one could say that governmental reason refers to a series of views, knowledges, and practices in which the problem of maintaining a hierarchical society's structure by the power of those who rule is centered on the question of how to manage the population.

Words are never innocent; we know that, of course. So, describing this problem as a problem of management, or as a problem of administration, or as a problem of subordination makes a huge difference. I believe that what Foucault was actually trying to locate in a period roughly around the middle of the eighteenth century was a transformation in the technologies of power that gave them a different focus, a series of different means, and also a different legitimization basis.

The focus: to control all by using predominantly the techniques of security. As we have seen, these techniques impose normalization by studying the population, by controlling specific tendencies of collective and individual behavior and action, and by reaching to the very depth of the population's biological characteristics and traits. What Foucault would term biopolitics is this technology of power that essentially aims at controlling life. That is why it is in this context that "problems like those of housing, of the conditions of life in the city, of public hygiene, of the modification of the relation between birth and mortality" (2007: 161) have emerged as political problems. As problems of governance, that is.

The means: knowledge acquired through the study of populations. Let us not forget that this knowledge is from the start a purposeful knowledge. It is meant to assist control. The positive aspect therefore, which Foucault has introduced to the discussions about power (which is usually predominantly considered as malignant and violent) by insisting that power indeed produces knowledge, should not make us forget this knowledge is motivated and mobilized by the project of normalization.

The legitimization: sovereign power is usually attributed to some kind of undisputable transcendental origin (including superiority based on the magical, or religious characteristics of rulers). Disciplinary power is predominantly legitimized as a technique that guides, fashions, and corrects the individual members of society according to society's predominant norms. Security power is connected to a legitimating logic that Foucault identifies with liberalism. The reproduction of population is connected to the considered-as-natural mechanisms of the market. Elevated to the organizing condition of social life, the market is for liberals something like the precondition of the population's existence and well-being. "The fundamental question of liberalism is: What is the utility value of government and all actions of government in a society where exchange determines the true value of things?" (2008a: 46).

As Foucault sums up his approach to the new governmental reason: "It is now a matter ... of modeling government ... on the rationality of those who are governed as economic subjects and, more generally, as subjects of interest in the most general sense of the term" (2008a: 312).

It is important to see here a peculiar shift of meaning. One thing is to consider the population as defined in its tendencies to act and behave by the biological characteristics that constitute the common ground of the "human" and another thing is to consider the market as the matrix of society. The collapse of this distinction under the metaphor of "natural" actually becomes the foundation of hegemonic reason in capitalist societies.

Let us remember Maurice Godelier's idea that "groups can 'spontaneously' consent to their own domination" provided that it appears "as a service rendered to them by the dominant" (2011: 157). Security, in its broadest meaning including the biological reproduction as well as the well-being of the society's members, is surely presented as a service to the dominated. This is where one can actually criticize the project of liberalism that Foucault identifies with a "self-limitation of governmental reason" (2008a: 20). Liberalism seeks to base the type of consent to which Godelier refers by assigning to the market the role of a natural process free from intentionalities of domination. Normalization, thus, becomes a project based on a kind of diffuse automatism of social relations: society considered as market or rather (which amounts to the same thing) market identified with society.

In contemporary societies, normalization (being a process at the center of government practices) should neither be reduced to the imposition of a preexisting norm nor to the forced obedience to rules established by laws. Normalization, although it may have recourse to the techniques of sovereignty and discipline, operates as a mechanism of consent through the technology of security power. Normalization naturalizes security as a scope accepted by all, whereas it is actually a set of mechanisms that only ensures the necessary security for the market to function. Exactly the reverse of the liberal dictum—it is security power that makes it possible for the market to dominate society rather than market mechanisms which guarantee the security of social reproduction.

Biopolitics, the term to mark this specific new condition of government rationality, practice, as well as its legitimizing matrix, is a politics focused on the management of life. Although the term has been developed by Foucault on a somewhat shifting ground, it is a term useful for understanding the inherent contradictions of contemporary normalization processes.

As Foucault suggests in the first volume of the *History of Sexuality*, biopolitics is about "distributing the living on the domain of value and utility" (1978: 144). Biopolitics marks a period in which "life emerges at the centre of political strategies" (Lemke, 2011: 33). Reducing the biopolitical condition to the exercise of a certain modality of power, namely bio-copower, may extinguish the field of contradictions characteristic of biopolitics. When life, the life of the society's members, becomes a stake at issue of political strategies, different political trajectories emerge. Biopower is obviously at the center of biopolitics of domination: It marks a crucial point in the development of capitalism (Foucault, 1978: 141) with "the controlled insertion of bodies into the machinery of production and the adjustment of the phenomena of population to economic processes." (ibid.). And this was made possible by regulating the forces and potentialities of life by ensuring that their development will not threaten the project of government.

Already present in this description of biopower is an impression of the biopolitical field as a terrain of contestations. Supporting life and its productive power does not necessarily guarantee life's docility. "It is not that life has been totally integrated into techniques that govern and administer it, it constantly escapes them" (Foucault, 1978: 143). Faithful to his idea that power and resistance exist and develop together, Foucault suggests here that resistance to biopower may actually develop at the same field that biopower aims to productively control. It is on this point that Hardt and Negri base their idea of the "biopolitical event" as the source of resistance of the multitude (2009: 56–63).

Foucault suggests that "the town posed new specific economic and political problems of government technique" (2009: 64). He refers to the problem of "the integration of the town within central mechanisms of power" (ibid.) in the period from seventeenth century to the beginning of the eighteenth. The emergence of the mechanisms of security is, according to him, the answer to this problem. What today seems to be an undisputable characteristic of big cities, namely the fact that city population changes due to global and national flows (generated by labor precariousness, investment opportunities, displacements because of war, etc.) was, according to Foucault, the main reason for developing the security mechanism of power in the eighteenth-century city governance. Choosing the term *milieu* (Foucault, 2008b and 2009) instead of territory (which can describe the space governed by sovereign feudal power), he opens a field of research that he did not actually develop: Was a distinct form of spatiality developed through the technology of security power that played a crucial role in the shaping of cities from the eighteenth century on? Could we project this question to contemporary urban form? Do contemporary big cities develop as milieux rather than as territories traversed by sovereign power?

It is important first to clarify the spatiality of milieu. Foucault explicitly refers to the origin of the term: Lamarcian ecology (Foucault, 2009: 20). We can see in this choice, not simply a descriptive word but the use of a term that understands the city as predominantly related to life. Security power is focused on controlling the life of urban populations. Studying this living environment thus becomes crucial. However, the multiplicity of the population's characteristics, its inner differentiations (including those that result from the flows already mentioned) as well as the complex interactions of city dwellers with the developing urban milieu require a flexible form of power that ventures to predict and regulate tendencies of urban behavior and action.

Returning to the initial question of urban ordering and to the role the normalization process has in this ordering, we may trace a line that connects the problem of governing urban populations to the technology of security. Today's big cities are treated by sovereign state's power as spaces of growing complexity and multiplicity on which total and uniform control seems impossible. Much in line with the logic of security power, states (and local states alike) study flows and develop statistical models in order to predict and regulate city life. But urban events, small of big, often escape such predictions and the control that aims containing them within patterns of action compatible with capitalist (re)production.

3

Spatial Practices of Repeatability

In contemporary cities, urban ordering develops through the mechanisms of normalization and domestication, as was so far suggested. Both mechanisms need to define an outside in order to ensure that urban ordering functions. For domestication this outside is wilderness, for normalization this outside is the abnormal (presented as a deviant other). Urban ordering is continuously confronting the wild and the abnormal, not simply by exorcising it or attempting to destroy it but also by extending and rearranging the areas of the accepted as orderly. Taming and normalizing practices and procedures are necessary constituents of urban ordering.

What seems to prevail in this contested terrain is a dominant hegemonic tendency to develop patterns of repeatability that ensure predictability. Since urban life, especially in vast metropolitan areas, is being shaped by a myriad of seemingly contingent factors, the project of urban governance needs to be able to predict and mold repeatable behaviors. Rhythmicality (albeit extremely complex in its motifs) seems to be the way to build urban order in a world of flows and formal diversity. Under this diversity, which is often presented by the apologists of current urban order as a proof of individual (and individualized) liberty, lies the patterning order of urban rhythms. But does this mean that repeatable urban practices, urban habits, and urban rituals are simply tools to sustain urban ordering? As I will try to suggest, repeatability may acquire a deviant, dissident, even insurrectionist power too. It is by exploring the power of repeated performances in urban life that we may locate the spatiotemporal potentialities of urban emancipation that emerge in today's metropolises. Let us then see first what forms do such repeatable urban acts take by focusing on the distinct patterns of space linked to those forms.

One crucial characteristic of performances is that they usually correspond to organized series of actions which can be repeated. Repeatability is at the basis of Richard Schechner's definition of performance as "twice behaved behaviour" (1985: 36). What actually constitutes performance (action-as-performance) is an effort to create and express something that may be recognized and repeated. Comparison between performances may establish patterns and thus convey meaning. This is easy to agree upon if we consider a simple example: a repetition of a certain noise, a pattern in noise, makes it a meaningful noise whose source and intention of meaning we tend to search for (even when we guess that it is a noise produced by a machine: What is this machine doing? What is the meaning of this rhythmical sound?).

The most general feature of human repeated behavior is that it mediates social relations. It is precisely this mediation that makes repeated actions expressive. For G. Agamben, "what characterizes gesture is that in it nothing is being produced or acted, but rather something is being endured and supported" (2000: 57). In his view, going beyond the Aristotelian distinction between "praxis" (an action that has aims beyond its execution by producing something) and "poiesis" (an action that is an end in itself, as is politics, for example, or the good deed), repeated acts expose the very possibility of communication. "*The gesture is the exhibition of a mediality: it is the process of making a means visible as such*" (2000: 58, italics in the original).

If in the performance of a gesture something endures according to Agamben, it is, we might say, the gesture's power to mediate. That is why it "opens the sphere of ethos" (2000: 57) as the only intrinsically human field, a field constituted by the communication between people. Gestures and repeated acts in general attempt to construct a communicable duration. This duration constitutes a field of common reference, an ethos: a habit that is jointly considered worthy of continuation. Communicable duration is itself a bond, whatever its content. It is not enough to see recurrent acts as carriers of messages to be read with the use of recognized codes. That would make such acts mere repetitions, more like the repeated on and off of traffic lights. If we want to capture the way in which repeated acts mediate the relationship between their instantaneous manifestation and the impression of duration they convey, we must see them in their rhythmicality. They affirm habits because they are always particular in the conjuncture of their occurrence while at the same time being recognized as familiar. This is probably what Deleuze and Guattari mean when they suggest that "it is the difference that is rhythmic, not the repetition, which nevertheless produces it: productive repetition has nothing to do with reproductive meter" (2004: 346).

The very process of performing gestures is characterized by the dialectic of duration and moment. In the present of its manifestation, performance acquires the value of a momentary suggestion, a gesture that interrupts the flow of time in order to draw attention to something.

Habits in Place

The Potentialities of Habits

Habit at first glance seems to be a means to ensure a future without surprises. In many theories as well as in usual commonsense thinking, habit is the opposite of change, the main obstacle to innovation. Habit is reduced to an acquired, unthought and therefore conservative behavior. However, equating habit to social automatism was strongly criticized.

According to Henri Bergson, habit is to be distinguished from instinct if one searches for the foundation of freedom within the essential characteristics of life. Oversimplifying his view perhaps, one may say that he proposes that habit is the necessary support of life that gives the living being the opportunity to become creative. It is as if unpredictable acts (acts freed from the constraints of instinct) can only take place as long as they are measured by and compared to habits: predictable acts.

In his work on memory, Bergson connects habits, bodily habits especially, to the ways we bring the past into the present. In its development as a pattern of action, as well as in its performances in distinct contingencies, habit in a way repeats a certain condensed and highly selective view of past actions. Habit, thus, is not simple repetition of past actions. It entails a decomposition and recomposition of acts, as Elizabeth Grosz—interpreting Bergson—suggests (Grosz, 2013: 228 see also Bergson, 1988: 80).

In *Matter and Memory*, Bergson distinguishes between two types of memory. "The first records, in the form of memory-images, all the events of our daily life" (1988: 81). The second kind of memory "no longer represents our past to us, it acts it; and if it still deserves the name of memory, it is not because it conserves bygone images, but because it prolongs their useful effect into the present moment" (1988: 82). It is by this second kind of memory that habits are being developed. As Grosz comments, "Habit is incipient action, action anticipated; it is memory accumulated in order to act" (2013: 228).

Habit treats the inherent unpredictability of the present (since life is flow, change) by responding to it through acts that are already known, therefore predictable because they are repeatable and repeated.

What is important in this approach to habit is that it "lies mid-way between an instinct and a consciously chosen action" (Grosz, 2013: 229). Habit is an unconscious, albeit highly labored, summoning of the past in service of the present.

Bergson's approach is not favorable toward habit. Following a long line of thinkers, he considers habit as an obstacle to individual freedom. As he further develops his thoughts in his last work, *The Two Sources of Morality and Religion* (1977), habit introduces between the members of a civic community "a discipline resembling, in the interdependence it establishes between separate individuals, the unity of an organism of anastomotic cells" (1977: 14). However, this unity is not natural. As it is based on a shared feeling of obligation, this unity establishes a kind of second nature (Brown, 2020) and constructs in every individual a part of its self as a "social ego." "To cultivate this social ego is the essence of our obligation to society" says Bergson (1977: 15).

Variation, difference between individuals, and the potentiality of freedom itself arise due to the possibility of choosing to ignore the obligation or to interpret it in different ways. This does not necessarily lead to the Deleuzian affirmation of difference as the result of a kind of creative or generative repetition. However, there seems to exist in Bergson's work a kind of connection between the repeatability of habits and the unfolding of life in time's duration.

We are used to associate memory with something that lasts. We believe that the shared memories of a social group try to preserve the impression of some lasting common characteristics, some traits that, after having become recognizably fixed, remain to characterize the group itself. Such a consciousness of perseverance seems to need its confirmation through a collective recollection of events taken to be the guarantee of a common reference.

Bergson attempted to reduce such duration-oriented human behavior to the very essence of human time. Seeking to question the techniques of subdividing time that science manipulates by objectifying it, he considered that he found in human time pure duration, the enduring force of life that insists on continuing. In his scheme, then, humans primarily experience duration. Time's division into parts or units, events, and moments is an instrumental action that conceals the very essence of the vital momentum, life's creative force (élan *vital*).

Gaston Bachelard, in his critique of Bergson, insists that "the only way we ourselves can feel time is by multiplying conscious instants ... Consciousness of time is always, for us, an awareness of the utilization of instants—it is always active, never passive" (2013: 50). "We do not know how to feel time except by multiplying conscious moments" (ibid.). "There is but one reality: the instant. Duration, habit, and progress are only groupings of instants—the simplest among the phenomena of time" (51). According to this perspective, duration is not a characteristic of time but constitutes an invention of consciousness that attempts to preserve and continue the unity of being. "Since the past is but a memory and the future but a prediction, we will argue that both past and future are essentially no more than habits" (30).

For Bachelard as much as for Bergson, such a discussion moves toward the search for a philosophy of the will. And the most important problem of such a philosophy is the problem of freedom. A philosophy of the will is essentially a philosophy of action. But a philosophy of action, and indeed of socially meaningful action, need not necessarily assume action as arising from an individual consciousness that sets ends. If social acts activate substrates of collective memory, it is because essentially collective memory is nothing more than a performed memory of duration. In its performances, collective memory becomes a constituent of the present. Thus, social acts in their present are, as Bachelard imagines them, restarts. "What persists is always what regenerates itself" (ibid.: 47). Thus for Bachelard "duration, always indirectly grasped, has no force other than that of its creative progress" (ibid.: 48). "Hence, as we stand before the tremendous wealth of choices offered by discontinuous instants linked by habits, we realize that it is possible to speak of *chronotropisms* corresponding to the various rhythms that constitute the living being" (ibid.: 42). Their time is the moment, the signifying, the fertile moment that each time produces the events. A "new beginning" (ibid.: 38) in the perspective of a philosophy of free will relates to a constituent contingency of action and to the opening of possibilities, to the emergence of novelty: "Rather than the continuity of life, it is the discontinuity of birth that ultimately needs to be explained" (ibid.: 39).

Bachelard would thus condense a view on habit that departs from the idea of pure repetition: "To seize habit in its essence, it is therefore necessary to seize it in its growth. Thus, by its incremental successes, habit becomes the synthesis of novelty and routine, and that synthesis is crystallized through fertile instants" (ibid.: 38).

The idea of "new beginnings" in the perspective of a sociology of action may mean that at any given moment in time actions must invent relations, express tendencies, while processing at the same time what memory can offer as resources, as knowledge and as the ground on which skills grow. Do these constitute fixed instructions of behavior that attempt to anticipate the future? In such a case, memory's sole role would be to offer a model to be repeated. And duration would merely be a form of repetition. To endure in this case means to remain the same. But in sociology, habit, hexis, needs to be problematized in its relation to the particular. The adaptation of a habit to circumstances requires changes. The schema of "new beginnings" can therefore indicate a process in which the invention of duration can be explained precisely in terms of the needs arising in practices of adaptation. And what is adaptation, after all, but a continuous production or, more correctly, renegotiation of the meaning of social actions?

Pierre Bourdieu seems to develop his thoughts on practice in a direction comparable to that of Bergson up to a point. He indeed considers practice as guided by stable and repeatable dispositions inculcated to individuals during their life in the context of a specific society (1992). What he refers to as habitus is the structured sum of those dispositions that characterize every socially constituted subject in a distinct moment of his and her history. And, like Bergson, he considers this characteristic structure as not easily accessible to reflection and conscious thinking. Habitus, "embodied history, internalized as a second nature and so forgotten as history" (1992: 56), works below the radar of critical knowledge, by becoming a kind of tacit knowledge (1977: 165–8). Bourdieu, however, greatly differs from Bergson on the matter of repeatability of practices. For him, habitus supports a kind of "regulated improvisation" (1992: 57 and 1977: 21 and 78), since society's members have themselves to find ways to use the acquired tacit knowledge in differing circumstances. That is why habitus is actually schematized in forms of possible behavior rather than in rules that exhaust the unpredictability of reality instructions of the type "when in A do B." Bourdieu describes this process as "conditioned and conditional freedom" (1977: 95).

Practices are not only characterized by the spaces that shape them but also, predominantly perhaps, by their tempo. Correspondences, mutual exchanges, reciprocal acts, and organized sets of practices depend on a feeling of time that is a crucial element of inculcated habitus. Repetition, thus, is not mechanical, neither does it refer to identical acts. It is rather a process that establishes rhythmicalities, which vary since they depend on different circumstances rather than on identical contexts. Tempo is what gives each practice its singular character although it is recognizable as having already happened in the past. A practice is "temporally structured" and it "is intrinsically defined by its *tempo*" (Bourdieu 1977: 8, italics in the original).

However, there emerge, in certain historical conjunctures, conditions under which habitus cannot provide the members of a society with solutions to problems of practice. Habitus then is opened to possible transformations. Bourdieu insists that "habitus helps to determine what transforms it" (2000: 149). This means that the power of habitus cannot simply be surpassed. And the important point is that the dispositions on which habitus is based exist "in a virtual state like a soldier's courage in the absence of war" (ibid.).

It is not by chance that Bourdieu uses the term habitus instead of the term habit: "I said habitus so as *not* to say habit—that is, the generative (if not creative) capacity inscribed in the system of dispositions as an *art*, in the strongest sense of practical mastery, and in particular as an *ars inveniedi*" (Bourdieu and Wacquant, 1992: 122, italics in original).

This approach helps to overcome the dilemma that transverses almost all discussions on the character of habits: habitus is neither a process of repetitive practices that are fully predetermined (and thus perceived as mere repetitions of the same), nor a process of idiosyncratic acts that are open to an unlimited possibility of differentiations. Habitus is a product of history and has its roots in the specific history of each socially shaped individual. That is why it may construct each one's history but also be opened by the challenges of history proper. And those challenges, either developed in social crises or in personal crises, may indeed produce new patterns of action and may develop practices which will contribute to the shaping of a different habitus.

Judith Butler is very well known for her approach to gender as performed and performative: "Gender is always a doing, though not a doing by a subject who might be said to preexist the deed" (1999: 33). This view, which puts an emphasis on the act rather than the identity of the actor, can be integrated to a theory on habits that sees them as recurrent performances rather than as indications of established identities. Of course, Butler focuses on issues of gender, and her aim is to oppose essentialist approaches to gender differences (including some feminist ones). She thus clearly states that "there is no gender identity behind the expressions of gender; ... identity is performatively constituted by the very 'expressions' that are said to be its results" (ibid.). From this follows that the gendered body "has no ontological status apart from the various acts which constitute its reality (1999: 173).

Gender performances are not simply acts that prove, so to speak, an identity while being recognized as instances of appropriate behavior for men or women. Gender performances are expressive; they are focused on expressing gender. What Butler insists upon is that it is those expressions that constitute gender identities. They are meant to be taken as expressions of an identity that is socially defined and taken to be a reality. Repetition of those expressive acts is necessary in order to ensure that one is the gender that he or she expresses. "Repetition is at once a reenactment and reexperiencing of a set of meanings already socially established; and it is the mundane and ritualized form of their legitimation" (1999: 178). Repetition, thus, constitutes a way of being as a member of a society that is "tenuously constituted in time (1999: 179). The question is: does this "stylized repetition of acts" (ibid.) depart, (or has the potentiality to depart), from a taxonomy of socially recognized identities or is this simply the means through which this taxonomy is reproduced?

To discover potentialities in the performance of recurrent expressive acts, one may focus on the individualizing opportunities inherent in the performance itself. One may perform a gender-expressive act differently from someone else, although the result may be taken to indicate the identity of a "woman." However, Butler's search is not in the direction of individualized performances that may open different possibilities of being (experiencing, feeling) a gendered self. She targets the inherent contradiction that makes gender performances open to different possible gender identities. And this contradiction lies in the discontinuity of "gender norms" (1999: 179) and the inherent impossibility of "compulsory heterosexuality" (1999: 180). No matter how often performances of socially sanctioned gender identities (or roles) occur, there will always be, according to this reasoning, a gap, a discontinuity, a failure that reveals "the temporal and contingent groundlessness" (1999: 174) of the identities themselves.

This idea may possibly be interpreted as follows: Social training aims at reproducing specific modes of behavior (and thinking) by grounding them on the considered-as-natural difference between man and woman. This kind of legitimation of the assigned roles based on natural characteristics needs to be proven again and again by the repetition of performances. Men and women need to repeat their gendered selves in order to prove their being men or women. Repeatability is both the strong point of social training and its weakest because repeatability is open to time and to the contingencies that may generate "de-formities" or even "parodic repetitions" (ibid.). If the ordinary is not simply what is there as naturally given but needs to recur in order to endure, then non-ordinary meanings and acts may emerge when repetitions unfold in wrong contexts (or in unpredicted contexts). Any kind of act, no matter how meticulously prescribed within codes of behavior, can never be fully predetermined since the context of its actualization is never fully predeterminable.

In Butler's analysis of speech acts, the fact that "contexts are never fully determined in advance" produces "the possibility for the speech act to take on a non-ordinary meaning, to function in contexts where it has not belonged" (1997: 161). This is how, for example, "the word that wounds becomes an instrument of resistance in the redeployment that destroys the prior territory of its operation" (1997: 163). Performative acts that acquire a dissident potentiality may *cite*, that is, repeat, in an unexpected context, a word or a typical gesture thus rendering it capable of producing a different or, even, reverse meaning.

Butler thinks that "this kind of citation will emerge as *theatrical* to the extent that it *mimes and renders hyperbolic* the discursive convention that it also *reverses*" (1993: 232, emphasis in the original). A lot can be said about the significance of theatricality in contesting norms of behavior, race, culture, ethnicity, and class. The important point is, however, that a kind of repetition of behavior through exaggeration, through hyperbolic emphasis on the exactness of repetition, or through minor deviations that expose discontinuities, may indeed reverse the meaning of repetition.

To generalize, performances may establish habits and thus express enduring identities but may also fail to repeat themselves or may take place in unanticipated contexts and thus produce unexpected effects. The conscious decontextualization of habit performances and the parodic repetition, which makes contingent failure its hidden programmatic accomplishment, are ways through which performances may signal change.

It is interesting to compare this approach that finds in repetition the potentiality of change and transgression with Virno's analysis of jokes. According to him "Jokers are the diagram of innovative action ... Jokes are the sociolinguistic diagram of the undertakings that, on the occasion of a historical or biographical crisis, interrupt the circular flux of experience" (2008: 73). Jokes play on a fundamental uncertainty, the uncertainty experienced in applying a rule since no rule may effectively determine the conditions of its application (2008: 119). This fundamental uncertainty is at the basis of creativity and decision: Innovation is always a condition that becomes possible due to this uncertainty. It is exactly in the same way that words and grammatical rules cannot predetermine the construction of a certain utterance, thus opening the discourse to a creativity supported by the contingency of its happening. "The point of honor of the witty remark lies in its ability to show many different ways one can apply the same rule" (2008: 119).

We may compare innovative action that arises in the creative potentialities produced by the essentially uncertain conditions under which every rule may be applied with the divergent parodic and decontextualizing appropriation of gender performances described by Butler. In both cases, it is not the heroic clash with the rules or patterns of imposed behavior that produces the possibility of divergence (or even "exodus" in Virno's terminology) but the innovative as well as the oblique and partially failed appropriation of norms that opens them to change.

The drama and the "dead end" of avant-garde action must be surpassed. Emancipation needs to cultivate new habits, in, against, and beyond the society of exploitation. Emancipation should not be identified with the creation of the new man ex nihilo, posing as the "uncontaminated," "pristine," and free man of the future. Performing potentialities means, thus, excavating through action the means and the scopes of human emancipation by challenging the imposed limits of the possible. And this of course may happen either through the slow transformation of everyday habits or in the sudden shocks of social ruptures and upheavals during which potentialities become visible while being performed. In such explosive circumstances, "naturalized" reality is revealed to be crafted by those who dominate.

Habit, unhinged from the regulating trajectories of automatism, can truly be an area of collective inventiveness. Lefebvre's comparison of habitual behavior with cyclical rhythmicality (in contrast to machine-like linear rhythmicality) as well as Bourdieu's approach to habitus as the source of regulated improvisation and vitalist and neo-vitalist views on habit that consider it as a force that enhances life's openness (opening living beings to new characteristics and capacities—Grosz, 2013: 233) actually converge on a reappraisal of habit: Habit becomes a dynamic process through which the future is neither merely a repetition of the past nor a totally alien unpredictable milieu. Habit actually creates potentialities, habit potentializes the present through a kind of unconscious, nonreflective relation with the past. Seen as a network of relations within a collectivity (a group, a society, etc.) habit actually intervenes inventively in this collectivity's future. To keep this process open enough, to allow adaptability not to be reduced to automatism, the collectivity needs to be alert and open to the potentialities that habits give rise to. Potentialities thus may become the forces that will shape new habits. Change will be crafted by the materials, the tools, and the creations of the past as they are redeemed in the performance of potentialities in the present.

Habits as Place-Making Practices

Bourdieu locates lived space as one of the most important sources for the inculcation of habitus. Insisting that we acquire our habitus not by explicitly learning to follow rules of behavior but through our body in all its abilities and capacities, he points out that space directs and shapes our postures, acts, and movements in ways that form patterns of repeatable practices. Of course, he does integrate with this approach to lived space an appraisal of lived time.

Bourdieu believes that habitus is being predominantly inculcated through the use of lived space in societies where educational systems are not as powerful and as organized as in the industrial societies. Space, the everyday space of the settlement and the house, becomes an educational system itself in which the young learn how to follow patterns of behaviors concerning their relations to the elderly, how to work, how to treat gender differences, how to use everyday objects, and so on. And they learn this with no explicit instructions referring to the moral or productive meaning of acts but rather through "structural exercises" (Bourdieu, 1977: 88) that predominantly arrange bodies in lived space.

Using a controversial distinction that is employed differently by different scholars of spatial theory, geography and sociology, habit may be linked to place rather than space. Habit is a place-making activity if by this we mean a set of repeated practices that not only are based on the idea that a certain space remains fixed and endures change but also performatively indeed ensure this non-change. This obviously goes against the reality of incessant transformations of spaces that unfold in the minor or major events of inhabiting. Places remain the same because they are experienced and understood as possessing an identity that prevails. Actually, there is no other way to define identity than to equate it with characteristics that persist, that endure, which means that they happen again, in the same way in time.

If we follow Gaston Bachelard, we need to analyze the importance of places in human dwelling by exploring a certain attitude that looks for "the space we love," "felicitous space," and "eulogized space" (Casey, 1997: 289; Bachelard, 1994: xxxv). As Bachelard describes his project in *the Poetics of Space*, "the images I want to examine are quite simple images of felicitous space. In this orientation, these investigations deserve to be called topophilia" (1994: xxxv). Bachelard, thus, suggests that being connected to a place is the result of a happy experience, especially of those happy experiences that mark an initial joy of identifying with the place we were born in. "The house we were born in is physically inscribed in us. It is a group of organic habits" (ibid.: 14). Happy memories seem to equip us with the means to find places, to inhabit places: The memory of the initial house we were born in provides us with a capacity of place making.

It seems that, for Bachelard, habit is not simply a pattern of behavior. It is more like an embodied disposition of inhabiting space and time. Memory and imagination activate these dispositions, and what is experienced in felicitous space is the "return" to an (imagined, sought for, remembered?) condition of happy, unthreatened, life. In a revealing image, Bachelard stages the degree zero of such happiness in the act of the mimetic animal hiding motionless by reducing its form to the form of its surrounding. This amounts to "carrying the tranquility of inhabiting to the point of culmination, not to say, imprudence" (ibid.: 132). Such an image of course points to a limit that is not even desirable for humans. However, it somehow condenses the ultimate, and completely maintainable, perhaps, scope of habit—to reduce life to its surrounding considered as fixed. In reality, this dream of total protection in complete stasis is only open to repeated efforts that try to adjust to an ever-changing environment. Of course, mimetic insects need to hide in environments that have certain characteristics, so their repertoire of mimicking is not perhaps utterly unfathomable. But their nonhuman behavior possibly reveals something of the impossible drama of habit: Never is one faced with circumstances that are being repeated *in toto*. So, habit struggles to reduce contingent differences to be understood as prevailing similarities, and changes to repetitions. Maybe Bachelard's idea of "organic habits," which stem from an initial happy home, gestures toward the impossible. Human life, however, struggles against such impossibility in a stubborn effort to persist in spite of everything that changes.

Topophilia may explain a certain attitude of seeking happiness in dwelling but it may certainly not exhaust the possibilities of being happy in the world. History and anthropology may provide us with a myriad of examples in which happy dwelling becomes a place-making activity with different, even contrasting priorities and dispositions. After all, to challenge Bechelard's presuppositions, for lots of people the house (or the place) they were born in was not necessarily a happy place. Place making is a socially developed capacity that may acquire different forms. What seems to be equally present in the development of such a capacity in different societies is the effort, the drama of habit: In habit and through habit people inhabit.

Habits, although usually understood as promoting stability and predictability, are essentially linked to a selective and inventive reappraisal of the past aimed at guiding future acts. Urban habits cannot be separated from the spaces in which they originated as reappraisals of past acts. And they are further corroborated as such spaces persist. Inhabiting the metropolis in this perspective might mean finding places that are suitable for the acquired habits of generating spaces to accommodate those habits. Habits rely on space, habits interact with spatial conditions, and, thus, habits shape space while being shaped by it through adaptation.

The question is: What processes allow people to develop habits that shape a different social condition? Are there forms of habits that enhance, support, and sustain the making of relations of cooperation and solidarity in equality? How do such habits possibly shape spaces of living together? And since the habits of the future draw upon existing habits, how do such transformations take place? As we will see, three areas of social inventiveness may possibly generate such liberating habits: the building of autonomous communities of commoning, the shaping of egalitarian cooperation practices, and the creation of new urban imaginaries.

Rituals and the "Magic Circle"

Ritual as Performance

Whereas habits are space sensitive and the repeatability of actions they promote adapts to specific spatial (and temporal, of course) conditions, rituals seem to be based on repeatable practices that tend to ignore, or at least put into brackets, spatial specificities.

Ritual performances create their own meaningful spatiotemporal context, a magic circle within which a coherent and total universe of meaning is constructed. Even the so-called commemoration rituals that at first glance seem to be site specific (celebrating a past event on the event's site) are actually unfolding in a space they create that temporarily transforms the commemorated site into a stage for memory performances.

It is Marcel Mauss in his path breaking work *A General Theory of Magic*, who brought attention to the fact that "the time and place of ritual are strictly prescribed" (2001: 56). And further developing this observation, he remarks, concerning the ritual practices of magic: "If the spot has no special characteristic the magician may draw a magical circle or square, a *templum*, around him and he performs his magic inside this" (ibid.: 58, italics in the original).

The act of the magician seems to be the act of anyone in charge of instituting or performing a ritual: It always becomes necessary to explicitly separate acts and words as well as space and time from the everyday flow of habitual exchanges. The "differentiated magical milieu" (ibid.: 61) Mauss talks about is marked off and circumscribed in ways that distinguish it beyond doubt from the experienced space of the community.

Bourdieu advances the logic of the magic circle one step further. He is particularly interested in the efficacy of rituals, their power that is, to produce real effects in the life and beliefs of those affected by these performances. Explicitly and repeatedly connecting rituals to a kind of preformed social magic (1991: 119–23), he puts an emphasis on the practice rather than on the attributed (or considered) meanings that are supposed to be established through rituals. Since practices for Bourdieu unfold according to an inherently practical logic which is not reducible to the logic of a distantiated observer, we need to understand ritual practices without reducing them to a model that condenses them.

"Practice is not *in* time but *makes* time (human time, as opposed to biological or astronomical time)" (2000: 206, italics in the original). You cannot, then, separate practice from the agent who performs it and, thus, you must take into account the ways this specific agent treats time as an integral element of practice. Tempo describes both practice and the agent. But such a capacity to treat time and tempo is not the result of an explicit knowledge or of a set of rules to be obeyed. Those who participate in a specific set of repeated and repeatable practices (ritual practices included) learn with their bodies ways of doing, which have been inculcated as bodily hexis.

Recognizing the limits and in this way ensuring the efficacy of ritual practice is something to be learned by participating in rituals and by being instructed on how to be able to do so through indications that are not reducible to reflexive thinking. We may easily deduce from this argument that recognizing the proper space of ritual and the limits of the magic circle (or, in Bourdieu's terminology, recognizing the area in which social magic is effective) is part of a social knowledge translated into body postures, body movements, and, we might add, types of shared experiences (for example feeling the cold of snow, the smell of grass, the taste of rice, the fear of a volcano, the joy of hunting, and so on, all of them meaningful within a specific society and a concrete social context—the smell of grass while ploughing, the joy of hunting in a society of hunters, and so on).

What Bourdieu adds to the concreteness of the magic circle is the embodied knowledge which constructs it and gives meaning to it, and at the same time, performs it, that is, brings it into existence each time the ritual is performed.

Catherine Bell, a religious studies scholar especially devoted to the study of rituals, also highlights the crucial role that demarcated distinct spaces play in the "ritual ways of acting." Ritualization is based on "the interaction of the social body with a structured and structuring environment" (1997: 209). A central characteristic of ritual acts is "the primacy of the body moving about within a specially constructed space, simultaneously defining (imposing) and experiencing (receiving) the values ordering the environment" (1997: 82). It is important to observe that although her approach to ritual comes from a different perspective (probably aiming to rescue personal autonomy in the context of religious rituals usually equated to a total immersion in a belief), she shares with many theorists (including Bourdieu, as we saw) an emphasis on ritual as practice rather than as a universe of meaning or a representation of a worldview (1992, 1997).

Rituals are repetitive performances. And as in the case of habits, rituals actually aim at shaping behavior. Only they do this in a different way. Habits are directly productive of actions. Rituals direct attention to the meaning of future actions. According to Luc Boltanski, rituals manage to enhance common belief in the constructed reality that each society produces and inhabits. But they are not to be equated with ideology. In rituals, "symbolic forms" and "states of affairs" are "indissolubly superimposed" (2011: 82). This is another way of saying that the symbolic dimension acquires the power to shape reality by being inseparable from it. The ritual of marriage creates a reality for the couple and the ritual of initiation creates the reality of a warrior, of a citizen, or of an elite group (of priests, of leading scholars, and so on).

An emphasis on stylization and a focus on form and ways of doing gives rituals the power to organize patterns of behavior by essentially condensing beforehand behavior's meaning. It is not easy to agree with Boltanski, though, that the emphasis on form is to be distinguished from an emphasis on the "functional consequences of what is done (and said)" (ibid.: 81). There are consequences that actually transform the status of certain people in rituals. Ritual practices are to be distinguished from the non-ritual ones not because they have no functional consequences but because they result in creating a kind of idealized setting, a magic circle, a laboratory for reproducing the essentials of a society's reality. And this process is a crucial social function, if we choose to use the term "function" for describing social life.

Byung-Chul Han explicitly connects the current diminishing importance of rituals (for him "the disappearance of rituals"), with the advance of neoliberalism. According to his approach, neoliberalism shapes a predominant "compulsion to produce" and an ethics of "communication without community" (2020: 1). Both those predominant tendencies destroy community bonds and develop individualism through a "narcissistic cult of authenticity" (ibid.: 21), "an obvious decay of the social" (ibid.: 18), and a "culture of interiority" in which the public expression gives way to "a pornographic exhibition of the private" (ibid.: 21). In place of such a diagnosed social condition, he proposes the rediscovery of play and ceremonial acts as forms that mediate and shape the social. "Rituals ... bring people together and create an alliance, a wholeness, a community" (ibid.: 6).

Interestingly, Han connects rituals to a closure in space and time. Hen contrasts the experience of closure with a continuously escalating demand for developed performances, production, "extensivity" (ibid.: 7), and seriality ("serial habitus") all of which characterize the neoliberal regime. However, closure, as he admits, is not "invariably positive," "given the possibility of violence associated with a fundamentalist closure of sites" (ibid.: 32).

Here lies a challenging potentiality of rituals rediscovered and reclaimed. How can ritual practices transcend the closure of a community as well as the closure of time (trapped in the eternal) in search of a creativity immersed in history? How can rituals support a rediscovery of history as a process of collective creativity in place of the dominant practices of consumption oriented exclusively toward the present? It seems paradoxical to ask for openness in processes essentially based on the production of repeated performances within a "magic circle" (Mauss, 2001; Hastrup, 2004; Bourdieu, 2000). These are processes that seemingly employ a kind for temporality that refutes change (time that stands still in Han's description) and a kind of spatiality that epitomizes spatial closure—a closure that ignores its outside.

Rituals in Change

There are three main ways through which ritual may be connected to change. The first one has to do with the expected, heavily controlled, and necessary change through which members of a society pass from one kind of social status or identity to another (this kind of change is broadly the one implicated in initiation rituals). The second one has to do with changes that emerge within a specific society and have to do with events related to unexpected (or not easily manageable) natural phenomena (plague, natural disasters, etc.). Prophylactic rituals or rituals that attempt to restore the social balance after such events can be included in this category. And, interestingly, healing rituals may be included too, since they mediate between a threat that has attacked an individual member and the community which will "reclaim" its temporarily lost member (sometimes through the mediation of a shaman or a sorcerer).

The last case includes the use of rituals in circumstances in which the society has experienced a major change due to an important crisis. This includes cases of radical restructuring of social relations due to a major social rupture coming from within the society (insurgency, revolution) or to one coming from "outside" (colonial takeover, war, forced displacement).

According to Bruce Kapferer, magic, sorcery, and witchcraft emerge in spaces of "disjunction, dislocation and discontinuity" (2002: 22 as referred in Della Costa, 2022: 11), "apart from everyday life" (ibid.). He calls these spaces "phantasmagoric" (ibid., also 2010: 244) and directly connects them with the opening of "all kinds of potentialities of human experience" (2010: 244). His approach may be used to support the idea that in those spaces set apart from the ordinary flow of everydayness, change may be tested as well as—depending on the circumstances—be reintegrated into the existing social order.

It is important not to confuse magic circle with context in general. As Luc Boltanski suggests, "The very idea of context, in the sense of conditions relatively independent of actions performed or words spoken, to which these actions and words should therefore be adjusted, at the price of variations based on interpretations, is, at least in principle, quite foreign to ritual" (2011: 88).

Whereas every act acquires its specific meaning and efficacy within a specific social context, ritual acts appear as meaningful only within a kind of contexts that are specifically defined for them. But that is not all. Ritual acts seem to acquire their power by affecting life outside the magic circle. This may possibly be done when ritual acts overspill the boundaries of the circle. But, interestingly, it is especially by being contained within the circle that ritual acts exert their power on the circle's outside. By being able to enter and exit those separated worlds, social members may actually compare, may make connections, or enhance distinctions. This for Kirsten Hastrup becomes a general characteristic of human action. For her, "social agents in general inhabit a comparable site of passage ... agents potentially expand the limits of the now" (2004: 111).

The spatiality of the magic circle cannot be reduced, then, to the spatiality of place, to a spatial arrangement, that is, which has the specificity of a defined context. Magic circle is locatable but its radiance depends on the social conditions that surround it as well as institute it. In search of the spatialities of potentiality, we may learn a lot from this particular performativity of ritual spaces. They are not mere stages of strange, "non-ordinary" enactments but temporary in-between worlds in which space is actually potentialized.

Bruce Kapferer attempts to theorize rituals as a particular kind of practice (although he avoids what he considers as an almost impossible task, the proposal of a definition), by focusing on what he terms as "the virtual reality to ritual" (2010: 244). This approach, explicitly referring to his own ethnographic work on healing rituals (in Sri Lanka), may possibly include all three types of change that rituals seem to deal with.

Rituals considered as virtual realities (neither simply illusions nor representations of reality) become for Kapferer "the means for entering directly within the habitus and adjusting its parameters" (ibid.: 245). If this is true, rituals have the power to accommodate change by providing participants with the means to shape behaviors that will deal with changed circumstances. If this is made possible under the strict protocols of initiation rites, there is however also the possibility that a sought-for change will make such rites become the incubators of deviance. Victor Turner was already exploring this potentiality in his exploration of liminoid phenomena as we will soon see.

Rituals in this approach are more than processes; they are considered as practices that develop a particular kind of "dynamics." Potentiality, thus, is developed within the performance of a rite both through the transformation of the perceptual and cognitive conditions of the participants as well as by "effecting radical adjustments and transformations or disjunctive transmutations of major historical significance" (ibid.: 239). Kapferer provides as an example the case of "the British appropriation of the annual festival of kingship [in Sri Lanka] to support colonial political interests. The festival was continued with the critical difference that it celebrated the British ascendancy over the Sinhalese" (ibid.: 240). In this case, the colonial rule was integrated into a preexisting cosmological and social order.

Kapferer's approach, however, is less convincing in his suggestion that rituals slow down "the tempo of ordinary life" (ibid.: 245) "[The] chaotic dimension (or chaosmos) of ordinary lived processes constitutes the reality of actuality" (ibid.: 244) as opposed to the virtual reality of the ritual. Ordinary life is far from being chaotic, however. The promises of urban order have already been described in this book. If chaotic is latently equated to the everyday experiences of precarity and insecurity, then ritual virtuality is reduced to a healing practice meant to reinstall compliance. The potentiality of change that could be connected to the idea of virtuality is thus reduced to a pacifying mechanism.

Here perhaps lies the link of ritual practices with performances of potentialization. Rituals predominantly accommodate change in ways that do not challenge a society's dominant order—what Victor Turner terms structure (1977: 166–7)—that supports the order of the sensible, the way Rancière understands it. But to do so they must face change. To contain change within the limits of the existing social order means to expose the society's members to a pre-fabricated, predictable, and thus repeatable change. In initiation rituals or, generally, in rites of passage, change is to be contained within an established set of identities and roles. However, as Turner observes, during the in-between period in which initiands are not any more what they were (boys, single, outsiders, etc.) but not yet what they are supposed to become (warriors, married, secret society members, etc.), a challenging experience emerges. Turner terms it "communitas" to indicate a condition of social existence that "breaks in through the interstices of [social] structure" (1977: 128).

This collective experience of the initiands unveils in a peculiar way the constructed nature of social identities, since they are exposed to a kind of reduction to a degree zero of social existence—"a strong sentiment of 'humankindness,' sense of the generic social bond between all members of society" (ibid.: 116)—in order to become ready to enter a new identity.

This might mean that accommodating change is not a totally guaranteed process. Social reproduction is exposed to the dangers of deviant behavior that might be developed in conditions of liminality. In Turner's reasoning, "No society can function adequately without this dialectics [structure-communitas-structure]" (Turner, 1977: 129). It may even be that social order (and urban order) needs to be reconfirmed through rituals but it can be challenged through "misfired" rituals too. In Boltanski's terminology, a ritual "fails" when "its artefactual mode of being" is exposed. Thus, the constructed character of reality becomes apparent "whereas [the ritual's] orientation is completely geared to the objective intention of reducing the differential between reality and the world" (2011: 88). For Boltanski, "world" is what exists and "reality" is the way a world is presented and lived within a specific society.

Turner talks about the "liminal areas," "which cannot be captured in the classificatory nets of... quotidian, routinized fields of action" (1977: vii). And he goes on to suggest: "The antistructural liminality provided in the cores of ritual and aesthetic forms represents the reflexivity of the social process, wherein society becomes at once subject and direct object; it represents also its subjunctive mood, where suppositions, desires, hypotheses, possibilities, and so forth, all become legitimate" (ibid.).

From such a reasoning grows Turner's view, which distances him from a merely functional approach according to which rituals are a "sort of all-purpose social glue": "As a 'model for' ritual can anticipate, even generate change; as a 'model of,' it may inscribe order in the minds, hearts and will of participants" (1982: 82).

In direct dialog with performance theorists as Richard Schechner, Turner puts an emphasis on the possibilities of deviance that arise in the context of liminal experiences. Attempting to locate the role of such experiences in the societies that emerged after the Industrial Revolution, he finds an essential characteristic of those societies that modify the potentialities of liminality: the harsh and definitive separation of work from leisure (1977). "One works at the liminal, one plays with the liminoid" (1977: 55). In this almost enigmatic phrase, Turner attempts to capture various levels of ambivalence. Liminal experiences are meant to reproduce structure. Work is predominantly structured in these societies and the reproduction of work habits and rules is corroborated by rituals that look a lot like the ones preindustrial revolution societies used to employ in order to ensure their own reproduction. One is tempted to compare, however, the potentialities of communitas in preindustrial rituals of initiation with the potentialities of communitas in the industrial controlled collective work (in the factory or in several service sector workspaces). While the conditions of communitas are necessary for the capitalist command of work to be effective, the experience of cooperation as we shall see carries with it the seed of sharing.

Leisure is presented as the opposite of work in "complex modern societies," as Turners labels them (ibid.). And in the activities of leisure a certain kind of playfulness emerges, reminiscent of the ludic element that was once an integral part of work and ritual activities. Where, however, a link to an almost obsolete past emerges is in practices of a free, non-commodified kind, such as "Mardi Gras, Charivari" and "home entertainments of various kinds." For Turner, these liminoid practices are often "cultural debris of some forgotten liminal ritual" (ibid.). As we will see in the chapter *Rituals in Community Building*, contemporary rituals may be a lot more than debris of the past. They may support both the reinvention of community through commoning and the liberation of cooperation from capitalist command.

A different approach to rituals may contribute to the problematization of their relation to the corresponding society's everyday reality. In a collective interdisciplinary work titled *Ritual and Its Consequences*, the authors "posit ritual action as a subjunctively shared arena, a space in between" (Seligman et al., 2008: 26). Stated in this phrase are two important claims. The first one is that rituals should be included in the area of the subjunctive. This means that they are meant to support the creation of possible worlds, "the creation of an order *as if* it were truly the case" (ibid.: 20, italics in original). The authors insist that this kind of human-made order, this effort to construct the shared impression of an ordered world (including nature and society, distinguished or not, depending on the worldview each distinct society develops), is in incongruity with the "lived reality" the participants of the rituals experience in their everyday life. The construction of "as if" necessarily entails a kind of creativity. According to the authors, "what constitutes society ... is precisely a shared 'could be', a mutual illusion of the sort that all rituals create" (ibid.: 23). Thus, "what we share as symbolic beings is potentiality" (ibid.). The experience of "as if" essentially constructs an area of possibilities and thus develops an exploration of "what if."

Creativity however, and especially the collective creativity that rituals entail, can either be reduced to a never-ending effort to collectively project order into chaos (a never-ending task according to the authors since the real world is essentially fragmented and chaotic), or understood as a force that may challenge and transform the reality of a specific society. Again, as in the objections raised concerning Kapferer's description of rituals' relation to an outer chaotic world, it is crucially important to distinguish between a kind of conservative or adaptive role of ritual practices from a potentially disruptive role that opens paths to social change.

Indeed, as the authors suggest, we need to go beyond Radcliffe-Brown's idea that rituals are only meant to support social cohesion as well as beyond Clifford Geertz's idea that ritual practices construct a coherent system of meanings, a worldview. In both cases the potentialities inherent in the workings of ritual are ignored in favor of a view that reduces rituals to mechanisms of social reproduction. However, "to think of ritual in terms of ... an endlessly doomed dynamic" (ibid.: 30) equates the repetitiveness of rituals to a tragic effort to bring order to a world otherwise perceived as fragmented and fractured. The power to impose a consoling order to a chaotic world is in this respect only temporarily successful; that is why the efforts of the ritual need to be recurrent. Opposing the idea that a worldview may be condensed and maintained in a ritual world, the authors suggest that the ritual worlds are necessarily tragic, because they always have to struggle against a shared experience of a world outside the magic circle that is inherently unpredictable, threatening, unruly, and fragmented.

However, reducing the lived experience of a society's members to a feeling of being in a chaotic world ignores the possibility of people feeling the kind of violence that comes from the imposition of a social (as well as spatiotemporal) order that excludes them, suppresses them, and exploits them. Rituals do not attempt to impose order on the allegedly unordered universe or perception. They may be either directed toward the corroboration of the existing order or open passages to a possible different order. In both cases, the subjunctive orientation is necessary. In the first one, rituals teach people how to act by transforming real threats to social order to symbolic ones so as to stage exercises in propriety (as in the ritualistic staging of war in games in which killing is only symbolic). In the second one, as we will see, the as-if mode opens the opportunity to envisage and to experience on a symbolic level different conditions of sociality that possibly gesture toward different forms of social organization. Turner's communitas may be describing such a possibility. It is not by chance that movements oriented toward social change establish rituals that rehearse the social relations of a society to come.

Catherine Bell sees resistance as a process that is intrinsic in the relation of every individual practitioner with the ritual she or he participates in. Basing her thoughts on Foucault's assertion that there can be no domination without resistance she suggests: "The strategies of ritualization clearly generate forms of practice and empowerment capable of articulating an understanding of the personal self vis-a-vis community, however these might be understood" (1992: 217). Resistance may take the form of "negotiated consent" allowing room for personalized interpretations or of "the pursuit of alternative ritual activities" (ibid.: 215). This is not to defy, though, that power ritualization has to support and reproduce dominant relations of power. Thus, "Ritualization can ... take arbitrary or necessary common interests and ground them in an understanding of the hegemonic order; it can empower agents in limited and highly negotiated ways" (ibid.: 222).

The second claim included in the phrase mentioned above is that the ritual world (contained in what so far has been termed as the magic circle) is a kind of intermediary area ("a space between"), mediating between the human and that which the human conceives as an outer world. The authors compare this area with the "transitional object," a term the psychologist Donald Winnicott uses for an object that mediates between the infant and its environment (1989). Within this area, cultural creativity unfolds. Potentiality arises because in the intermediary area of ritual, the repeatability of words and acts is a part of the effort to adjust to situations that change. The comparison with the transitional object lies in the fact that as in the use of this object, a subject is constituted through a necessary illusion: that the world out there is both distinct and at the same time the subject's creation. What the authors seem to suggest is that the ritual as-if has a similar illusion at its basis (this time a shared one), which becomes the driving force of a collective creativity. Between total innovation and total obedience to established canons, rituals provide the canvas of cultural creativity that ensures the autonomy of each individual act: Instead of being a set of prohibitions and dictates (thus being an imposed order of behavior rules), rituals, according to this approach are, one could say, laboratories of propriety. They may of course also be treated as means solely to ensure the strictness of the canon (the order they project to lived chaos). According to the authors, this reduces ritual to practices of "endless compulsive repetition" (ibid.: 41). One could say that in this case rituals try to totally efface the constitutive tension between social reality and performances of the as-if mode. Opposing this reduction of ritual acts to mere forced repetition, the authors suggest that ritual is "a recurrent, always imperfect project of dealing with patterns of human behavior—patterns that are always at risk of shifting into dangerous directions—or of unleashing demons [that is, the threatening chaos of the world]" (ibid.: 42).

The authors of *Rituals and Its Consequences* as well as Turner in his work insist that rituals are meant to sustain order. The first consider this order temporary—fictitious but with real effects on people's lives—and, essentially, a never-ending process. Turner sees this kind of order as part of a dialectics that reproduces social structure. In both cases, however, ritual is considered to carry the potentiality of change. Collective creativity is to be found in the adaptive and conservative role of rituals as well as in the openings to change that rituals inherently carry. It is important, however, to keep from these approaches the idea that rituals are practices, forms of repeated collective action. They thus should not be reduced to the rules of conduct they often establish, to the moral canons they support, or to the messages they articulate. Being constituent elements of social praxis, they necessarily engage in relations with other modes of praxis. That is why ritual workings cannot be understood by reference to the closed worlds they themselves create. Actually, the effort to create a closed world, a magic circle, is what gives rituals the power to deeply intervene in a society's life. The spatiality of rituals and their rhythmical temporalities are forms of performed closure. But this kind of closure paradoxically opens social life to the possibilities of change. Rituals are potential laboratories of social change.

The anthropologist David Graeber in his study of existing egalitarian societies (2004, 2007) locates a role of rituals that seems to support the idea that what is at stake is not a process of peaceful social reproduction but rather a dynamic condition in which ritual practices constantly and repeatedly confront an inherent and unavoidable social tension (2004). For him, egalitarian societies (or anarchistic ones as he sometimes describes them) are not unaware of the dangers that may destroy their core values (mainly equality and consensus), which are predominantly attributed to the accumulation of power, wealth, or means to exert violence by certain of their members.

That is why in those societies ritual worlds are full of images of malignant and nonhuman entities at war with themselves or overlooking social life to violently punish those who depart from the society's egalitarian ethos: A kind of "spectral violence seems to emerge from the very tensions inherent in the project of maintaining an egalitarian society" (Graeber, 2004: 32). This violence is projected in the ritual performances as extra-human. And this seems to be one among the ways an essentially present and always real danger haunting such societies is confronted with. Thus, according to Graeber, "spectral zones are always the fulcrum of the moral imagination, a kind of creative reservoir, too, of potential revolutionary change" (ibid.: 34).

"Counterpower," for Graeber, works in these societies as a mechanism that prevents the development of relations of subordination and hierarchy. It is important to see this process as immersed in the workings of collective imagination that through the mechanism of ritual "as-if" both develops images of an egalitarian society (to be created or sustained) and treats the real danger of such society regressing to a system of domination—one more indication, then, that ritual is not a world of representations but a world of actions that make representations effective in shaping potentialities. Ritual acts are performances and have a performative power: They create potentialities and events in the lived world.

Rituals may be appropriated and transformed the way habits are. The creation of the magic circle may thus be employed to construct on a symbolic level a community that challenges dominant taxonomies and hierarchizations. Questions of course arise as to whether a community may use the modes of social reproduction to transcend, bypass, or challenge the existing social relations. Central to those questions is the problem of collective identity: Don't "alternative rituals" fall in the same trap of enclosure, albeit in new identities (rather in those belonging to dominant taxonomies)?

Such questions can only be answered in concrete and focused studies of the ritual's interaction with the constitution of the deviant communities. Do these communities simply find a place in existing taxonomies or do they bring an element of crisis that suspends the efficiency and the legitimizing power of such taxonomies? And, furthermore, what kind of relation develops between the ritual magic circle and the community's reality? Is this reality reduced to the "artefactual" world presented in the ritual or is it potentialized through the symbolic performances that actually indicate possible realities in the making?

Tracing Trajectories

Following and Leaving Traces

In search for the temporal aspect of potentiality, we are bound to face the idea and experience of time's discontinuity. Societies tend to reproduce themselves by maintaining their characteristics although their members of course are born, live, and die. This truism includes the kernel of experienced time's ambiguity: Although men and women experience discontinuity in the fundamental phenomena of individual existence, namely birth and death, their own life appears to them as if it unfolds in continuous time. As long as we exist, we feel that we continue to exist. The fundamental experience of discontinuity is death but, always, the death of others.

Many works of human societies are devoted to commemorating this experienced rupture of time by somehow integrating it to the continuity of social time. And it is by no chance that these works are indispensable to the workings of social reproduction.

It was Adolf Loos, the architect, who described as the originary act of architecture the arrangement of stones to mark a place where someone is buried. "If we find a mound six feet long and three feet wide in the forest, formed into a pyramid, shaped by a shovel, we become serious and something in us says, 'someone lies buried here.' That is architecture." (mentioned by Aldo Rossi, 1982: 107). Stones are there as traces of a burial site as well as to indicate, to show something. The message may be different depending on the corresponding society's view on death or afterlife, but it is a message that boldly addresses those who are exposed to it.

Discontinuity experienced, continuity emphatically stated. Time is processed socially: no one may doubt without consequences the way collective experiences are processed by practices which again and again mend time—the existence of the collective as continuity against the individual existence as discontinuity.

Potentiality arises where and when continuity is questioned, challenged, and suspended. Or even when continuity is shuttered. However, this is not equivalent to the existential discontinuity. It emerges within the socially constructed continuity but it carries the threatening but also seductive (for the imagination) power of individual existence's discontinuity. Potentiality is a death of certainty that is somehow propelled by the certainty of death. Or is it that potentiality makes an appearance when the certainty of death is exorcised by the certainty of life? Because life is change, life is always becoming.

Traces seem to be anchors of experience. The moment we discover them, they testify to something that has happened. Something that already belongs to the past, even when it is just moments before we discovered the traces left. Traces anchor in time both the experience of their discovery as well as the experience that they are thought to refer to. Traces, thus, are treated not as means to stop time but as means to articulate time by distinguishing what is important (for those who discover them) in the past from what at the present of the trace's recognition seems unimportant. This act of articulating time makes traces powerful weapons in society's struggle against the individual experience of discontinuity. By articulating time, traces testify to time's continuity. In contrast to what seems an obvious affirmation, namely that traces stop time, traces actually are one among the many ways societies have at their disposal to construct time's continuity. Without traces, time does not pass. Without the ability to recognize, to name, to inventory, to transmit traces, time is suspended: Strangely, thus, we seem to reach the other "end" of a circle. The act of recognizing a trace seems to be the recognition of a burial site and the same time, our ability to recognize traces collectively defies death.

The anthropologist Tim Ingold considers human existence as "place binding" rather than "place-bound" (2011: 33). "It unfolds not in places but along paths. Proceeding along a path, every inhabitant lays a trail. Where inhabitants meet, trails are entwined, as the life of each becomes bound up with the other" (ibid.). This approach sees human interaction as a crossing of trajectories that leaves traces and thus through repetition establishes meeting points, "knots" in Ingold's terminology. A place, then, is a knot, and a house "is a place where the lines of its residents are tightly knotted together" (ibid.) Borrowing Lefebvre's term "meshwork," Ingold, thus, suggests that the human world (much like the world of animals) is woven by all those patterns of texture that characterize human movement.

According to this approach, the capacity to recognize and follow traces is connected with the capacity to leave traces. Joint action or individual actions converge to a continuous exchange of traces—traces found and traces produced. And traces are in this way perceived as being addressed to those following them (and are meant to be addressed by those leaving them). Tracing is, thus, predominantly connected to potentiality: to the potentiality of encounters (that sustains Ingold's knots-places), to the potentiality of finding ways to targeted scopes, and to the potentiality of discovering different worlds and ways of being.

The act of recognizing traces does not necessarily entail the presupposition that traces were made in order to be recognized. To gain a certain kind of knowledge related to their living environment is capacity that humans share with animals. We also know that nonhuman beings in certain cases leave traces on purpose (as for example in the case of marking a territory with urine). So, animals too produce material indicators to be recognized by allies or enemies. However, the act of recognizing traces as intentional gestures destined to communicate something to other humans creates a different, distinctively human context of action. In such cases, traces seem to acquire a different relation to time. Traces are taken not as markers of something that happened which then retreated inescapably to the past but as something that remains as pending in the present. Such traces ask for a response. The past weighs upon the present. We may, then, understand potentiality not as the characteristic force that opens different paths toward alternative futures but as a force that opens the past, makes the past a question for the present to answer. Not merely through interpretation (locking the past to a chain of continuity that has "meaning") but, crucially, through acts. The moment we respond to traces considering that they address us, considering that they are there to convey a message to us, traces become a powerful means to engage with the past.

W. Benjamin suggests that "trace is appearance of a nearness however far removed the thing that left it behind may be" (1999: 447). Nearness can be taken here to represent both an actual spatial proximity as well as a metaphor concerning time (the recent, near past). And then, all this is but an appearance. It is a certain subject who each time enters to this nearness because of the trace. And "in the trace we gain possession of the thing" (ibid.). Bringing a "thing" near in time and in space through the recognition of its trace is a way of "holding" it, controlling it, making it part of one's own possession. Isn't this an aphorism that includes, as if in an all-encompassing gesture, Benjamin's approach to the past? If we can get possession of past "things," we can actually "redeem" the past. We may return to the past not simply to interpret it but, predominantly to bring it to the present, and thus explore potentialities that were not actualized then but possibly may flourish now.

W. Benjamin considers the bourgeois house interior of nineteenth century as an arrangement of objects that predominantly endeavor to keep traces. Keeping traces of the past, in such a context, is some kind of ritual repetition of an impossible effort to stop time. Not by literally stopping time, of course, but by containing the experience of time in the illusion that nothing changes as time persists.

It seems that a certain mentality of the bourgeois ruling class is characterized by an obsession to preserve all the possible material indications of belonging to this class. If the feudal classes and the aristocracy had to remind everyone of their descent considered as a past with the power to define the present, the middle classes could only exhibit their possessions as markers of belonging. Objects then, especially those showcased within the bourgeois house, were meant to be exhibited as markers of indisputable ownership.

However, there has been a crucial turning point in the expression of bourgeois power to control time (and thus in bourgeois society's reproduction): the modernist myth of progress. Instead of bourgeois power being legitimized as a guardian and owner of the past, in the modernist myth bourgeois society is projected as the owner of the future. Progress incessantly devalues the past: New things, new ways, new looks dominate the progress-bewitched imaginary.

What happens to traces, and to trace collecting obsession in the context of the modernist myth? Probably everything becomes a potential indicator of change. "All that is solid melts into air" as the well-known phrase goes (Berman, 1982). However, progress represents itself not as a random exploitation of traced potentialities but as a linear course toward the future, which, always retrospectively of course, seems to have been coherently directed toward a specific scope: the betterment of humanity's life (a scope obviously highly ambiguous, nevertheless accepted by almost all). Traces of the future would thus become markers of specific potentialities, inherently existing in the present and waiting to be discovered.

Such an approach to traces will eventually lead to the use of traces as a means of "promoting, managing and orientating change" (Boltanski, 2011: 129). However, the modernist imaginary should not be understood as a mere reflection of the processes of capitalist modernization, which surely staged the phantasmagoria of progress.

Modernist imaginary, as concretized in futurist and constructivist performances and as expressed in Dadaist and surrealist writing, manifests itself in the explosive denial of the past rather than in the canonic depiction of "progress."

Contrary to the aberrations and unpredictable consequences of such modernist imaginaries, the management of change (and of course not its denial) became—from the period we call modernity to today—the mainstream approach to the problem of comparing past and present. Benjamin's suggestion has been heretical albeit modernist. Redeeming the past potentialities in order to open the door to a radically different future stands opposite to the predominant ideology that considers the future, no matter how different, as following the tracks defined by the processes of capitalist reproduction.

Pervasive Connectivity: Instant Tracing?

Nowadays, connectedness is the perverse substitute of solidarity. Technologies of telecommunication and telepresence keep us connected in an endless streaming that permeates our everydayness. What makes this pervasive experience dangerous and outwardly alienating, though, is the substitution of well-thought exchanges by automated, almost unthought-of responses. Connectivity of this kind expects immediate reactions and demands answers and acts that have to adjust to incessant and rapid flows of information. Messages are already reduced to a few words (from e-mail to X, a world of meaning is reduced to almost stereotypical gestures of taking sides). Tele-commands need to be transferred quickly, in real time (as if the time of lingering, of waiting, of pause is not real at all!) in order to be effective. The real-time responses in warfare conditions are to a large extent transferred to automated systems—no human decision can be quick enough to avert the enemy's attacking missiles. Video games often simulate such conditions—after all young generations will have to develop capacities that depend upon immediate reflex-type decisions. What Franco Berardi, the Italian philosopher, terms as "the externalization of the self" is "a sort of psychotic deterritorialization of attention" (2019: 131). Connectivity educates the senses through this kind of learned instant adaptation to outer stimuli.

The dominant paradigm of connectivity replaces the collective intelligence of tracing. Trajectories that establish connections are replaced by instant interfaces. Time needed for a trajectory to be followed is not empty time. Traces are being evaluated again and again as the trajectory is being formed. The relation between expected findings and mobilized means is being examined while the path is actually being defined through tracing rather than the path indicating the traces to be followed. In short, tracing always demands a kind of improvisation and inventiveness even when it is supervised by social mechanisms that try to impose a strict repeatability of acts (inflexible itineraries). In other words, tracing necessarily opens experience to potentiality even when routine acts are expected to be executed by following repeatedly projected traces. Contrarily, in total and instant connectivity traces are replaced by signs and the latent or explicit inventiveness of tracing is replaced by the automatism of instant response.

There is a certain structure of individuation that is developed through the connectivity paradigm. Dispersed along networks of instant communication, the self becomes more like an agglomerate of signals transmitted rather than a narrative to be crafted by a will for coherence and endurance. True, the will to remain the same may create monsters: Adherence to identity has been at the foundations of essentialist discriminations (racism, nationalism, etc.). However, aiming to create a narrative of the self while performing it may be a modest way of accepting changes of the self that are part of the self's developing relations with the "other," the "others." Signals may only mark instantaneous changes, or even, simulations of change as in the case of fake internet personas. Narrative gives to change the time to unfold, to be tested, to be criticized as well as to be sensed. Time unfolds in corporeal as well as in mental gestures addressing the otherness of others.

Individuation shaped by narrative time is replaced by a quasi-individuation expressed in instant time. It is just one step away from the swarm-like behavior that makes stereotypical responses the substratum of socially inculcated mass obedience. Connecting in such a case becomes the means to coordinate responses without the subject of response retaining the power to differentiate, to disagree, and to reflect upon options. This is a tendency that is integrated to the automating advancements of connectivity. For example, the ideal of the smart house or the smart city already includes everyday "care" systems that decide according to algorithmically processed parameters: What is missing from the refrigerator, what time you must take the bus, when do you need to take your medicine, or who is to cross your door. Innocent and useful information is being processed, some might say. The crucial question is how is information processed (with what kind of presuppositions taken for granted) and what kinds of decisions are reduced to automatic recurrences. Behind the complexity of the ultra-connectivity of the smart city model lurks a model of urban governance that reduces political decision to management options.

Perhaps in, against, and beyond the universe of connectivity, mutuality and cooperation may emerge as long as the mad dream of the unlimited freedom to connect is shown to be a pervasive form of behavior engineering. In the endless exchanges of collective narratives-in-the-making, different "we" may craft a common world. Shared time and shared space may thus develop into collective art works as long as connecting will be performed as a form of creative solidarity.

4

Challenging Urban Order

Collective Inventiveness

Social reproduction gets shaped, as we have seen, through the spatiotemporal practices of trace production (and reading), habit acquisition (and activation in specific circumstances), and the participation in rituals. Those kinds of practices are predominantly based on the repeatability of actions and the production of meaning that repeated actions establish and support.

However, traces may also be directed toward the future or produced in order to redeem a pending past; habits may be transformed (or challenged) by emerging new ones, and rituals, either expressed as "artefactual modes of being" or appropriated as collective experiences of possible words, may become matrices of new social relations and generators of deviant social meanings.

The invention of traces, the transformation of habits, and the opening or appropriation of rituals' magic circle are ways to perform potentialities. Such potentialities are not being developed as pure externalities in comparison with the closed worlds of tracing, habitual, and ritual behavior. And they are not merely actualizations of inherent possibilities lying dormant at the heart of reproduction processes. They rather become active constituents of social life when they are performed. They challenge established social meanings and extend the limits of the possible because they emerge in practices—they unfold through action. Performances of potentiality develop within the inculcated capacities of social members and are characterized by a shared ability to invent. Inventiveness, however, in this context, is not the power to construct and envisage the absolute "other" but the ability to construct and envisage a beyond by using the means to the present. Inventiveness is more like the ingenious practice of *bricolage* than the sudden discovery acts that are mythologized both in a certain history of art and a certain history of science. Let us remember that Levi Strauss uses the image of the *bricoleur* to describe how "savage thought" or "mythical thought" works: The *bricoleur* is "someone who works with his hands and uses devious means compared to those of a craftsman" (Levi Strauss, 1966: 16–17).

Tim Ingold persistently develops an approach to culture that describes it as an area of creativity and improvisation rather than as a closed world of constructed patterns of behavior. Interestingly, he distinguishes a kind of creativity that is combinatory from a kind "that is inherent in the flow of life or consciousness" (Ingold, 2007: 48). For him, the second kind is the one that may free us from a predominantly dominant modernist belief that connects creativity to total innovation. As he and E. Hallam suggest, classical aesthetics, from Renaissance on, developed an important change in the understanding of creative act: "from a formulation in which to create is to be part of an ongoing process, to one that 'reads back' from the finished product to the capacity that produced it" (Ingold and Hallam, 2007: 18).

Being part of an ongoing process means taking part "in the never-ending and non-specific project of *keeping life going*" (Ingold and Hallam, 2007: 48 emphasis in the original). Ingold's view then must be understood in the context of an approach to culture (and social life in general) that explores them as always in the making. They are thus considered as areas of improvisation and inventiveness that shape life itself (from the biological to the social), transcending the dichotomy between nature and culture.

A helpful point in the distinction between improvisation and innovation is "that the former characterizes creativity by way of its process, the latter by way of its products" (Ingold and Hallam, 2007: 2).

This is why the predominant modernist support of design considered as essentially innovative process misses the point. The production of form always includes improvisation no matter how clearly the scopes of design are stated. Rather than the attribution to design of a will to predict (and thus to direct the future) we need, suggest Ingold and Gatt, to be able to foresee through improvisation: "opening pathways rather than setting targets" (Gatt and Ingold, 2013: 145). This is how "design can be open-ended" (ibid.: 146). Designing the future, thus, is more like exploring potential paths to collective aspirations rather than fixing a specific image of a longed-for destination.

We need to distinguish, however, creativity and inventiveness considered as a means to adapt to varying circumstances and survival demands from creativity and inventiveness that seek ways out of predominant social life patterns. True, there is no clear distinction between these two processes if we try to find what distinguishes them by trying to locate inherent characteristics. Specific historical contexts mark collective or individual creative acts as potentially counter dominant. In Ingold's approach, the problem of hegemony and suppression is downplayed in search of a general theory of culture and society that sees them as worlds in the making. And this approach is useful for overcoming ideas that present structured social worlds as fixed and self-repeating. However, creativity and improvisation may express differing potentialities of change within specific sociohistorical contexts. It is of course important to observe, as probably is becoming apparent in the way this book's argument unfolds, that improvisation is not the power (or the gift) of extraordinary individuals but a capacity that is, as Edward Bruner puts it, "a cultural imperative" (in Ingold and Hallam, 2007: 2). This means that at the very root of cultural reproduction (culture-as-reproduction) lies the power to invent, to seek, or to experience change. According to the view that creativity is combinatory, improvisation and inventiveness introduce change by discovering and producing new combinations of already existing aspects of social life and values. Provided that those aspects are not taken as inert and fixed entities but themselves as already exposed to the dynamics of social life, this combinatory logic may support theorizations of potentiality that are compatible with this book's argument. The Benjaminian flaneur, who connects fragments of the city as he meets them in his chance wanderings, is close to the surrealist artist who depicts chance encounters of objects in order to reveal a deeper reality, the reality expressed in dreams. As we will see, combinatory improvisation shapes the habits of cooperation and the work of the craftsmen.

But improvisation that attempts to follow flows and to create while meeting demands that emerge in the flow of life is equally a potential source of change that may threaten urban and social order. It is rather important to retain both modes of improvisation as sources of potentiality.

Could collective inventiveness gesture toward a different urban future? And what kind of future? What I will attempt to show is that the performance of potentialities that is grounded on the deviant appropriation of tracing practices, habits, and rituals may construct instances of a different world based on equality and solidarity, provided that these performances unfold in the context of urban commoning.

Urban commoning is an area of collective improvisation that emerges within practices of everyday life in contemporary cities. Urban commoning is often linked to survival tactics of the urban poor as they try to cope with limits and discrimination barriers that each one cannot confront alone. It thus involves both types of creativity, connected as it is to combinatory inventiveness of resource uses as well as to the skillful appropriation of opportunities that arise within the flow of urban life. What makes urban commoning potentially threatening to urban and social order are its nonindividualist ethos and its corresponding patterns of cooperation. As we will see, collective inventiveness, when developed in urban commoning, may give rise to forms of social organization that challenge dominant capitalist market rules and neoliberal governance. Urban commoning, thus, may support changes that are of a different level: systemic changes.

In order to trace such a possible trajectory of social change, the following suggestions will be developed:

1. Performances of potentiality may break the vicious circle of social reproduction by destroying the polarities on which urban ordering is based, namely the polarity wild/domesticated and the polarity abnormal/normal.
2. The patterning of behavior based on the above polarities is challenged by the creativity of urban commoning (sharing the city and shaping sharing through the creative reinvention of the urban). This creativity will be explored in three distinct domains of metropolitan life
   a. The reinvention of urban communities
   b. The development of cooperation and mutual aid practices
   c. The arising of new urban imaginaries focused on the right to collectively produce a shared city—the city as commons.
3. By linking to a long tradition that sees the struggle for a just and egalitarian society as directly connected to the reinvention of the urban (what Lefebvre called "urban revolution" and Benjamin "the disenchantment of the city"), an effort will be made to disengage emancipatory aspirations from visions of building the future (and thus the future city) from scratch. Real existing cities have become in certain moments of their history concrete spatiotemporal performances of emancipatory potentialities: Paris in 1871 and 1968, Buenos Aires in 2001, Oaxaca (Mexico) in 2006, Athens in 2008 and 2011, Tunis in 2013, Portland in 2020 (Black lives matter), Moscow in 1917, Munich in 1916, Havana in 1959, San Cristobal (Mexico) in 1994, Cairo in 2011, Cali (Colombia) in 2021, Santiago (Chile) in 2019, and the list may be extended to include more. There is an important lesson to be learned by following and studying the diverse multiplicity of the urban challenges to dominant urban ordering, which actively produced instances of a different urbanity. In such a prospect, the city becomes a collective work in progress based indeed on the reinvention of urban communities, the reclaiming of the emancipatory power of cooperation between equals, and the reflective reconsideration of urban imaginaries of change.

This is not a way to celebrate historical contingency and the seductive longing of surprises in history. Although the moments in which urban practices develop as performances of potentialities are not easily predictable, there are indications each time of the confluences that might produce serious ruptures in urban order. What is crucially important is to have the means to recognize the potentialities that develop in those ruptures and the will to contribute actively to the changes they may engender. As for emancipation visionaries, they (we?) need to be more modest. We need to judge and choose when facing changes, but, as the Zapatistas say, we make the road to emancipation as we walk. And this is surely not a yellow brick road, but the muddy road opened within and in spite of the miserable urban everydayness in which so many people are sentenced to live. And this road does not lead (or is fantasized to lead) to heaven but to another earth, that is, to a transformed earth.

Beyond Ordering Polarities

As we saw, metropolitan urban ordering is based on the control of two distinct polarities both instituted by the dominant definition of the sensible (in Rancière's terminology) as well as through policies of urban space production. The polarity of wild versus domesticated and normal versus abnormal essentially structure a field of high complexity (urban life) with the aim of governing this complexity in accordance to the structural priorities of neoliberal capitalism. Definitions of the wild and the abnormal may shift according to differing social contexts (within this system). Wilderness and abnormality, however are always meant to be expelled from the metropolis.

We have already encountered M. Sahlins's position, which suggests that at the basis of Western reasoning and disputes about the appropriate form to governing lies a strong belief that considers human nature as essentially and primarily malignant, wicked, and aggressively selfish (2008). The threatening wild, thus, is not simply outside society and in constant need of being contained and confronted but also at society's very foundation. Society, in such a dominant worldview, is a taming project par excellence.

Big city life is understood as a continuous challenge to the project of urban ordering, mainly due, according to this approach, to an always threatening eruption of human nature's alleged selfish animality. The everydayness of the urban poor or the marginalized populations is often stigmatized as "uncivilized," which means more close to nature than society. Taming this threatening wild nature means, depending on the occasion, either direct state violence (like shooting human "animals" from helicopters in the so-called pacification policies in Rio de Janeiro favelas) or projects that offer opportunities of "civilized" (or dressed as civilized) integration.

Treating designed natural environments as consoling albeit highly controlled ways of reconnecting to nature may become the means to re-signify wilderness through mass consumption. The "wild" thus becomes a harmless simulation of the demonized anti-urban wilderness.

A different approach on this matter characterizes cultures that essentially differ from the Western canon. If nature, human nature included, is not considered as the absolute (and threatening) other of civilized life and humans are believed to live in a world of interactions between different subjects (including what Westerners understand as nonhuman), then wilderness cannot be conceived as the necessary outside of the city. In Amerindian cultures, animals are humans too and live in societies (Ingold, 2002; Viveiros de Castro, 2014). "Perspectivism," a term coined by the anthropologist Eduardo Viveiros de Castro, attempts to capture this approach to society and to co-living, which sees a continuum rather than a separating rupture in a world of mutual involvement. Could this potentially become the source of a new urban ethos? Viveiros de Castro warns us against the danger of exoticism in the case of succumbing to the Western myth of the "noble savage." "We" may never be in the place of those "others," although we may fruitfully criticize our world using elements from those other worlds. Thus, "anthropology's role ... is not that of *explaining the world of the other* but rather *of multiplying our world*" (Viveiros de Castro, 2007: 266, emphasis in the original).

AbdouMaliq Simone explores a nuanced and ambiguous path to question and challenge urban order by effectively connecting practices that seem to overflow the polarities of urban ordering: "Blackness ... calls attention to the very existence of forces indifferent to the sustainability of the urban as a place of inhabitation" (Simone, 2016: 189). According to Simone's reasoning, there is an important moment in the constitution of urban modernity that he describes as the "constitution and appropriation of blackness" (2020b: 759). Blackness refers firstly to the actual history of slavery: The constitution of West's free subject (being recognized as free citizen, inhabitant of the city) is contradistinguished with the nonurban, nonhuman status to the Black slave. Especially focusing on the work of Hegel, Susan Buck-Morss explicitly underlines "the paradox between the discourse of freedom and the practice of slavery" (2009: 23) that characterizes early modern West. The slave, an emblematic outsider of the urban order, is connected to the wilderness of natural life (with no restrictions, no civilization, and no productive ethos—"Blacks are lazy"). By being tamed, the slave can only be used as a domesticated animal in the plantations of colonialist rule.

"Generic blackness" (2016) refers to the common ground of nonhumanness attributed to expendable populations. Regardless of color, such populations are kept at a distance from the normalized urban territory to be exploited without being included in the "official" city.

Generic blackness acquires for Simone a potentiality of recomposing the human, of developing forms of being and living that defy normalizing and taming processes. And this he locates not only in attitudes of dissent and revolt but also in attitudes of indifference to being part of a world that excludes them. Generic blackness thus includes practices developed under the radar of normalization, practices that develop relations based on an opaque everydayness. Opacity characterizes ways of living that cannot be reduced to the neoliberal calculation logic, that escape predictability but are also immersed in tormenting precarities. These patterns of living endure, according to Simone, in ways that shape unpredictable forms of interaction and care.

Simone seems to suggest that within the urban and its ongoing "extensions," a nonurban (or beyond the urban as planned) ethos develops that defies its simple reduction to an alternative urban culture. However, in his reference to the Black Power movement (and the current renewed interest for its history) he explicitly shows how important for the Black community's empowerment were initiatives for building schools, nurseries, mutual help committees, "circuits of information exchange and collective religious worship" (2016: 192). In such efforts based on activating the memories and skills of Black people, care was, according to Simone, the central uniting element (ibid.). And, of course, this process directly reflects a remaking of the city from below—the city as the collective *oeuvre* of its inhabitants as Lefebvre proposed.

Indifference and opacity may thus be considered as the substratum of politicized practices that reclaim the city by explicitly challenging the normalization polarities. Actually, it is because of these undetectable and the not easily describable practices, which neither clash with nor succumb to subjugation, that explicit resistance may emerge. And this kind of resistance is indeed rooted in the everydayness of opacity that may possibly give rise to forms of organized deviant or unpredictable living which remake collective life. On this fertile ground inventiveness grows—not as an individual capacity to explore ways of survival and personal profit but as a shared capacity to develop relations of sharing.

5

Reinventing Urban Communities

Autonomy as Community *Autopoiesis*

Commoning is usually considered as a form of goods distribution that is based on rules of sharing rather than on practices of individual appropriation or profit-oriented transactions. In such a prospect, conditions of power arrangement and collective choices related to culture are expected to shape commoning since they will directly influence the priorities and the scopes of sharing.

If however commoning is to become a process that directly challenges the logic of social organization that characterizes contemporary capitalism, then relevant practices are expected to produce emergent forms of an alternative social organization. Alternative forms of goods and services distribution are merely one part of an overall process of power relations rearrangement (Stavrides, 2016 and 2019).

Could we then possibly attempt to trace one of the fundamental aspects of such a rearrangement, the reinvention of community in the prospect of sustaining a potentially emancipating project? As this chapter will try to show, the reinvention of community through commoning will be the result of a collective culture of sharing based on the power of collective creativity unleashed in the context of the project of autonomy.

Creativity will be explored as a collective process that challenges the limits of the possible, which are crafted by dominant values and norms. The art of rule-making will be considered as a crucial part of this process that establishes autonomous open communities. Culture is the contested terrain on which such inventiveness potentially flourishes. That is why a critical reassessment of modernity is needed in order to open current urban imaginaries to different visions of the relationship between land and community. If community is a tender rather than the owner of territory and community rituals are means to establish bonds of sharing and equalitarian conviviality, then commoning becomes both a material force and a value establishing process that creates common worlds. As the chapter concludes, cultural commoning may become a crucial shaping factor for the reinvention of communities characterized by equality and solidarity.

One way to understand the project of autonomy is to compare it to what has been known as the autopoietic process which, according to certain biologists, characterizes living beings. Autopoiesis actually attempts to describe a certain level of autonomy that characterizes the unfolding of life: Tracing a path between the opposing views that either overemphasize the role of environment in shaping life or the role of inherent characteristics that simply develop, this theory suggests that autopoietic systems are at the same time open to their environments and "operationally closed" (Varela, 1997; Maturana and Varela, 1980). This means that interaction with the environment takes place under certain structural conditions that characterize the living entity, which is opened to such a relational condition. Autonomy is a context that does not describe an organism able to reproduce itself no matter what its environment is constituted of. Autonomy refers to a constitutive nucleus that responds to changes in the environment in ways that tend to reproduce the organism's mode of interaction.

As F. Varela explicitly specifies, an autopoietic system is a "minimal living organization" that "continuously produces the components that specify it, while at the same time realizing it (the system) as a concrete unity in space and time which makes the network of production of components possible" (1997: 75; Maturana and Varela, 1980).

Two important propositions are crucial for this approach to life, to the "living." First, autopoiesis is a process that constitutes the organism's identity, "a unitary quality, a coherence of some kind," which, however, "is not meant as a static structural description" but as an ongoing process within the boundaries of an "operational closure" (Varela, 1997: 73; Maturana and Varela, 1987). Second, "reproduction is not intrinsic to the minimal logic of the living ... Reproduction is essential for the long-term viability of the living, but only when there is an identity can a unit reproduce" (Varela, 1997: 76).

When considering an organized human community as a living organism, we employ a kind of analogical thinking that we need to reflect upon with a certain precaution. Bearing this in mind, the central question arising from a need to explore autonomy as a project of social emancipation is this: Which relations and what elements of community life are to become the anchors of a community's autopoietic self-creation if this community is to liberate itself from the dominating power of a social environment that actively aims at controlling community life?

By accepting the fact that inside a community, antagonisms of different kind exist, we already partially question the validity of the autopoietic metaphor. Changes may occur not only through the community's interaction with its outside but, essentially, because community itself includes forces and actions that develop toward opposing scopes. The "living organism" in this case is potentially torn apart from inside. There is, however, a kind of force that may retain a community's "coherence" without equating it (as Varela rightly suggests in his model) to an identity. This force necessarily reinvents community as a process of negotiations that limits the opportunities of power accumulation by some of its members while aiming at an equalitarian future. We may recognize this force in practices of commoning that support equality and mutual support without eliminating differences (Stavrides, 2016 and 2019). To be more exact, this kind of transformative force will develop through negotiations that will create a common ground between different perspectives, provided that these perspectives converge in sustaining this common ground as a shared guarantee of equality. For some non-Western cultures, this kind of common ground may be defined as an area of complementarity and harmonious coexistence. It is by no chance that such a possible common life-world is described by some of these cultures as *Buen Vivir* (living well) rather than *Vivir* (living). Living well directly challenges the limits of a model aimed at understanding bare "living."

By critically employing the autopoietic principles to community's claim for self-reproduction, we may actually distinguish between two possible opposing projects. One tends to barricade a community from outside influences by emphasizing the community's power to preserve intact its integrity, while the other tends to see community as a collective entity that claims its right to change in ways and directions collectively chosen, produced, and supervised. In the last case, the autopoietic structure is not a condition inherently connected to community's reproduction but a collective choice made in the direction of the collective emancipation project.

In other words, autonomy is in a constant struggle to develop itself in confrontation with powers that tend to control the community's life. It is not always external powers—what Cornelius Castoriadis describes as the forces of heteronomy (Castoriadis, 1987). Forces developed within the community may also tend to block any change—forces we might call conservative. Autopoietic autonomy should then be clearly connected to a change that aims at transcending community's reflexes for self-preservation.

Roberto Esposito (2013) introduces the term "immunization" to describe the process through which communities develop these self-preservation tactics. Interestingly, for him the same process that is employed to protect the individual members of the community forms the very obligations that bind them to all the others.

Esposito locates a constitutive contradiction in immunitary dynamics: "That which protects the body (the individual body, the social body, and the body politic) is at the same time that which impedes its development" (2013: 85). The way out of this contradiction lies in a kind of compromise: Immunization needs to be effectively controlled so that it will not reach a point that will threaten the community coherence itself. And this may only be accomplished, according to Esposito, if community members struggle to ensure the expansion and maintenance of the common (2013: 89). Here lies "the possibility of a positive, communitarian reconversion of the ... immunitary *dispositif*" (Esposito, 2006: 54, italics in the original).

In this approach, the common lies at the heart of community's reproduction. Offering an etymology of the word community that supports his claim, Esposito sees *munus* at the word's root. Munus means duty, post, and gift. "What predominates in the munus is ... reciprocity or 'mutuality' ... of giving that assigns the one to the other in an obligation" (2010: 6). Thus, community, "isn't the subject's expansion or multiplication but its exposure to what interrupts the closing" (ibid.: 8). Community is constituted by the obligation to give and to assume responsibilities (ibid.: 5). Opening oneself to others through offering essentially means sacrificing the individual safety that immunization promises. Immunity encloses, and community tends to open individual or shared enclosures toward the proliferation of the common.

Of course, the immunity metaphor, which directly refers to a biological mechanism of protection as part of an organism's defense against recurrent outside threats, has its limits as every metaphor does. When applied to societies in general or to particular communities specifically, the metaphor of immunity needs to be nuanced and related to the historical context. How do specific organized groups of people collectively recognize threats to their collective existence? In what cases perceived or imaginary threats cause splits in the corresponding communities? How is openness experienced and practiced as a force that expands obligations and offerings in different arrangements of power relations?

Autonomy as Collective Creativity

For Gustavo Esteva in "genuinely democratic politics," "the art of the possible consists of extending it: the art of making the impossible possible" (2015a: 140). In what seems at first glance a poetic reaffirmation of hope for changing society is in reality a clever statement regarding the limits of social order. Reversing the well-known motto, Esteva seems to suggest that instead of developing the art of finding solutions within the framework of a given society (and democracy allegedly is meant to provide us with this capacity), we need to develop the art to transcend such a framework. Thus, inventiveness and creativity will not be used in order to adapt to the defined social reality but to challenge it, to extend it and to go beyond it. The possible should be disentangled from the dominant framework of imaginaries and behaviors that tend to circumscribe it.

Rancière (2010) understands politics in a similar way. For him, politics emerges when the dominant framework, the order of the sensible, is challenged by those who were not meant to have the right to speak, think, and express themselves within this framework. Restaging and thus rearranging the distribution of the sensible opens the road to emancipation for the dominated ones.

Interestingly, Rancière also talks about art by connecting it with the power of politics to transcend the limits of dominant reality. However, he chooses to put an emphasis on the "aesthetic experience" that refers to the specific condition under which art "produces a gap with regard to ordinary forms of experience" (Rancière interviewed in Batista, 2017: 251). Distancing himself explicitly from didactic, pedagogic, and self-proclaimed critical forms of art, Rancière (2006) supports artistic acts and works that open up possibilities of experiences not already included in the field of the possible defined by the dominant ones.

However, the opening up of the field of possibilities develops, according to Rancière, not only because creativity expands and transcends the limits of the sensible, but also because those who "receive" the artworks are equally creative (2009). The "emancipated spectator" is the one who uses artworks to express, narrate, and depict his or her own stories. Emancipation in this prospect has to do with the opportunity to integrate the creativity of others (producers, artists) with the creativity of one's own life that acquires, thus, the power to transcend the limits of the possible.

Comparing the two approaches, we may conclude that art (literally, as an instituted form of practice or, generally, as the capacity to inventively create) may be used to explore the possible without even accepting the limits within which the possible is defined according to the dominant forms of the sensible. Viewed either from the perspective of the creative producer or from that of the creative receiver, art may potentialize experience, as well as the means we have to attribute meaning and value to experience. As collective creativity unfolds, the distinction between production and reception as well as that between active creators and passive interpreters is decisively challenged.

Art, then, should not be reduced to practices of representation but should be primarily described as a form of engagement with the existing inhabited worlds. Artistic practices may transform materialities (textures, sound effects, bodies in motion, images concretized in different media) into activators of experiences that do not necessarily fit into the dominant order of the sensible. Even in the case of works that are of a predominantly immaterial kind (music, songs, literature), their reception always unfolds in conditions in which materiality is important. The reception of artwork, in general, is part of a process that gives art the power to challenge established approaches to experience, to generate experiences, or to attribute unexpected meaning to familiar ones. Works of art, then, actively interfere in the social production of perceived reality (the socially crafted area of the sensible) and in the ways this reality is made meaningful in concrete social relations.

Under different lines of reasoning but following similar paths sustained by emancipatory aspirations, Esteva and Rancière use the notion of autonomy in close connection to practices of individual and collective creativity. Esteva explicitly relates autonomy to the creative power of the collective unleashed by the democratic self-government. In contrast to "ontonomy," which is "the regulatory system based on a cultural tradition itself" (2015a: 143 n.15), autonomy "appears when the members of the current generation modify existing rules or create new ones" (ibid.). In autonomy, thus, collective creativity expands the limits of the possible.

Rancière talks about "aesthetic autonomy" as "what makes the work available to anyone and thus no longer the expression or signature of its creator" (Rancière interviewed in Batista, 2017: 250). Autonomy frees the work, the product of someone's creativity, from the burden of its creator's intentions.

Couldn't this approach to creativity be also applied to the art of rulemaking? Not connected to a prevailing authority that gives them form and determines their jurisdiction, rules become part of a process of an ongoing creativity. But if rulemaking may be compared to the art of autonomous creation, could it be also related to Agamben's suggestion that "one day humanity will play with law just as children play with disused objects, not in order to restore them to their canonical use but to free them from it for good" (Agamben, 2005: 64)? This is a possibility based on Agamben's idea about the "coming community" in which "singularities form a community without affirming an identity" and "humans co-belong without any representable condition of belonging (even in the form of a simple presupposition)" (Agamben, 1993: 86). As Catherine Mills rightly points out (2008), Agamben's coming community is directly related to the play with law through which the constitutive experience of historicity is made possible. By playing, humans experience truly human time, the time of *Kairos*, the time of contingency, as they are freed from the burdens of sacred time that prescribes the future and interprets the past. Such an experience is meant to give "onto a new communism, in which nothing is shared except the power and possibility of life itself, and life escapes the caesuras and impotence to which law has relegated it" (ibid.: 26).

Creativity lies, in this prospect, not in the power to collectively explore possibilities of devising new rules that would redefine the common but in the unleashing of the pure, unrestricted, and indeterminate potentiality of life itself that will characterize the acts of the "whatever singularities." Playing with rules is just part of this essential playfulness of life that unfolds against the restrictions imposed by law.

Deactivated rules, rules having lost the power to direct and punish behavior, may possibly become toys in the hands of a self-liberating humanity even in the form of a revealing joyous play of obsolete roles (more like children playing pirate adventure games). Such a capacity to inventively play with rules may indeed enhance collective creativity. After all, since antagonistic societies teach their members how to always be fighters by offering them a series of war games, why should not egalitarian societies play with past laws enriching in this way shared imaginaries of collective emancipation? However, to play with the deactivated products of history that used to explicitly aim at controlling the future (as the laws do by prescribing what should not be done) should not be equated with the romanticized potentiality of "whatever" singularities "sharing nothing except the being-thus of happy life, in which all belong without any claim to belong" (Mills, 2008: 26). As opposed to Agamben's formulation, collective rulemaking creativity needs to be developed in a constant and reflexive redefinition of a mutually imagined and produced common ground.

In line with Rancière's suggestion who proposes that we need to suspend or, rather, to transcend the distinction between producers and receivers, we may understand autonomy as a process in which the power to create rules belongs to those who try to collectively define a shared future while being both coproducers and individual interpreters of these rules. Sovereign laws are meant to last and to control the future by banishing certain acts. But rulemaking, understood as an act of commoning, opens the potentiality of change by opening the process itself to a community that keeps on inventing itself.

Esteva insists that autonomy is not the grand project of a political proposal aspiring to have a universal validity. "In the barrios and pueblos of the world, in Africa and Asia as in Latin America spaces of freedom have been spawning where autonomy and the art of living are being exercised more fully" (Esteva et al., 2013: 140). Autonomy seems to be emerging according to this logic in the context of everyday survival efforts of populations living in the peripheries and poor neighborhoods of metropolises. But, people on the margins (in many cases forming the majority of the relevant megacity population, as for example in Mumbai) do not live in conditions of autonomy simply because the state has no interest in imposing its laws and providing its services to those vast "neglected" urban areas. Struggles to preserve "autonomous ways of living" (ibid.: 136) emerge in such places against invading "development projects" or harsh militarized interventions to control the "dangerous classes." There is a positive potentially emancipatory element in the autonomy of the marginalized populations. And this, according to Esteva, and to other thinkers and activists, can be envisaged as the emergence of "the new commons" (ibid.: 136). As Esteva describes them, "They are contemporary ways of life, sound spaces for comfortable living, sociological novelties that activate traditions and reappraise modernity" (ibid.: 142).

Collective creativity, directly or indirectly related to art, redefines, extends, and develops the common. Both the immunitary dynamics and the autopoietic hypothesis not only offer the means to explain an organism's self-reproduction (be it a living being or a community) but also suggest ways to understand interaction between organisms. Communities may employ collective creativity to explore and develop relations with what lies outside: The common may thus become the fertile meeting ground of different collectivities. Potentializing experience, challenging the limits of the possible, and questioning dominant reality will in this prospect become not only forces that make communities change but also practices that open communities and build bridges toward what used to be considered as the "outside," the "other," alien or even hostile.

Beyond Tradition and Modernity?

Emancipatory potentialities are being produced in urban life through a constant cross-influence of two main sources: tradition and modernity. Tradition may be activated by reference to past experiences or collective memories that certain urban populations carry from their recent rural past. Interestingly, such traditions cannot be transferred wholesale to the urban context: Urban space and urban networks as well as the prevailing neoliberal ethos privilege individuality instead of community, alienation instead of a feeling of belonging. Such populations, therefore, have to re-invent community and to readjust habits of cooperation and sharing. Above all, they have to deal with extensive and unpredictable forms of differences instead of taking for granted a homogeneous body of dwellers sharing familiar and slowly changing (if at all) living environments. Autonomy in such a context would mean the potentializing of traditions (and not of "tradition") in order to collectively craft a common ground of negotiations.

On the other hand, reappraising modernity would mean taking into consideration the vast changes that communication, information, production, and mobility technologies have caused in urban life conditions. We know that the modernization project has emerged in the context of capitalist exploitation of people and resources (both in the colonizing and colonized world). The two principal spaces in which such exploitation unfolded were the factory and the plantation. Both were rationally organized so as to develop and augment production and both were closed and highly controlled spaces in which people had to work hard under surveillance.

The planation was of course a productive machine based on a rationalized extractive ethos. Its structure represents a view toward nature that aims at maximizing profitable production at the expense of ecosystemic relations necessary for the reproduction of nature. Clearly distinguishing between the resources to be used and the "useless" elements of the ecosystem to be discarded, the plantation is a homogeneous world that corresponds to the linear rhythmicality of capitalist production. That is why it is considered by Arturo Escobar as "the most effective means for the ontological occupation and ultimate erasure of local relational worlds" (2020: 74).

Plantations emerged from the early years of colonialism as spaces under heavy surveillance in which slaves and indigenous people were literally driven to death through cruel and unlimited forced work. They evolved to today's vast areas of intense cultivation, which rely on climate-destructive technologies and on health-threatening conditions both for those who work as well as for those who consume what the plantations produce. Local relational worlds included natural ecosystems in the dialectics between nature and the human-made worlds. Such relations may regulate coexistence or, even, discover the merits of complementarity.

Commenting on the Haitian revolution, which was mainly led by the insurgent plantation slaves, Susan Buck-Morss highlights the use of the plantation work disciplinary model by the new regime to establish a labor system "employing freemen as wage laborers" (2009: 95). This, according to her, established the continuity of an "agrarian militarism" based on the figure of the male-slave-turned-to-soldier (literally in military service but also metaphorically in the case of disciplined labor) (ibid.).

Although in modernist utopias they were envisaged as integral parts of a new urban condition, both factories and plantations were located at the periphery of cities or far away from them. We may even consider the factory and the plantation as essentially anti-urban production machines. It was the so-called socialist utopias that tried to integrate workspaces to the city in the prospect of developing a decentralized network of self-sufficient settlements (by descaling factory units at the same time). And it was the Garden City type utopias that tried to keep cultivated land near the urban nuclei as part of an organic city development.

According to Virno's (2004, 2008) and Hardt and Negri's (2005, 2009) analyses (among others), the city has become a vast and polymorphous site of capitalist production. Production process itself (still centrally dependent upon the exploitation of labor) has been expanding to even include private house spaces (as in the case of tele-work). And, as we will see in the next chapter, production processes include forms of cooperation and cohabitation as necessary constituents of exploitation mechanisms.

Reappraising modernity in such a context would mean carefully exploring the new conditions of exploitation and the spatialities that they gave rise to as well as the mutations of the modernist imaginary. W. Benjamin was one of those to first call for this reappraisal, claiming that an inherent emancipatory potential had to be reclaimed in an effort to redeem the modernist project. In his reading of urban modernity, large cities are not simply symptoms of the modernity's hopes and failures but, crucially, shaping factors of modernity's reality. That is why he searched in large cities in order to locate the potentialities of the modernist project that were blocked or perverted by the capitalist command of the modernization process (1983, 1999).

Reappraising modernity need not be limited to those who have been accustomed to modernity's dominant, hegemonic normality. Different collective life traditions had to face the invasion of urbanized modernization in their communities. Resistances, especially developed by colonized indigenous populations, were never simply obstinate struggles to preserve their traditions intact. Zapatista communities, to take a highly indicative example, distanced themselves from a possible Maya fundamentalism while at the same time embracing emancipatory ideas coming from the West. The result was (and this is still a work in progress) a kind of reinvention of community that struggles for autonomy neither with the aim of preserving an absolute otherness nor with the scope of establishing borderlines demarcating an "outside" and an "inside." Directly inspired by such an effort, Arturo Escobar suggests, "that we all need to make serious efforts to *vivir entre mundos*, to live in between, with and from multiple worlds, as we attempt to recommunalize our daily experience" (2020: 115).

Zapatista territory is connected to specific self-governed communities that take care of it and protect it from the "bad government," as they call it. Such a renewed understanding of Mayan territoriality contributes to the reinvention of indigenous communities by the Zapatista movement. What shocks most of the outside visitors is that the territory of an emancipatory rebellion that clashes with the Mexican state's policies and control mechanisms cannot really be defined by a borderline to be drawn on a map as well as on the ground (Stavrides, 2019: 47–54). Appropriation of feudal land and the use of existing road networks are forms of expanding the territory of autonomy and developing a network of autonomous settlements in cooperation.

Another interesting treatment of tradition in the prospect of community reinvention can be found in the renewed momentum the *Buen Vivir* indigenous culture has acquired. Buen Vivir (living well) is a view of life in which the indigenous Andean peoples express a harmonious respectful coexistence of human communities with nature. Buen Vivir includes an understanding of community's commonwealth as the result of relations of cooperation between its members based on solidarity and complementarity. Cooperation is supported by an ethos that permeates both the human relations as well as the relation of the community with nature. "Production and work is done with respect for and in harmony with nature" (Prada, 2013: 146). Since, however, nature is not considered as a resource but as a sacred entity, as the mother who provides and must be taken care of, "pacts with it are renewed through ritual" (ibid.). For Andean people, the ritual reaffirmation of Buen Vivir relations is a way of establishing such relations of mutual care between community and nature.

Community, thus, is not the collective owner of natural resources (including land) that are to be found in this territory. Community is more like a tender of its territory, attached as it is to it not only out of need to dwell and survive but also through links that relate community to its past and its future, its ancestors and its collective aspirations. Commoning in this case is more like an extensive participation in exchanges within and through nature that aim to be just, sustainable, and based on mutual care.

Buen Vivir principles were in a way integrated to the constitutions of two Andean countries, Ecuador (in 2008) and Bolivia (in 2009). The Ecuadorian constitution explicitly states, "We hereby decide to build a new form of public coexistence, in diversity and in harmony with nature, to achieve the good way of living [buen vivir]." In Bolivia, indigenous people form the majority of the population. In Ecuador, the presence of indigenous population is less dominant in terms of numbers but equally powerful in terms of culture. But, as R. Prada explains, the adoption of Buen Vivir "as a state and government objective" (ibid.: 147) rather attempts to create a meeting place, an area of agreements based on the ethics of pursuing harmony through complementarity. Cooperation thus is elevated to a governance model that will lead to a "plurinational state" that is meant to guarantee and protect an inclusive and equalitarian pluralistic society.

In many efforts to implement this new legal condition, Buen Vivir principles clashed with extremely strong elite interests as well as with taken-for-granted hopes in "progress" through "development." True, rural communities in these countries had the opportunity to protect their established customs of collective care for land and their ritual and practical ways of expressing a bond with nature that explicitly clashes with the predominant extractivist ethos (De Sousa Santos and Meneses, 2020; Acosta, 2013). Urban communities also have the opportunity to use the same legal guarantees to protect their neighborhoods and shared spaces from an advancing urban extractivism (including gentrification, urban expansion, public land grabbing, aggressive "touristification," etc.). The integration of the Buen Vivir approach into constitutional legislation has performative effects in practices that reinvent both urban and rural communities in the context of decentralization, horizontality, and plurality of social organization forms. However, progressive governments in both countries did not choose to confront fundamental inequalities and to limit existing power asymmetries. Without attacking the development model based on extractivism, they also became complicit with a governance ethos that gave no room to movements and to organized communities determined to act as organized contesters of developmentalist priorities. Communities can only be reinvented by themselves through the practices of commoning that will reconstitute them.

In spite of its beautiful resonances of eternal peace and cooperation, *Buen Vivir*, considered as life in harmony, needs to be integrated to a politics of overcoming capitalism and hierarchical forms of governance with a careful reconsidering of the idea of harmony. This might mean returning to the initial image of the able craftsman that lies at the etymological root of harmony. Indeed, the word comes from a description of a craftsman's knowledge and practice. For the ancient Greeks, harmony (*armonia*) describes the process and the successful result of joining a ship's planks. Crucial for this is the way joints themselves are made. The word actually comes from *armos*, the Greek word for joint.

Fitting the planks for the construction of a ship indeed is a work of skill: You need to know how to do it but you also need to know how to improvise, by taking into consideration the circumstances of the shipbuilding, the available wood, tools, people to help, and so on. Cooperation is crucial in this process—so harmony has to do with testing and establishing human relationships. Joining together, fitting together is not simply adjusting material and human "resources" to a fully predetermined scope.

True, the result of such a process seems to be in accord with uses of the word that connect it to an accomplished successful result: a ship, a well-governed universe, life in equilibrium. However, harmony can become the word to describe the process of fitting rather than its end-result. An able craftsman actually invents joints or uses them inventively in order to produce the fitting of adjacent planks (or of tiles in a stone floor, etc.). The joint, this in-between element, is there (hidden and exhibited) to express a craftsman's magic: What connects is based on a separation that is being worked upon in order to make possible the joining. Couldn't this be an apt image for a world that may include many worlds oriented toward collective emancipation? Couldn't we see all those movements struggling for a more just world in cooperation with nature as able collective craftsmen?

Working for devising joints but actually on shaping the contours of various worlds so that they can join in for the construction of a shared liberated life can be a task for the future and the present urban communities. Urbanites need to collectively invent those joints that create both the social bonds within any specific community and those that create bridges between communities. The image of the urban archipelago may be reduced to an agglomeration of urban enclaves in which collectively stigmatized or collectively privileged dwellers live by being attached to identity enclosures (to enclosures-as-identities). The social wisdom epitomized in the craftsmanship of social joints has the power to transcend the closure of homogeneous (or violently homogenized) urban communities. To reinvent such communities would mean to learn how to build relationships of complementarity and cooperation.

Should urban craftsmen (craftsmen of an inclusive urbanity) try to produce a fixed urban and social order in which everything is in balance? No, we need to keep from the metaphoric potential of the word harmony its link to the process of exploring the fitting. As we struggle, fitting is always a negotiated, inventive, and precarious practice. Respecting differences, while seeking for an agreed-upon common ground that will make possible relations of mutual care, equality, and solidarity, is an ongoing process. We need to become the able craftsmen of a future that is in the making. Let us then abandon an Arcadian vision of harmony that projects into the future a totally balanced social order and let us support harmony as a project of crafting this common ground of liberation and coexistence. Let us explore the ways human societies can coexist and cooperate with natural ecosystems by realizing that ecosystems themselves are dynamic processes of rearrangement and adaptation to changing circumstances. Harmony, then, is a process of co-living that is not closed to a predetermined repeatable future.

A Politics of Being-in-Common?

Establishing community bonds, grounded on a relation of mutual definition with the land on which the autonomy project flourishes, challenges both the Arendtian tradition that considers public space as the "space of appearances" as well as Jean Luc Nancy's ontological grounding of "being-in-common" in a space of mutual exposure.

According to Hannah Arendt's approach, the space of appearances becomes the locus of politics since it is constituted by individuals acting together in the presence of others. "Wherever people gather together [the space of appearances] is potentially there, but only potentially, not necessarily and not forever" (1958: 199). Arendt's distinction between the social, the private, and the political, attributes to public space a potentiality that is activated when people do not act under the pressure of needs or particularistic motives. Public space is inaugurated as a pure space of freedom produced by the creativity freedom engenders in pluralistic societies. Space, thus, is more like a scaffold for potential political activities rather than a shaping factor of the relations a community builds within itself and with its outside.

Buen Vivir communities, for which there is no actual outside but only expanding relations between partners (including what the West would call nonhumans), actually reproduce themselves as they coproduce their living environment with forces, entities, and agents that are deeply interrelated. A clear-cut distinction between nature and culture is not accepted. Arendt's view ignores the inherent connection between the social and the political considered as the multifaceted engagement with community's governance.

Buen vivir principles transverse all areas of common life and thus define community as an extensive field of relations between living beings. Complementarity rather than antithesis is at the root of this cosmovision. A reinvention of community inspired by such principles can develop out of practices of expanding commoning that depart from the capitalist plundering of resources and the ruthless exploitation of humans and nonhumans alike. A relevant politics of community autonomy, thus, establishes forms of living together that are based on mutuality, cooperation, and respectful and balanced relations with nature. In order to search for a politics for community building, it is better to look at the potentialities of the social rather at the exceptional presence of the political, understood as a demarcated area of common life (as in Arendt's hypothesis). The social with all its latent or potential resistances is where a politics of commoning emerges as a force to reclaim what should be discovered and sustained as the source of the common.

Jean Luc Nancy, let us recall, understands the "being-in-common" as constitutive of the existence of humans. For him, being-with-others should be understood with an emphasis on the constitutive "with" (2000). It is here that his problematization of the political is grounded: "The political is the place where the community as such is brought into play ... the place of a specific existence, the existence of being in common" (1991: xxxvii). Being-in-common does not mean for Nancy being similar. Quite the contrary: being-in-common is the condition in which singularities may coexist and expose themselves to each other by sharing a common ground, a "stage," the "space of a co-appearing" (2000: 66–7). As in Arendt, the space of coappearing is more like a receiver of action rather than a concrete shaping element of action, a perceptible, reflexively made meaningful, and often ritually established and reproduced constituent of action in the context of community.

Putting an emphasis on the openness and contingency of shared spaces is a prime concern of both Nancy and Arendt, as Mustafa Dikec rightly suggests (2015). What however both fail to notice is that a "we" is being crafted in the materiality of concrete relations with land as well as with those with whom this land is shared. This view directly challenges Western dominant ideologies from within the context of today's multicultural megacities. Public spaces as well as spaces developed through commoning (common spaces) are spaces performed and performative. They participate in the construction of social bonds and shared worldviews while they support all aspects of social life. Being-in-common is a spatiotemporal set of performances. To reinvent community through commoning might then mean to explore a possible politics of being-in-common.

In Buenos Aires, during the days of 2001 uprising, neighborhood assemblies had become "space[s] of experimentation on the possibilities of producing popular and autonomous forms of administration" (Colectivo Situaciones, 2002: 170). Thus, "in the assemblies people put forward practical hypotheses of re-appropriation—no matter how partial—of the living conditions" (ibid.: 168).

Isn't this a well-stated synopsis of what it means to collectively reinvent communities by exploring the very core of commoning? For this potential community reinvention, which is to distance itself from enclosed (including self-enclosed) communities as well as from state-controlled or market-developed community simulations, it is not enough to reappropriate what must be and has been the commons. Emergent communities have to rethink about the commons, to reevaluate forms of defining what is to be shared and how, and to thus reinvent commoning by reinventing open communities of equality and mutual support. Autonomy describes the practices and the ethics of such communities and it should not be confused with "self-sufficiency" (Escobar, 2017). Rather, it is about constructing an "archipelago of conviviality" (a term of A. Gorz to which Esteva, 2015b refers) that may be described in condensed form by the motto of the National Indigenous Congress of Mexico: "We are a web when we are separated and an assembly when we are together" (in Esteva, 2015b: 86).

Collective Habits Invented

Individual habits usually articulate an individual identity. A person is identified by his or her habits. Collective habits, however, identify a group, a community.

They circumscribe a coherent whole by identifying the group's members as those who have the same habits. Those similarities that are recognized and regarded as crucial may be elevated to the group's distinctive features.

Both individual and collective habits give the impression of an identity. What is an identity after all if not the impression that certain characteristics of behavior continue to characterize this behavior by being repeatedly expressed?

Habits support continuity, give the impression of similarities, characterize by supporting identities. What if however habits become the focus of collective creativity? What if new habits emerge in the process of exploring the potentialities of shared life beyond the limitations imposed by inequality and individualist ethos? What if habits become an area of emancipatory commoning?

Habitual performances are performances that bring into memory similar ones that took place in the past. But at the same time they are unique in the context of their present execution. Collective and individual memories offer fields of comparison between an act being performed and acts that have been performed in the past. The unfolding of a habit is diagnosed because we are capable of drawing similarities between acts happening in different moments in time.

Each act that appears as being repeated is capable of representing a series of similar acts that share something in common. Any performance, thus, may be seen as an example that precisely illustrates a pattern, a rule.

The example aims to reveal a category and, in the case of recurrent performances, a category of similar behaviors. It thus identifies a set which it represents. But in order to represent this set, the example needs to be temporarily outside the set. It is an example only in so far as it is no longer a member of the set. The only way to remain within the set is to retain its specificity, that which makes it distinct from the other members of this whole. By becoming exemplary, the example loses its specificity. If "to believe" is to be used as an example of a verb, the specific meaning of the act of believing becomes totally irrelevant. Agamben insists on the etymology of the word example: "beside, in spite of, para-deigma" (1998: 220). The example shows a class, a whole, only when it steps out and stands beside that class or whole.

The "whatever singularity" to which Agamben refers (1993) is a singularity precisely because it constitutes neither a repetition of a type nor an absolute difference. It is a singularity that has the characteristics of an example. Being a member of a "coming community" means not being reduced to a repeated and repeatable character but, rather, being able to communicate "without being tied by any common property, by any identity" (Agamben, 1993: 11). This is the conclusion to which Agamben leads his reasoning about a future community in which pure belonging will be freed from the burden of shared identities. We may, however, lead this reasoning to a different path: What if this power of performed acts to remain distinct while appearing as familiar and recognizable reveals the potentiality of establishing shared habits of emancipatory co-living? What if rituals, habits, and tracing practices (the shared repetitive performances that we will soon explore) don't simply corroborate established identities but possibly open collective creativity to the invention of new patterns of living in common, and of living in common without the need of being similar or same?

Urban communities develop urban habits. Are there not patterns of inculcated behavior that are specifically metropolitan? Don't the inhabitants of large contemporary cities develop capacities to face the particularity and the unprecedented space–time conditions of the urban environment they live in? A kind of metropolitan habitus is inculcated through the repetitive experiencing of metropolitan space. Knowing how to cross a street, how to drive on a congested avenue, how to estimate where certain goods are located in a supermarket, how to avoid "dangerous places," and so on, is part of a knowledge that is often learned through the body. And this knowledge supports recurrent practices, as it condenses in everyday habits.

"Using" the city, living in a big city, does not rely simply on explicit instructions but crucially depends on the development of appropriate habits that become corroborated when the performances they support produce gratifying results.

Urban habits rely on a kind of spatial knowledge that reflects the spatial typologies that the imposed spatial urban order supports. The more this order manages to naturalize its logic (convincing the urbanites that this is naturally the only possible way of arranging space for an urban society), the more urban habits tend to become fixed. An acquired urban habitus (specifically shaped by the corresponding urbanite's social characteristics) becomes the most important means of urban survival.

In moments of crisis (personal, local, or social) habits are confronted with circumstances, which their adaptive repeatability cannot treat effectively. Urban space plays an important role in such cases. To follow Lefebvre's distinction, spaces that challenge established habits may be either "produced spaces" or "appropriated spaces." In produced spaces, new social relations and modes of human interaction are being tested. Such spaces result from great social upheavals that destroy existing conditions of domination. What Lefebvre calls "trial by space" (1991: 416) is for him a necessary ordeal the ideas about social change have to go through. So long as these ideas about society manage to produce their corresponding space, they will manage to produce change.

Appropriation, on the other hand, is a more complex process. Lefebvre warns us not to confuse appropriation "with a practice which is closely related to it but still distinct, namely diversion (*détournement*)" (ibid.: 167). In diversion, the existing spaces created for specific social uses are reappropriated to accommodate new emerging collective needs especially by those whose needs and aspirations could not (or were not allowed to) produce their own space. In diversion, true production is replaced by a kind of ad hoc adaptation and thus it is possibly postponed. On the other hand, appropriation is a creative process: "It may be said of a natural space modified in order to serve the needs and *possibilities* of a group that it has been appropriated by that group" (ibid.: 165, emphasis added). It seems that the distinct characteristic of such spaces is that they preexist: Modifying them means, for the corresponding social actors, to actually shape them in a process that Lefebvre compares to the creation of works of art (ibid.). Appropriation, thus, becomes also a way of producing space, since it employs inventive practices that transform given spatial conditions. Such practices are clearly different for Lefebvre from "a master's project" that produces "dominated" or "dominant" space—a kind of space he considers as opposite to appropriate space (165).

Tempo, scheme transfer, and the need to chart change on a map of seemingly predictable forthcoming events gives to habits a role that clearly defies the clear-cut distinction between pure innovation (and therefore surprise) and absolute sameness (and therefore reassurance).

True, dominant elites try to reduce habit to automatism. Especially nowadays, this effort is supported by the development of technologies of predictability and productive ordering (of time and space) by those programming technologies which process sensory data (and control responses to those data through algorithmic scenarios).

Consistent to his diagnosis concerning the current phase of capitalism as "semio-capitalism," Franco Berardi understands automatism as predominantly connected to semiosis, the production and fixing of meaning. For him, "automaton" "produces meaning by following rules that are compliant with the digital machine, and can act effectively only within the semiotic universe of connection" (2019: 110). For Berardi, thus, automatism, which includes both the responses of individuals as well as those of mechanized systems, is based on connectivity. Connectivity enhances and develops the effectiveness of machine systems (and especially data processing systems) since their construction is actually based on relations of connectedness. In the case of people, however, connectivity replaces singularity and differentiated individuation. Transposing this view to the discussion on habit, we may discover the historically specific form through which habits are shaped in contemporary societies of advanced capitalism. Automatism in the production of meaning and in the creation of predictable responses to produced meanings reduces habit to a kind of "second nature" based on "neo-instincts": "Connective neo-humans tend to be more and more integrated through swarm behaviour" (ibid.: 109). Human interactions are ruled by automated responses.

Habit, both as means to reproduce existing urban order and as a series of emerging patterns of behavior that challenge this order, is, as we saw, a place-making capacity. Places are spatial arrangements that appear as possessing a certain recognizable identity and characteristics. This means that they appear as spaces which retain a certain social meaning.

In the process of shaping spaces for inhabiting, people actually transform them into places: Habits are those networks of practices that establish the use, meaning, and value of specific places for specific social contexts. Places endure as social constructs through the habits that dwell in them.

We need to be beyond the idea, however, that this place-making process should be necessarily linked to the reproduction of existing social identities. Habits may be invented and pursed as a means to challenge social identities. Places produced and reproduced through imposed habits may be transformed through the emergence of alternative habits. We need to disentangle the term "place" from a literature that tends to ignore the historicity of social struggles and thus connects place to allegedly inherent qualities of certain spaces. And we also need to recognize the multileveled complexity at work in place-making activities, which simultaneously involves materialities, geometrical relations, arrangements of power, and symbolic mechanisms.

Habit is place-sensitive—it shapes space while attempting to control the flow of time through its repetitiveness. The status of place, and therefore the conditions under which people recognize and inhabit places is, of course, depended upon the particularities of the society they participate in. Current "semio-capitalism," to borrow Berardi's term, somehow tends to vaporize the material basis of place. It is not however that we don't live any more in concrete spaces, perceivable and describable in their materiality. Rather, our relations to space become more and more ephemeral, flexible, and often unpredictable. For some, this is an indication of uprootedness. And for some others, this is more like a promise of liberation presented as stemming from the merits of nomadism. As Zygmunt Bauman has clearly shown, however, nomadism is for some people an advantage and a privilege while for others it is a burden, an unavoidable fate (1998, 2000). All of them however develop habits.

The difference lies in the ways their habits create place. Repeatability is the basis of performance. For someone thus to perform a place, to make a place, is to be able to compare it to a before. For the jet traveling elite, the business class area of airplanes may acquire the status of place. The expression to "feel at home" possibly condenses the feeling of being at a place that we know how to inhabit. Home becomes the most persistent metaphor of places inhabited by habits. In terms of tracing a firmly grounded imaginary especially for those raised within a sedentary culture, Gaston Bachelard (1994) seems to have a strong point. We tend to carry in our body a kind of home-seeking disposition. And we tend to employ those dispositions even in circumstances in which "home" is fleeting, always departing, or suddenly sinking beneath our feet.

Habitual performances become creative by repeating acts that have proven to be transformative (of matter, of relations between objects, of relations between humans, etc.). Beyond and against a well-established imaginary of total innovation, primarily supported by the modernist ethos and especially praised as the most important source of modernist artistic creation, performances can be inventive by integrating change to recognizable patterns of acting.

A few important lessons may be drawn from the history of the establishing of new habits as a way of creating a new society.

It was the so-called utopian socialists of nineteenth century who first explored the possibility of developing new arrangements of everyday time and space as means to produce new forms of social organization. Robert Owen's experiments in New Lanark, Scotland, included an Institute for the Formation of Character, a place in which the education of children and the reeducation of working mothers was to be explicitly developed. Owen was one to the first to pursue the idea of a model urban structure as a means to shape new values and habits through living together. In New Lanark, this vision was made partially possible because it had been connected to the effort to build an ideal working and producing community around Owen's owned textile factory. Although his plans to actually construct such a community in New Harmony (Indiana, United States) did not succeed, Owen's ideas developed a legacy according to which the creation of a new co-living environment, distinct from the existing cities, was considered as the necessary condition for creating new egalitarian habits. Of course, Owen was firmly convinced that "environment and not heredity shape character decisively" (Heynen, 1982: 33).

Owen based his thoughts on a rational approach to social harmony. Charles Fourier, the other great utopian socialist of nineteenth century, was more focused on the liberating development of passions (Stavrides and Travlou, 2022: 5). According to this approach, a better world would be a "world organized according to the 'dictates' of the passions" (Beecher, 2012: 94).

In his *Theory of the Four Movements*, he explicitly connects the "progress in Civilization" with "sensual luxury." And he concludes, "Can there be any doubt that the civilized order is incompatible with reason, when you say the latter's purpose is to moderate the passions" (Fourier, 1996: 184)? "The more developed Civilization becomes, the less respect there is for austerity and moderation" (ibid.: 185).

Fourier's suggestions about a new community, concretized in his proposals for the *phalanx*, were thus based on a kind of a combination of passions. His complex inventory of passions supports his classification of personality types. The Phalanstery, the model community-building city, would include a complete spectrum of those types in a new ideal community. This was for Fourier the way to reach the ideal number of people comprising the community as well as the ideal combination of sexes, professions, and ages. The passions of the community's members were meant to support the motives for co-living—well-being and pleasure. A suggestion highly debatable indeed. However in Fourier's contribution to the utopian longing for a liberated community, we may trace a reasoning about habits that departs from an analysis concerning their attachment to social control and opens the way to an analysis of human relations beyond the presuppositions of moral philosophy.

An array of measures taken and a set of legislative decisions made during the days of Paris Commune (1871) indicate the importance of changes that directly shape collective habits. Usually, such measures are described as actions related to new forms of governing, which of course they also are. However, it is important to observe how such revolutionary decisions directly influenced the organization of social everyday life itself.

Take the issue of education, for example. The Commission for Public Education headed by Édouard Vaillant aimed at rendering education "not only secular ... but also free and compulsory" (Abidor, 2015: 404–5). If this is a declaration of values and a political program, its immediate results had been affecting many people's lives. First of all, the parents themselves. They were called in meetings to express ideas and to organize the reforms in the education system. For them this was indeed a change in their everyday routines and a potential new role in their relation with their kids and school. Children too must have had opportunities to develop new habits. Many of them were previously left without care in the streets of Paris (due to poverty and the calamities of war). Reorganized social spaces, as were the Commune's schools, would give to those children an inclusive non-paternalizing environment of democracy and equality.

An emblematic statement used in the Commune's Federation of Artists manifesto is, "We will work cooperatively toward our regeneration, the birth of communal luxury, future splendors and the Universal Republic" (in Ross, 2015: 91). Kristin Ross attempts to capture the quintessence of the Commune's political imaginary in the term "communal luxury" (2015). This declaration is first of all connected to a new way of understanding the role of the arts by reestablishing their links with the community and by abolishing any hierarchical separation between low and high art. "The demand that beauty flourish in spaces shared in common and not just in special privatized preserves means reconfiguring art to be fully integrated into everyday life," Ross comments (2015: 92).

There is also a kind of everyday ethics inherent in the imaginary of communal luxury. Everyday habits of conspicuous spending and of wealth exhibition performed by the affluent are condemned. Not only measures of fair redistribution were taken by the Commune (by raising salaries and by controlling rents for example), but also a kind of communal ethics of sharing was developed. Ross, linking William Morris's thoughts (an enthusiastic supporter of the Commune) to this reconsideration of discrimination habits by the Commune, has this to suggest: "Senseless luxury, which Morris knew cannot exist without slavery of some kind, would be replaced by communal luxury, or equality in abundance" (2015: 98).

David Harvey considers the Paris Commune as "the greatest class-based communal uprising in capitalist history" (2003: 219). Insisting on the working-class orientation of the community creation that unfolded during the days of the Commune, he connects the Parisian uprising with a confrontation between the neighborhood institutions and networks of solidarity developed by the working class on one side and the Haussmanian rejection of "any version of community that involved the socialist ideal of a nurturing body politic" (ibid.: 229). In a city in which a vast restructuring of public space was in progress (Haussmann's great projects), the Commune was a reinvention of community through new forms of self-government and the rising of new collective habits based on a culture of solidarity, equality, and mutual help.

The case of Oaxaca Commune is perhaps less well known. From August to November 2006, the city of Oaxaca in Mexico was occupied by protesters and was organized as a veritable urban commune. Starting from a massive teachers strike against a neoliberal education reform, Oaxaca occupation became the ground of a series of social experimentations in urban self-management and autonomy.

"Barricades became sites where people shared information and grievances … [T]hey became mobilized political units that would eventually serve to resist the federal police's siege of the capital later that fall. This level of popular mobilization and organization led many to declare the movement the 'Oaxacan commune'" (Dilingham, 2021: 186).

The Oaxaca uprising had its own political and social roots and belongs to an important series of struggles against capitalist neoliberal governance. The teachers strike, which became its igniting event, also has its genealogy in many similar struggles and, as most of them, was faced with brutal repression (the eviction of the teachers' encampment from Oaxaca's central square was the event to trigger the uprising). What is however the most distinct characteristic of this uprising is the fact that it unleashed an impressively creative popular power that actually transformed the city for seven months to a dense network of self-governed urban communities.

It is undoubtedly important to study the alternative forms of governance developed during the days of the occupation. The role of Asamblea Popular de los Pueblos de Oaxaca (APPO) and the alternative institutions of popular participation have rightly become the focus of political analysts and movement thinkers. It is, however, also important to trace the ways a different kind of everydayness was created by the people themselves during the occupation.

The barricades, initially constructed in order to organize the Commune's defense against the police (Federal and Regional), became the condensers of a reinvented everyday life liberated from the routines of capitalist reproduction. They became a "mobile utopia" according to Katerina Nasioka (2017: 103), "an open urban utopia" (ibid.: 102).

The everyday distribution of food, cooking and making coffee, sharing news, and attending educational workshops were among the many things that happened in the barricades. The barricades, according to Barucha Peller, "were home to a myriad of reproductive activities in which historically feminized labor became the basis for transformed social relations" (2016: 72). They were part of a network of "transformed and transformative spaces" (Nasioka, 2017: 107) that were spreading in the occupied city.

Gustavo Esteva adds another important point to the role of barricades as condensers of community organizing. People from popular neighborhoods "formed, in the majority of cases, by illegal land occupations by squatters" (2010: 985) participated unexpectedly in the movement (along with some from the middle-class areas). Carrying the experience of a "communal social fabric" (ibid.) those people actually took part in the development of a shared social consciousness that often led to the defense of a distinct kind of urban autonomy.

Everyday habits, related to work routines or to household care, were thus replaced by new ones. Practices that were considered as private or family-oriented became public. And as one would expect, this had introduced serious difficulties in the reproduction of gendered roles even within the movement itself. "Men," as Peller claims, "attempted to uphold the gendered division of labor and force women back into the home" (2016: 72). But women determined to contribute to a reclaiming of everyday life with dignity and equality kept on fighting for gender equality, expressed especially in the rotation of everyday duties and responsibilities and in the sharing of housework.

Interestingly, the barricades of the Paris Commune had a quite different function, according to Kristin Ross. Instead of being condensers of an alternative everydayness, they were of a mainly "strategic use." The Parisian barricades were not "to be used as a shelter ... but to prevent enemy forces from circulating" (Ross, 2008: 37). In the street fighting, Communards would move through passageways and from house to house. For them, as Ross concludes, "the interior becomes the street" (ibid.: 38). This is perhaps one more indication of the close interdependence between community bonds of mutual support and the arrangement of neighborhood spaces (a maze of interconnections that would puzzle any "outsider," including of course the Versailles army).

In a very bold and decisive gesture, thousands of Oaxaca's women took over the state television and radio station, *Canal Nueve*. In a contemporary city, the manipulation of information and news by the dominant media is a crucial factor in shaping views and everyday routines. An occupied media station that transmits news created and presented by the people themselves is a major change. What is amazing is that the occupation was not even predecided. After a huge demonstration ended at the station, the demonstrators made a demand for a 15-minutes broadcast, which was flatly refused by the station's director. This successful recuperation of public media (which lasted until the riot police took back the station), was part of a series of initiatives that established a network of self-managed radio stations in the city (Nasioka, 2017: 104). Belonging to a community of struggle meant—for the insurgent people of Oaxaca—having the opportunity to communicate and become informed through exchanges that traversed the occupied city.

Oaxaca commune developed its own patterns of liberating everydayness. Collective habits based on mutual care and solidarity shaped all of the city's reinvented routines, including education, health care, food distribution, information exchanges, leisure activities, garbage collection, and traffic regulation. Not losing sight of the need to be always ready to confront military and paramilitary attacks, the people of Oaxaca managed to take the life of the city in their hands.

Community Building by Inventing Rituals

In certain indigenous languages in Mexico, the word for community and territory is the same. In Tzotsil and other Mayan languages, the word used is *jlumaltik* (Baschet, 2018). However, this does not indicate an attitude of possession. Land is the common ground to be shared by all. *Pacha Mama*, mother earth, does not belong to anybody. To say therefore that community and territory are the same thing means that there can be no community without a land to which it is embedded.

This somehow reveals the powerful connection an indigenous community has to its territory not only as a means to sustain itself but also as a constitutive element of the operational relations this community has with its surrounding environment (both "natural" and "social"). A. Escobar suggests that a community's territory is to be understood as "a system of relations whose continuous re-enactment re-creates the community in question" (2017: 173).

And if in rural communities these relations are developed through practices of cultivation, farming, livestock raising, and so on, in urban communities these relations are developed by producing the city in its everyday uses and rituals.

Community's relation to space is multifaceted. It activates practices of care and exchange, processes of production and social reproduction, as well as the construction of shared worldviews. Those shared worldviews explicitly construct community bonds either by strengthening inherited ones or by opening the field to rearrangements in power geometries. In such a context, rituals contribute to the reproduction as well as to the reconstruction of community and can be taken to constitute powerful means of community reinvention.

Let us explore the possibility of rituals playing with the magic circle's closure—of rituals that develop the potentiality of open communities through their performed closures. Seen from a certain perspective, the *Mística* ritual of the Brazilian Landless Rural Workers Movement (Movimento dos Trabahadores Rurais Sem Terra—MST) is an interesting example.

MST is a movement with a long tradition of struggles including, predominantly, land occupations. It is a very well-organized movement, and it has successfully established self-governed settlements mostly close to large areas of collective cultivation that are in most cases recuperated *latifundios*.

MST "has been advocating an alternative way of life. It is a struggle that goes beyond land redistribution" (Issa, 2007: 85). So, MST is organized not only to develop the strategy and tactics of struggle but also to promote within its members a collective identity that makes them builders of a new kind of community. The occupation, the temporary camp, and the settlement become important areas of living together in which this emerging collective identity is being shaped. In such "interactive spaces" (Hammond, 2014: 383) MST militants share experiences and aspirations and learn from each other's stories. They become empowered and even raise the identity of the landless poor to a positive marker. Commenting on an activist's words who proudly proclaims "I am a Sem Terra with capital letters," J. Hammond notices that "not only does she invert the status of landless from pejorative to proudly acknowledged; she converts it from an attribute to a noun, from an incidental characteristic to the essence of *what she is*" (ibid., italics in the original).

Mística rituals play a very important role in the formation of this emerging identity, which actually radiates as a kind of call to action and participation to all those who will potentially join MST. Mística rituals are not merely identity performances, however. Comprising expressive acts as diverse as theatrical pieces, flag waving, collective singing, organized sceneries for assemblies, poem reading, commemoration of movement's struggles and heroes, symbolic arrangements of objects (seeds, candles, rural workers' tools, etc.), Mística rituals actually lack strict formal rules. Nevertheless, they are recognized by MST members as important empowering experiences that give them the strength to continue in struggles that are difficult, dangerous, and not always successful (Figures 1 and 2).

Interestingly, one of the movement's leaders, João Pedro Stedile, declares that MST is open to "all truths, not a single truth" (quoted in Issa, 2007: 128 and in Hammond, 2014: 375). Such an approach clearly differentiates MST's cultural and ideological formation from other explicitly Marxist, anarchist, or populist movements. Without being a religious movement, it has

Figure 1 *Mística* ritual during the 6th Congresso Nacional do MST, in 2014 at Brasília (DF). Courtesy of Oliver Kornblihtt (Midia Ninja).

Figure 2 *Mística* ritual during the celebration of thirty years of MST in 2014. Courtesy of MST Maranhão.

managed to appropriate both Catholic ritualism as well as indigenous and African religiosity producing an almost animistic amalgam of belief in the "sacredness of nature" (Issa, 2007: 90).

We must keep in mind that Liberation Theology has been the source of many anti-dictatorship and anti-capitalist movements in South America. Distancing itself from a preaching mode that promised a better world after death, Liberation's priests were fighting for a just world in which everybody could live. And, surely, their ethos of humility and respect for nature became a strong example to be followed by the rural poor.

"Mística is a vision of the future, the way you're part of something bigger" (MST activist interviewed in Flynn, 2013: 186). Mística rituals are oriented toward the transformation of existing social conditions. This differentiates their characteristics and their effects from rituals meant to ensure the reproduction of a certain status quo.

Employing Nicolas Bourriaud's theory of relational aesthetics (2002) Flynn considers that mística performances "are capable of producing 'micro-utopias,' temporary communities of intersubjective encounters" (Flynn, 2016: 65). In a way and following Bourriaud's approach, Flynn disconnects mística from a grand plan to prefigure an emancipatory future and puts emphasis on the performative aspect of the ritual—the ways it affects concrete people's lives and aspirations by producing diverse experiences of political subjectivation. It seems, however, that both tendencies are present in mística, exactly because it lacks the formal rigidity of a social reproduction ritual. Mística is transversed by the microutopias of everyday transformation as well as by visions of an emancipatory society, albeit envisaged not as an abstract "beyond" but as a world crafted from the concrete experiences of struggle. Delinking mística from the collective emancipatory project that characterizes MST struggle is a kind of "depoliticization" of the movement's scopes. After all, Bourriaud's relational aesthetics is heavily criticized for taking for granted that any kind of relationality necessarily involves democratic forms of sociality (Bishop, 2004; Kunst, 2015). Without concrete forms of relations that attempt to open possibilities of a different social organization, participation and collaboration may shape relations focused on the temporality of the present without challenging the future.

Mística shares with order-maintaining rituals the essential characteristics of ritual action, which are: the definition of a magic circle within which performances acquire their meaning, a certain pattern of repetitiveness and the power to mobilize images and shared experiences in order to produce shared emotions, to strengthen (and develop) shared beliefs, and to reaffirm (and develop) communal bonds. However, mística is not the work of chosen experts capable of conducting the ritualistic staging (a role that in many analogous cases is given to magicians, priests, group leaders, etc.). Members themselves are meant to prepare performances of mística for different occasions. There is a debate among the researchers considering the "institutional" status of mística. Do the movement's leaders or MST's Cultural Committee or simply the elders somehow paternalize mística performances, thus depriving them of spontaneity and improvisation?

Stédile's remark supports the view that mística is genuine popular creativity. "We realized that if you allow mística to become formal, it dies out. No one receives orders to be emotional; you get emotional because you are motivated as a result of something" (Stédile and Fernandes, 1999: 130, cited by Flynn, 2013: 180).

In a way, mística is closely connected to the "performative aspect of the [occupation] camp" (Flynn, 2013: 178). The experience of taking part in the occupation of land, of sharing the dangers, and of being part of a community in struggle has both a tactical and a pedagogic role. So does mística—it is meant to transcribe in a symbolic language these experiences by enhancing at the same time the shared values that make them possible: humility, loyalty perseverance, dignity, determination, sacrifice, and a strong belief in scopes that go beyond individual aspirations and needs.

A kind of magical efficacy is present in rituals (both in dissident ones as well as in those that align with the prevailing social order). It is important to distinguish ritual practices from performances that aim at representing a scope, a set of values, a series of past events, or a symbolic landscape of future life. In ritual acts, both the participants in the performance and those who are less involved (although there are never mere spectators in a ritual event that addresses the corresponding community) are engaged, moved, and transformed. Even the most temporary effects have a lasting impact on the members of the community. Otherwise said, rituals are not artistic events (like happenings, for example) although they employ elements of artistic expression and creativity. Rituals matter. They are meant to shape modes of behavior, to justify collective scopes, and to shape identities and patterns of action that influence social life well beyond the magic circle. Dissident rituals, thus, do not only express dissident values and scopes but actually shape dissident acts and practices, and thus exert pressure on the boundaries of urban and social order. Ritual repetitiveness does not merely put an emphasis on a message to be communicated to the community itself. This is not about an act of addressing an audience so as to ensure that its members receive it and interpret it.

During the days of President Fujimori's administration in Peru (a president accused and convicted for corruption), a very interesting ritual practice unfolded: people of the democratic movement were washing the country's flag in public performances that took place every Friday in Lima's Plaza Mayor as well as in many other cities (Vich, 2004; Lane, 2007). The most obvious way of interpreting this gesture is to consider it as the articulation of a message: Fujimori had "dirtied" the country with his corrupt government and the false elections that made him Peru's president. And the flag was of course meant to represent the country itself. Repetitiveness, however, produces effects, not only meaning. Democratic activists were actually empowered by their acts, and their presence became part of a dissident setting that kept on challenging and confronting Fujimori's propaganda. Reminding people that they live in a dictatorship disguised as democracy was not the transmission of information, it was a call to action. It was a kind of performance that, although enacted within a ritual magic circle, acquired a certain crucial efficiency: It intervened in the struggle to oust a dictator. Reducing this series of repeated acts to the status of a message misses the point of ritualistic efficacy.

A lot has been said and written about carnival and the ritual aspects of carnival feasts. What is useful in the context of this work, though, is to trace the potentialities of contemporary urban carnivals in relation to the reinvention of urban communities.

Let us first see some examples. The first two come from Athens. The Metaxourgeio carnival and the Exarchia carnival. Both are self-organized with the free participation of people and have no relations to state or market sponsorships. As in most cases, the preparations for the day of the carnival parade take a long time. Discussions, rehearsals, and an atmosphere of living together as a gratifying experience characterize those meetings.

Although lifestyle media present Metaxourgeio carnival as an effervescent eruption of spontaneity, a lot of preparatory work is done to make sure that the parade will evolve in an inclusive and organized way. The parade's itinerary is carefully planned and the spots in which different street bands will wait to enter in the parade are carefully chosen. The idea is to commence and end the carnival's colorful procession at the same central square of Metaxourgeio. It is in this square that at the end of the day a huge effigy of the "carnival king" is set to fire while people are dancing and singing around the ritual bonfire.

People participating in the organizing meetings as well as those who join the parade every year seem to consider themselves as a kind of urban community that explicitly distances itself from the neighborhood's gentrifying atmosphere. In a way, Metaxourgeio carnival is an active protest against official carnival feasts (organized by the municipality of Athens), which tend to support gentrification and become tourist attractions. A feeling of being part of an albeit temporary community that encourages individual improvisation (all costumes are inventively crafted by reused materials) seems to prevail in Metaxourgeio carnival. This is an open community of commoners that dissolves after the feast (although several of its members continue to support each other as urban activists) only to reemerge next year.

In Exarchia, a neighborhood widely known for its youth alternative culture and for being a melting pot of dissident and anti-systemic practices, the yearly carnival parade is more explicitly politicized. In the posters pasted in the neighborhood in 2023, the carnival was announced as a feast against gentrification and opposition to the state's effort to construct a metro station at the very alive central square of the neighborhood (although other options were available).

Most of the banners and effigies carried in the 2023 parade explicitly referred to the anti-gentrification movement's slogans or ridiculed dominant policies of brutal police interventions (Figure 3). The central square now totally occupied by the police and the metro construction site used to be the final point of the procession and the place for the burning of the king carnival's effigy. These last years this is not possible. And an almost unavoidable confrontation with the police (provoked or not by anarchist activists) has resulted in an abrupt ending of the carnival feast.

Figure 3 Poster announcing the Exarchia Carnival celebration: "Against Gentrification and Touristifcation. Let's Keep Exarchia as a Neighborhood." 2022. Author's photo.

Preparations for this parade are equally important in shaping bonds within a community. This community is active in many ways, struggling to preserve the unique character of the neighborhood. Members of an Initiative of Exarchia Citizens are the constitutive core of this community, which is generally open and tries to integrate people working, studying (in the nearly School of Architecture), or staying in the neighborhood.

A comparable community reinventing ritual is taking place in Naples. In this city, an interesting experience of urban commoning has resulted from the cooperation of distinct initiatives of urban commoning with a municipal administration eager to support them without patronizing them (Stavrides, forthcoming).

An important area of intervention in the city's commoning potentialities is the organizing of what they call a social carnival (*Carnevale sociale*) by some of the urban commons initiatives. Flooding the streets of the center of Naples, *Scugnizzo Liberato* initiative organizes a procession with festive characteristics, which explicitly demonstrates the potentialities of neighborhood communities. It is because in the occupied former adolescent prison now called Scunizzo Liberato (freed adolescent in Neapolitan dialect) various activities throughout the year create ties especially with the young population of the neighborhood that this open community can give a strong contemporary social meaning to carnival rituals. Instead of being primarily a self-managed cultural center, Scunizzo Liberato is a condenser of neighborhood life and a space free for all. This kind of urban activist context makes it possible for a community to reaffirm as well as to reinvent itself in public performances, including the social carnival ritual. Obvious ritualistic elements as the masks, the costumes, and a staged playful derisory attitude toward expressions of the neoliberal status quo are employed to support bonds of affect and meaningful relationships in the neighborhood. At the same time, carnival parade becomes a kind of demonstration in support of the commoning initiatives.

In the case of the *Lido Pola* occupation at Bagnoli, a former industrial area in Naples that is heavily polluted and neglected, social carnival acquires a more straightforward political momentum. One of the main struggles of the Lido Pola urban commoning community is opening the beach to everybody, considered as a common good. The carnival procession has its theme connected to this struggle. Being mainly a working-class area, Bagnoli bears a stamp of proletarian activism on the festive demonstration. Lido Pola community, by definition an open "community of reference" (Stavrides, ibid.), acts as a catalyst in synergies between environmental housing rights and cultural initiatives active in the area. The social carnival ritual seems to unite those initiatives in a festive atmosphere that corroborates bonds of belonging to a rather homogeneous urban setting. And what is perhaps crucial in the context of Neapolitan life, such performances help movement activists to build a popular support that distances itself from the strong networks of mafia-type solidarity established by the local *Camorra*.

One more area in which we may detect the potentialities of urban ritual in processes of reinventing urban communities is the rituals connected to practices of commensality. Eating together in large organized events has in certain cases become the means to corroborate an open community of struggle in an oblique confrontation with the dominant policies of urban governance.

In Istanbul, an important struggle to preserve a park at the center of the city by a very rich and diverse set of initiatives was brutally suppressed by the police (Stavrides, 2019). The camp of the protesting occupiers was destroyed and people were chased all over the city's central avenue, İstiklâl Caddesi. Among the responses to this brutal suppression of the movement was the one organized by Muslim activists at the same avenue. Since for Muslims it is customary to eat only after the sunset during the days of Ramadan, these activists organized a huge shared meal-taking place at a very long table at İstiklâl. Police could not intervene since this initiative had the appearance of a customary Ramadan shared meal although everybody knew (and participated for this reason) that this was a meal of protest. A community of struggle managed to convert a ritual of commensality (which is anyhow a community strengthening ritual) to a ritual of protest and commoning-through-struggle.

In Diyarbakir, one of the major Turkish cities in which an uprising of the predominantly Kurdish population took place, one more instance of insurgent commensality unfolded. At the ruins of a neighborhood almost razed to the ground by the Turkish Army that suppressed the uprising, collective meals were organized during the days of Ramadan. The meal was prepared collectively and served literally on the ground, on blankets and carpets arranged between the ruins. Organized by various initiatives of the city (including the local Union of Architects), this ritual meal had the power to transcend its religious origin and to express a feeling of solidarity in an urban community that was heavily suppressed (Figure 4).

Ritualistic behaviour may be used in raising the self-esteem and morals of a community's members. It may also create, albeit on a symbolic level, a different social context and a different set of social relationships potentially leading to new forms of social organization. Reinventing community by developing new rituals based on commoning both supports and expresses the shared values that constitute a common world. And, as has probably become evident throughout this chapter, no commoning practices and performances can unfold without literally taking place. Shared land, common ground, common space. These become the concrete (material as well as symbolic) conditions under which space commoning becomes a shaping factor of communities that reinvent themselves through commoning.

Figure 4 A collective meal during the days of Ramadan between the ruins of a neighborhood in Diyarbakir. 2017. Author's photo.

Traces that Support the Reinvention of Community

The rhythmicality of tracing practices may support and reproduce a feeling of belonging to a community. The shared knowledge necessary for the members of a community to navigate themselves through their living environment (be it a city, a village, a settlement, or a territory) is based on the recognition of recurrent signs. And culture-specific narratives often codify a certain area of knowledge.

However, we should not reduce such a shared capacity to the reproduction of a homogeneous social world. Differences in space and variations in prescribed trajectories supply a shared canvas for actions that characterize different subjects within a community. Different tracing skills as well as differing scopes, albeit related to the following of common trajectories, open a socially inculcated capacity to the potentialities of differentiation within an established community. In the case of open communities of commoners, these potentialities become a propelling force for commoning practices. Heterogeneity—as long as the search for common ground remains—will only make commoners more inventive and obliged to develop trajectories of encounter rather than lines of flight.

Migration has been studied as a process that is predominantly an experience of dislocation. Refugees and immigrants are mostly considered as people who have been forced to depart from places they had considered as their homes. However, we need to admit that a lot of different historical cases of migration were often reduced to a generalizing model. What were the conditions under which people were forced to move? What were they hoping to find when crossing borders? Were all under the same pressure? Did some choose to do so while others had no other option?

Sara Ahmed criticizes analytic narratives of migration that tend to present the process of dislocation and movement as essentially defying the closure of identity. According to her, in Ian Chambers's work, which is in search of an "authentically migrant perspective" (Ahmed, 1999: 334), "experiences of migration, which can involve trauma and violence, become exoticized and idealized as the basis of an ethics of transgression (ibid.).

If, according to Ahmed, Chambers ignores the real conditions of migrant experience, Rosi Braidotti ignores the historical specificities of nomadic life only to construct the figure of the contemporary nomad as a subject of choice. But such a choice, when it is possible, mostly characterizes people who have the privilege to move around the globe "because the world is already constituted as their home" (ibid.: 335). "By refusing to belong to a particular place, the world becomes the global nomad's home" (ibid.: 337).

In both cases, as discussed by Ahmed, movement, either presumed as voluntary or not, becomes a challenge to identity. Migrants and nomads allegedly depart from the closure of shared identities, free themselves from the limitations of a place-bound community, and so may become the appropriate figures to represent a nonessentialist stance.

The experiences of migration and nomadism are a lot more complicated than in such schematized representations (although we must recognize that the theories developed out of them are intended to advance a useful criticism of the dominant identitarian politics). Ahmed's proposal is to question the very center of these and similar theorizations, namely the meaning of home: if home is rather considered as "the lived experience of locality," then "the lived experience of being at home" can be thought "in terms of inhabiting a second skin." Therefore, "movement away is always affective" (ibid.: 341).

Introducing the affective stance to the exploration of migrant experience makes it possible to understand this process as a process of "estrangement" (ibid.: 343). And since estrangement is taken to be related with a particular space and time, the sharing between immigrant experiences is based on differences that manage to communicate. Although Ahmed thinks that it is "through an uncommon estrangement" that migrants possibly develop communities, it seems equally true that they manage to create a common ground on which community develops out of their different, individual experiences.

Of course, there are other things beyond affective experiences that shape migrant communities, especially those of migrants who were forced to leave the place they used to live in. However, the idea of home as second skin helps us understand the feeling of homelessness as a concrete bodily experience. Traces that possibly mark trajectories of forced movement are thus felt traces, traces felt with one's own body. And often those traces may become literal marks on the body, scars (obvious or hidden) that mark out such trajectories in memory.

Could migrant communities be considered as meeting places of such bodies-trajectories? Of such embodied trajectories? Narratives then, when shared within the community, do not only include the necessary mythologized recollections of a lost home, but also the recurrent recognition of traces. When building homes in displacement, migrants possibly retrace the itineraries of their displacement rather than only long for a fixed elsewhere. And when they manage to return (or when they return only to leave again) it is perhaps the recurrent motifs of their movement that give them the power to struggle with estrangement.

A special albeit indicative case of refugee experience is that of the displaced Palestinians living in Gaza. Trying to understand their acts and narratives that keep on returning (literally or in an imaginary way) to the lost home, Ilana Feldman suggests that they "practice (or perform what we might say) "home as a refrain" (2006). "By articulating and enacting relations with home that at times worked with distance and at times brought it closer, the Gazan refrain of home was able to survive the ruptures of Palestinian history and continue to work to provide some sense of security for people" (Feldman, 2006: 18).

Following the different practices of border-crossing by the displaced Palestinians, Feldman traces the importance of a spatial practice that is repetitive. Traces followed during these repetitive enactments of a right to be in the places from which they were expelled were based, as it seems from Feldman's research, on shared narratives. Collective memory was thus performed in acts of crossing borders and following routes toward a lost home.

The idea of refrain as a repetitive act of utterance that produces a feeling of security and "brings chaos at bay" comes from Deleuze and Guattari (2004). And it is connected to a complex conceptualization of territory and territorialization. In the case of Gazans, however, the very idea that a feeling of security stems from repetitive acts and narratives seems not able to capture the potentialities of those acts. Repetitive acts of course are related to the strong shared determination to not abandon the scope of returning "home," and show "a denial of deterritorialization" (Feldman, 2006: 31). But they equally express a struggle for self-determination in a confrontation with colonialism. Exposure to risks (vey literal and deadly ones) cannot be equated to efforts to establish a feeling of security or to establish a kind of order (the rhythmicality of everydayness) in chaos (the unpredictable responses of the powerful). A Gazan community was (and still is) based equally on a collective desire to return and to a "struggle for political liberation" (Abreek-Zubiedat, 2022: 120). What seems to be important for community empowering tracing practices is that those displaced people mark again and again the trajectory of return by performing traces of the future that they collectively desire.

In many cases of refugee camps, researchers and activists have documented the ways refugees themselves are marking their "home" by introducing to otherwise anonymous emergency shelters (containers, tents, mass-produced "houses") marks of individuality (Katz, 2022) (Figure 5). These marks not only trace a path to an individual home (often temporary) but also institute privacy within a "zone of indistinction" (Agamben, 1998), the refugee settlement, in which the private and the public lose their distinctive meaning. Irit Katz suggests that such acts of appropriation of the "bare shelter" are "potentially political" (2022), since according to Arendt's idea (which Katz adopts), politics may only emerge if there is a clear distinction between the private and the public realm. One need not necessarily agree with Arendt's view in order to see the political meaning of resistance expressed in acts of appropriation, which, importantly, are often beyond the satisfaction of the so-called elementary needs and rather express the belonging to a community (political, ethnic, religious, and so on).

In a different context, when refugees had the opportunity to equally participate in the shaping of the conditions of their stay in a country they managed to reach, traces of belonging as well as shared marked trajectories in the city were collectively crafted. A characteristic example is the City Plaza occupied hotel in Athens, which housed a self-managed open community of refugees and activists for thirty-nine months (2016–19).

During the so-called refugee crisis that started in 2015 and made Greece one of the most affected European countries, a very important refugee solidarity initiative emerged in Athens. An unused hotel at the city's center was squatted by a group of activists with the intention of giving to refugees a shelter of dignity and security. The building had the infrastructure to support around four hundred persons and soon became what one of the activists characterized "a peculiar transit village" (Lafazani, 2017).

Creating a community of mutual support and equal responsibilities was not an easy task. Different people coming from different countries, following

Figure 5 Refugee camp in Skaramangas, near Athens. 2019. Courtesy of Zoe Stavridi Michalopoulou.

different religions and with different cultural backgrounds had to devise ways to live together in a culture of sharing, solidarity, and equality. However, as Eleni Katrini's ethnographic work shows, "City Plaza formed a unique collective identity amalgamated from many individual stories, identities, and the participatory interactions between them" (Katrini, 2020: 42).

We may discover in the process of forming such a feeling of belonging (albeit temporary since many refugees were planning to be in other European countries when allowed to do so) a kind of continuous exchange of gestures and messages meant to establish a common ground of trust and mutual support. "The hotel's service-like atmosphere was altered by decorating the walls with artwork, photos from their home countries, solidarity statements, and photos of current and past residents" (Katrini, 2020: 44). One may interpret those acts not only as efforts to appropriate a building that was designed and structured for a very different way of living but also as gestures for leaving traces of presence and belonging. A presence that had no guarantees of permanence (often not even aspirations for that) and a kind of belonging that was not easy since it was not established on common identities or habits and beliefs. Such traces were possibly memory markers

Figure 6 City Plaza occupied hotel: a refugee self-managed shelter. 2017. Author's photo.

of trajectories followed or of home places left behind. Crafting a community without the preexisting guarantees of similarity or homogeneity may indeed employ gestures that establish shared references, or even more important comparable references (Figures 6 and 7).

The way spaces were marked by recurrent recognizable practices of use became an important aspect of building such a heterogeneous open community of commoners. As suggested by Nikolas Kanavaris (2022) and Katrini (2020), the experience of threshold spatiality played a crucial role. Katrini puts an emphasis on the building's numerous windows and balconies that established a kind of osmotic relation with the neighboring buildings. These encouraged relations with the neighbors and even transformed an initial hostility to a friendly and supportive approach by some of them (2020: 46).

Also, the frequent use of the side street (safe and not open to traffic) for events that attracted the presence of neighbors further established recurrent acts of opening and sharing with the neighborhood. In these cases, too, temporary traces of presence (including ways of dressing and acting that would identify some as "foreigners") contributed to the expression of an inclusive community.

Figure 7 City Plaza occupied hotel poster.

Kanavaris describes the ways distinct places of the hotel were defined within the building as "privacy empowering thresholds" (2022: 181). Among them, the "private zones and households" were not defined the usual way a private family space is defined, that is, by markers of ownership that prohibit trespassing. "Due to the lack of extra space, private rooms and households would keep their doors open and the required extra space was found in the corridors or in the everyday spaces on the first floor" (2022: 183). A curtain was put in place of the room doors: a gesture that ensured a certain degree of privacy, an osmotic threshold that allowed the easy movement between room and corridor (especially for children playing). This marker of privacy, this symbolic gesture that attempts to bridge such different cultures and diverse, acquired everyday habits, seems to have contributed to the establishing of a commonly accepted way of living together. And this contributed to the establishment of a culture of sharing and mutual respect. Privacy is a very important constituent of co-living in communities of commoning. To negotiate privacy's limits and symbolization in the context of commoning communities is a crucial task for such communities as they create themselves.

Traces collectively recognized and produced may support the development of communities of struggle. These are traces that explicitly mark public space and gesture toward the potentialities of collective struggle.

For many years, starting from 1980, the Mothers of the Plaza de Mayo (Las Madres de Plaza de Mayo) have been performing a specific demonstration at the central square of Buenos Aires (in front of the presidential palace) asking for justice and the truth about their disappeared boys and girls during the Videla dictatorship. Every Thursday they still march around the square as if to establish their presence and to sustain collective memory in the heart of the city.

This repeated practice has ceremonial elements and aspects of a commemoration ritual. We may however also observe a kind of tracing performance that gives to the movement of those participating a kind of community feeling strengthened by the movement's circular pattern. Marking a specific urban space with the repeated presence of their bodies, Mothers and their supporters trace a different kind of public space. Space created to show, to express a demand. Space marked through an itinerary that has its power due to its circularity. No ending for the demand of justice. Because all those accused are not punished. Because all those who disappeared, killed, have not returned. The traces marked by the bodies of the protesters are there to create a circle of shared memories and of unsatisfied collective demands.

In Montevideo, Uruguay, the victims of the dictatorship are remembered every year in a huge demonstration that follows a specific itinerary at the city's center. They call it the "silent demonstration" and it is remarkably silent: "El día en que el silencio grita" (The day in which silence screams).

This gives to the movement of people a certain ceremonial character comparable to one of the Mothers of Plaza de Mayo. The annually repeated demonstration has specific stop points, in front of a building with a giant screen projecting the faces and names of the victims of the dictatorship and the national monument of Plaza de Libertad at its end. A trajectory of remembrance that is also a trajectory of demands for justice. The motto at the head of demonstration leaves no questions: "Our heroes walk with us. Against the impunity of yesterday and today. The state is responsible."

What the Buenos Aires Mothers do with their bodies in circular movement, the protesters of "the silence that screams" do in procession, which performs an itinerary of memory. In both cases, it is a collective performance that, through a specific recognizable and repeatedly followed itinerary, creates a community of struggle. Whereas for the Mothers, this community has its history and keeps on reestablishing itself in various ways (the Mothers have also established a university focusing on liberation and social emancipation movements), for the protesters of Montevideo this community of silent grieving is reactualized in an annual rendezvous. In both cases images of the "disappeared" are carried by their surviving relatives and friends. Surely those images contribute to a feeling of having to face the same violence and of being angry for the impunity of the dictatorship's monsters.

A last example that I have extensively presented elsewhere is that of Fernando Traverso's bicycles (Stavrides, 2016: 203–7). This artist has developed an idea of a kind of metastatic trace to be imprinted upon the buildings' walls of different cities in which instances of injustice and brutal violence have caused murders of people. The idea came from the cruel experience Traverso himself had when he was waiting for an illegal resistance meeting with a close friend—he just saw him pass by on his bicycle without stopping. In an obvious effort to not reveal Traverso's participation in the resistance, his friend chose to sacrifice himself since he realized that he was being followed by the dictatorship's agents. Traverso created a stencil image of the bicycle in natural size and chose to paste it on walls as a way of commemorating his friend's murder along with all the victims of dictatorships and state violence. He thus performed this gesture in various cities—including Athens and Madrid—which experienced periods of military dictatorships. Traverso's performances were based on the invention of traces in places where traces of such crimes have been lost or have never

Figure 8 F. Traverso placing his stencil bicycle at a wall of the Alexandras Prosfygica social housing complex. 2009. Author's photo.

been discovered. The disappeared ones were the ones whose traces were covered by their torturers and murderers. So, the stencil bicycle became a trace of the past but also a trace of the future. A kind of promise to fight against any future attempt to limit democracy. A kind of declaration that boldly asserts that no one is alone against those who suppress democracy and attack resistance movements (Figure 8).

6

Cooperation as Commoning

Cooperation Captured, Cooperation Liberated

If the formation of communities is a process that shapes the potentiality of urban space, the development of cooperation in and through urban space is an equally crucial process of metropolitan potentialization. To follow the ways such a development indeed affects metropolitan city life, we need to start from an analysis of cooperation at work. Is cooperation a process that necessarily connects to labor and thus to "productivity?" Or should we understand it as a set of values and patterns of activity embedded at the very core of social organization? If this is so, we need to explore cooperation both in the context of the cultural presuppositions of the West (capitalist West to be more precise) as well as in the context of cultural presuppositions that have been grounding different forms of social organization. To go beyond current metropolitan order and the kind of social order it supports and shapes, we need to see what other forms of social worlds give meaning to cooperation (and thus to social relations).

In the context of the dominant Western reasoning concerning development and productivity, cooperation appears as a necessary force provided it is being properly controlled and directed. Channeling cooperation away from the direct control of those who cooperate is not simply a kind of autarchic choice that characterizes sovereign power. Surely directing cooperation from outside is a sign of social despotism that has reached its culmination in different periods of history including both serfdom and slavery. However, in capitalism, as Marx explicitly shows, workers "as cooperators, as members of a working organism ... merely form a particular mode to existence of capital" (1990: 451). "Their cooperation only begins with the labor process, but by then they have ceased to belong to themselves" (ibid.).

In such a production process, what distinguishes the worker from the surf and the slave is that he or she has, at least theoretically, the power to bargain for the sale of his or her labor power. "Agreement" on a certain wage is, thus, an agreement that does not include the merits and advantages of cooperation. No matter how, depending on the historical conditions under which agreements are being made, collective actors (as for example unions) may shape better or worse agreements for the workers, what remains true from the time of Marx till today is that "the socially productive power of labor develops as a free gift to capital" (ibid.) when and if capital directs cooperation.

It is at least on two levels that cooperation's potentiality is captured and exploited within the economy of the capital. First, the worker bargains for a potentiality to work. Work capacity is within the worker's body as a form of potentiality. Moreover, this potentiality is trapped within conditions that are determined by the work to be executed as described by the employer. At the same time however, the worker may be in possession of various other capacities and abilities that are not described as necessary for the tasks in which he or she is to be involved. For example, a bus driver may have acquired a competence in mathematics or have developed knowledge of a foreign language or become experienced in child raising. Some of these capacities may make the bus driver's labor more productive. But he is not going to be paid for those extra performances (unless of course he is paid according to his "productivity"—a form of agreement that opens a different chapter in exploitation conditions).

The idea is that whereas potentiality is in every human being related to the sum total of his or her capacity, and, moreover, to their synergy, wage or compensations are fixed only in consideration with distinct predescribed employer's expectancies. Easily one can deduce from this condition that essential attributes of social education (including language, affective relationships, survival tactics, etc.) are not even counted as potential employee's capacities.

On a second level, the social knowledge connected to cooperation is, as Marx suggests, not included in the bargain for a certain worker's potentiality to execute a certain work. Otherwise said, cooperation is a captured and exploited potentiality.

Many refer today to a knowledge-based economy (Rossi and Tola, 2019; Vercellone, 2007. This does not mean that knowledge and the development of organized areas of socially accumulated knowledge (like the ones related to universities and scientific laboratories) became productive only in our times. The difference is that certain kinds of socially produced knowledges explicitly depend on cooperation and cooperation's potentialities.

These potentialities may well be developed without the need of a commanding or orchestrating center. "Inside the enterprise just as in society, the mobilization and the co-operation of collective knowledges is increasingly fundamental, the only elements able to release and to control a dynamic of accelerated change" (Vercellone, 2007: 33). Is it possible, under these conditions, to consider different kinds of shared knowledge developed and maintained within cooperation, as potentially clashing with the terms imposed by capitalist appropriation?

According to some, cognitive labor is becoming today the main force of value production. In a way, this diagnosis seems to have been already announced in Marx's famous "fragment on the machines" in *Grundrisse*: "social knowledge has become a direct force of production" (1973: 706). Fixed capital (machines and technical infrastructure explicitly or implicitly employed in production processes) consists actually of *"organs of the human brain, created by the human hand*; the power of knowledge objectified" (ibid., italics in original). However, there seems to be a qualitatively different form of cooperation involved in processes in which knowledge is not used to create "machines" but is directly integrated into production. Information and data processing, thus, is an area of production that is greatly depended upon knowledge transfers and combinations of disparate fragments of cognitive inventions. This kind of cognitive cooperation obviously depends upon information processing machines and networks but such arrangements cannot work without cognitive cooperation in turn. The possibility of rearranging the priorities that trap this kind of cooperation into knowledge enclosure practices lies in actively reaffirming the essentially social character of such a knowledge production. What Marx refers to as "general social knowledge" (ibid.) corresponds to today's intellectual labor as developed through contemporary networks of intellectual cooperation.

This kind of cooperation, as the anthropologist Marylin Strathern suggests, depends upon *"techniques of distribution* [that] *do not just disseminate what has been created elsewhere, but have themselves a creative or productive potential"* (2005: 16, italics in original). Comparing this process to the collaborative creativity inherent in Papua New Guinean ritual exchanges, Strathern tries to show that cooperation may produce value (it may actually produce values translated into "money" as in the exchanges she describes), but is not necessarily connected to individual appropriation (and, thus, to individual profit). In the world of exchanges she describes, consecutive acts expand and transmit ritual skills and knowledges that add value to such products of social creativity by keeping the flow, the movement of "knowledge" going (ibid.: 16–19).

In a world distinct from the Western cultural and economic presuppositions we may thus encounter the possibility of value production (and "validation" as a general form of instituting value in whichever culture) in "nonproprietary regimes" (ibid.: 15).

F. Berardi rightly insists that cognitive knowledge needs to emancipate itself from the entanglements of the "networked information machine" (2019: 218). And he asks, "Can knowledge truly be disentangled from the semiotic grip of the economic paradigm?" (ibid.: 221). The answer lies exactly in the appraisal of potentialities lying at the heart of this form of cooperation. Is it a kind of cooperation that only develops under the rule of capital (and capital's management and distribution technologies) or is it a kind of cooperation that may develop autonomously due to its inherent characteristics? If the latter is true, cooperation's autonomy is only canceled by capitalist enclosure and a kind of direct appropriation analogous to material dispossession.

In Hardt and Negri's view, "rather than providing cooperation, we could even say that capital *expropriates cooperation* as a central element of exploiting bio-political labor-power" (2009: 140, italics in original). Let us not forget that for Hardt and Negri, the biopolitical refers to the current transformation of the life conditions to an area of capitalist value production. In other words, according to this view, members in this society are not exploited as workers only but in the totality of their human capacities. It is not any more that certain capacities are not paid for even though they are connected to specific forms of labor (directly or indirectly). It is that the totality of human relationships (including care, knowledge exchanges, discourse performances, and so on) are turned into areas of profit making. And, of course, this fact directly influences the way subjects are being shaped.

It seems important to distinguish between the two possible poles around which this thesis oscillates. It is either close to the model of "extractivism" (considered as a general metaphor for plundering including knowledge grabbing, and thus to the idea that something is captured by the capital either because it exists as a resource in "nature" or because it is produced prior to its capture) or to the model of total capitalist domination in which not only work relations and economy are under capital's command but also subject formation and modes of life.

Can we really take sides prioritizing one against the other of those models? Probably the answer comes from studying the ways disobedience and insurgency challenge this tendency of capital today to totally control (and subsume) both social production and social reproduction. As we will see, contemporary movements not only demand access to resources or decent ways of living but also develop forms to social organization that are in direct or indirect clash with the dominant ones. Often, while directly testing and challenging the limits (or, as some will say, the ambiguities or contradictions) of dominant power geometries, such movements produce hybrid (contradictory as well as precarious) conditions that permit the reappropriation of the products of cooperation (intellectual as well as material). These are in effect collective interventions in the processes of subject formation.

It seems that such efforts have a certain genealogy which, according to Dardot and Laval (2019), may be grounded in struggles to develop a "workers common." Cooperation relations that develop to the level of constituting different forms of social organization within, against, and potentially beyond capitalism may have differing results depending on the conditions under which they emerge. It is important to distinguish between such relations developed in the process of organizing alternative patterns of everydayness by the urban poor, and relations developed under conditions of urban insurgency.

What various socialist thinkers of late nineteenth and early twentieth centuries have been advocating for is the centrality of cooperation practices and experiences in the development of socialist ethos. As Dardot and Laval show, Marcel Mauss was one of the most devoted defenders of such a "cooperative socialism" (2019: 267) that would arise in direct connection to the development of cooperatives. In the *Cooperative Manifesto* of 1921 (to which Mauss's contribution was crucial), cooperation becomes "a general program of social reconstruction" (referred to in Dardot and Laval, 2019: 271). What divides different thinkers on the value of "cooperativism," though, is the location of the defining characteristic of cooperatives. Are they forms of organization of work and production that advance a specific model of economy or are they laboratories of emancipation in which participants learn how to organize their own self-government? An emphasis on the economy of cooperatives may lead to an expectancy that economic relations may change without changing political relations (relations of power and governance). An emphasis on the pedagogic role of cooperative experience will lose sight of the importance real changes in the lives of real people will acquire for the development of a different society based on solidarity.

The Potentialities of Cooperation Habits

Cooperation liberated from capitalist command and oriented toward the creation of emancipatory ways of living together—is this possible? The example of a network of cooperations in Venezuela, CECOSESOLA, may help us in locating the potentialities of the cooperativist conditions that nevertheless have to face inherent contradictions in the context of a capitalist urban society.

CECOSESOLA (2007, 2010) has a long history dating back to when a cooperative was founded in the city of Barquisimeto in Venezuela to provide funeral services to the population of the city. Back then, the initiative looked a lot like any other cooperative, apart of course from the fact that the service provided was an urgent social need that the private sector found not worthy of investing in. A crucial next step was taken when in 1976 CECOSESOLA decided to assume the responsibility of a bus community service (operating 127 buses in the city of Barquisimeto). This was the first time that CECOSESOLA "was giving a service without a preferential treatment to its own associates" (CECOSESOLA, 2010). A choice was made at that time to integrate members and the users of the service. Cooperation transcended the boundaries of a purely economic endeavor based on collaborative work and became a force of urban community empowerment. Popular assemblies in neighborhoods developed relevant demands and forms of organization to support what was becoming a self-managed common: public transportation.

It is important to observe here that the nature of work directly influences the potentialities of transforming cooperation to collective decision-making and, finally, to practices oriented toward commoning. Administration (including supervisors in workshops, route coordinators, etc.) often seems to be a technical issue since a certain level of efficiency appears to depend upon quick and well-informed decisions to be executed on a routine basis (especially in the case of bus schedules). However, forms of organizing cooperation are inadvertently linked to forms of power distribution within working conditions. CECOSESOLA activists realized very early that if cooperative work is to become an educating process to promote values alternative to individualism, then administration procedures should reflect such a scope. "Couldn't organizing be a … simple integration of wills fed by mutual trust, that finds order by being true to the organization's history and purpose?" (ibid.).

Both education and decision-making become aligned with a process of collective transformation meant to create conditions of living together "in harmony, solidarity and respect" (ibid.). Rotation of duties and equality in participation, thus, creates the potentiality of producing forms of social organization that explicitly diverge from capitalist ethos and the hierarchical distribution of opportunities and privileges. This reflects back to the seemingly technical problems of cooperation: when CECOSESOLA chose to develop a network of food fairs (in 1984, initially mobile ones in converted buses) the very problem of organizing such fairs was treated as a problem of horizontal distribution of tasks and responsibility. Following the principle that those who participate in decisions are responsible for the outcomes of these decisions, CECOSESOLA made it possible to ensure participation without the need of centralized administration. Food fairs were economically successful but were politically successful too. And it was in the recent pandemic crisis that such networks became operative in the support of the most vulnerable and the deprived.

The main idea behind a reflective reappraisal of CECOSESOLA experiences is that participation, cooperation, and active involvement in decision-making is generated "by progressively sharing the collective criteria that emerge consensually from [the] get-togethers" (2010). Holding meetings becomes the catalyst of an emerging culture that may be described as a culture of emancipatory commoning: In the context of this culture trust, responsibility and mutual help develop within cooperation.

As was made clear during a prolonged visit to CECOSESOLA areas of activity in Barquisimeto (in 2023), assemblies for programming collective tasks and for appraising results characterize the everydayness of the cooperatives. A special emphasis is placed on the complete sharing of available information so that everybody may shape an opinion on the matters discussed and on the equality of all opinions as long as they accept the basic premises of CECOSESOLA. The motto that is written on the wall of the assembly areas is characteristic: "Construyendo confianza en la diversidad" (Constructing confidence in diversity) (Figure 9). It is impressive to observe the way discussions unfold with no moderators and with speakers waiting patiently to hear without interrupting and using time

Figure 9 A CECOSESOLA assembly. Barquisimeto, Venezuela. 2023. Author's photo.

sparingly for their contribution. This kind of deliberation ethics is directly linked with the everyday practices of collaboration based on the rotation of duties and the acts of mutual care. This kind of commoning culture made possible an unbelievable achievement of CECOSESOLA: the construction of a self-managed hospital that was made possible by the participation of the cooperative's members in the discussions about the building's planning and design, by the work of many in the construction process, by the collective effort to raise money for this without relying on the government or on rich donors, and by the collective organizing that maintains the everyday functions of the hospital offering health services to all at affordable prices. They even dared to challenge the hierarchical structure of mainstream hospitals that is based on the authority of doctors. It is not that they don't accept expertise knowledge but they don't allow the experts to gain absolute and unchecked predominance over those with whom they work. And for decisions that have to do with the management of the hospital and the human relations developed within it, everyone is equally responsible and everyone's opinion is equally needed (Figure 10).

Out of these experiences of cooperation that develop by establishing a shared ethos of commoning, this community of commoners that develops services open to all has the right to ask: "Will there be a day in which we

Figure 10 The CECOSESOLA hospital. Barquisimeto, Venezuela. 2023. Courtesy of CECOSESOLA archive.

will be so interconnected that these get-togethers, as we conceive them today, will no longer be necessary? Are we becoming some sort of collective mind?" (ibid.). A far cry indeed from the nineteenth century of socialist visionaries who saw cooperatives as a school for socialism (Dardot and Laval, 2019).

Cooperation may in such a prospect support skills and habits of working together that overspill the boundaries of the labor process. Such habits include recurrent practices of limiting the accumulation of power (and thus limiting opportunities of any personal appropriation of collective work) and of ensuring the sharing of knowledge. Trust and care may only develop through repetitive acts that give them form and reality. And solidarity will never become the fertile ground for a just and emancipated society unless trust and care permeate the everyday habits of emancipated commoners.

Freeing work from capitalist command may lead to various forms of diffuse cooperation. Networks of exchange and skill sharing may enrich individual competence and inventiveness as well as a feeling of belonging to a community of creative workers. Homemaking can be considered as a complex sociocultural process that may enhance such a collective, albeit diffuse, creativity.

Depending on the cultural and geographical context, homemaking may be more connected to a quasi-industrial reproduction of recognizable examples (to be inhabited by the many in contradistinction with the outstanding examples destined for the affluent few), or to typologies evolving through shared skills of building craftsmanship.

Decoration has been condemned both by modernist pioneers as well as by religious reformers. Equated to an ethics of aristocratic exhibitionism and ostentatious expenditure, decoration was interpreted as a sign of decadence and backwardness.

Decoration has also been praised. Especially in today's consumption culture, choices in ornamentation are being presented as the essential ways to identify styles of living. Emblematic signs of specific consumption trends are integrated to otherwise similar products (from cigarettes to cars). Packaging is elevated to the most important art of marketing and advertising images further situate marketable products in a desire provoking décor. Prestige, distinction, and taste are to be attributed to those who know how to distinguish and appreciate the most appropriate decoration for any occasion.

There can however be a different attitude toward decoration that distances itself equally both from functionalist fundamentalism and from lifestyle ornamentation. While attempting an interpretation of a phenomenon that is surely more complex than it seems, let us use the facades of Brazilian Nord Este houses as an example of such an approach.

Art Deco decorative motifs applied to the facades of humble houses in this Brazilian region (invented as well as modified and reappropriated) are used to give a singular identity to otherwise quite similar houses. Beyond the differentiated facade an easily recognizable typology of house layout prevails. And this typology has been used both in small villages and towns.

A plausible interpretation of this gesture's genealogy connects it to the houses built for workers near the factories that were established in Brazil by following the spatial arrangement and architecture of similar complexes in Europe. The decoration of those row houses was "imported" following the prevailing tendencies of the period (twentieth-century Art Deco).

One can easily connect this gesture to an emerging, albeit highly contradictory, proto-modernist aesthetics in which the stylization of geometrical forms prevails. Initially imported from Europe as a style to represent a modern prestigious ethos of progress Art Deco decorative patterns were both contrasted to neoclassical ornamentation (usually connected to an aristocratic romantic legacy) and to the vernacular picturesque motifs (attributed to the expressive traditions of the "lower classes").

Interestingly, Art Deco patterns were used by popular masons and builders to decorate the facades of peasants' or low-middle-class houses. Probably following the preferences of the corresponding homeowners, each house is actually "named" by its distinctive decoration, which often changes colors as the facades are repainted on various occasions (especially to celebrate the day of a patron saint) (Figure 11).

The mechanism of appropriation, understood as inventive adaptation, is set in motion here in order to create singular spaces out of (and not in place of) rows or neighborhoods of similar houses. Obviously this is not an example of deviant or dissident urbanism. It shows quite clearly, however, that urban craftsmen may appropriate proto-modernizing symbolisms and imagery in ways that reform the relations between tradition and modernization. It would be a hasty oversimplification to equate this appropriation to pure imitation, or to connect it to a colonizing of popular imaginary by imported images. Ornamentation is not simply used in the packaging of otherwise identical products aiming to enhance and differentiate the consumption of forms. Ornamentation should be rather understood in this case as an area of popular creativity arising from shared skills and shared aesthetic preferences.

The powerful and the dominant may express their disdain for this minor, even condemned as "vulgar," art, while privileging their own aesthetic sublimation of power that they take to be the work of "true artists." However, this kind of popular ornamentation may be understood as expressing what Sergio Ferro, a Brazilian architectural theorist, has described as "the song of

Figure 11 Nordeste vernacular Art Deco facades. Penedo, Brazil. 2018. Author's photo.

free labor" (2016: 102). And this takes us a long way far from the Brazilian Nord Este to the Paris Commune (1871).

The shoemaker Napoléon Gaillard, a devoted Communard, "had himself photographed standing in front of the barricade he designed on the Place de la Concorde, in effect 'signing' his creation" (Ross, 2015: 87). This "artist-shoemaker," as he wanted to be called, reclaimed the right of craftsmen to be equally included in the realm of art making together not only with the sculptors and the painters but also with the "ornamentalists" (ibid.: 85). Kristin Ross helps us understand the importance the pathbreaking declaration of the Federation of Artists had in its inclusive definition of the arts. Not any more accepting the distinction between humble decorative arts and glorious *beaux arts*, "the Federation's members exhibited no concern whatsoever over what was to be counted as a work of art, nor over any aesthetic criteria for judging the worthiness of an artisanal product. They did not presume to act as judge or evaluator from an artistic point of view, acting rather as the driving force of a mechanism capable of assuring the liberty of all" (ibid.: 90).

Much in line with this approach William Morris, who is wrongly interpreted as a conservative nostalgic of Middle Ages craftsmanship, defined art as "man's expression of his joy in labour" (in Ferro, 2016: 102). Ferro, who also refers to Morris's definition, insists that liberated work is creative and inventive. Work subordinated to the priorities and expected profits of the employer loses the essential potentialities of creativity that connect it to common life and to shared competences and dreams.

As the famous Brazilian singer Caetano Veloso (born in this region) recollects, those houses used to be repainted each year, often in different colors from those in the previous year, on the occasion of a patron saint's celebration. "It is as if someone buys a new dress. The city is dressed up as if in the decor of a popular theatre (theatre naïf) with all those houses re-painted. It is simple: this is the joy of life, the desire to be even more beautiful, in the eyes of the others, in the eyes of God" (Mariani, 1988: 233).

Could it be that the builders of the Nord Este facades had the opportunity to sing the songs of a popular art that explores the poetics of ornamentation at the crossroads of traditional forms and appropriated "modern" ones? Could it be that they develop their own version of shared communal luxury? And, perhaps, the future culture of liberated work will also liberate ornamentation both from the aristocratic ethos of distinction and from the lifestyle ethos of current consumption culture.

Rituals of Cooperation

Cooperation may become productive in different ways. What however distinguishes those different ways is neither the production process itself, nor the end result of coordinated work and the complementarity of skills involved. Of course all these aspects are very important if one wants to calculate the output—a more or less economy-focused way of reasoning. Cooperation however is in all societies a lot more than an economic, productive activity. It directly involves and shapes human relationships, it either strengthens or dissolves bonds that are being put to test due to coworking conditions (as for example family bonds, ethnic, cultural or religious alliances, and so on).

Furthermore, cooperation often has to face problem-solving conditions, conditions that pose dilemmas and require decision-making arrangements. As we have seen in the case of CECOSESOLA, assemblies and "get-togethers" (as they call them) may become an integral part of the cooperation process. And the quality of horizontality explicitly affects the quality of egalitarian relations developed in the corresponding cooperation practices.

For the liberal urban thinker Richard Sennett, cooperation is a form of relating to others that does not have to rest on shared characteristics apart from those directly involved in the task at issue (2012). Differences, especially present in big cities with widely differentiated inhabitants, permeate any kind of workplace. And any kind of workplace may explode if such differences make working together intolerable. Sennett proposes the term "sociality" as a kind of "limited fraternity," which may describe relations of cooperation without presupposing shared identities. "That limited fraternity arises when people are doing something together rather than being together" (2019: 260). "Sociality appears when strangers are doing something productive, together" (ibid.).

Sennett is right in one thing: Cooperation does not need to presuppose uniformity, homogeneity, and shared identities. Often, we tend to confuse an idealized cooperative work with an ideal community. And sometimes solidarity and equality in and through shared labor tends to presuppose sameness. However, differences are by no means to be taken as threats to cooperation. Quite the contrary, differences may enhance cooperation, by bringing forward a complementarity of skills and ideas. The question is in what ways differences are negotiated, in what ways common ground is created and possible confluences or synergies are being developed. For Sennett, who is explicitly skeptical about the cooperative workshop-dwelling utopias of Fourier, cooperation will have to retain the task-focused relations between people, which will produce an inclusive urban culture. For CECOSESOLA people, however, cooperative relations feed dreams of a different emancipated society. And they offer opportunities to test such dreams, to observe the potentialities of equality they create, and to sustain the opportunities of mutual care they give rise to.

Creating the common ground on which cooperation may flourish is not simply a process of arrangements that convince participating individuals to engage in the process of working together. Rational choice theories are full of naïve assumptions forgetting that conditions are shaped by power asymmetries and that the so-called choices are rather a complex set of interactions based not only on calculation thoughts and information but also on emotional responses, ethical convictions, and existing social bonds.

That is why rituals play such a dominant role in shaping cooperation practices. To remember Durkheim's fundamental diagnosis, "Rituals are ways of acting that are generated only within assembled groups and are meant to stimulate and sustain or create certain mental states in these groups" (2001: 11). "No society can exist that does not feel the need in regular intervals to sustain and reaffirm the collective feelings and ideas that constitute its unity and its personality" (2001: 322).

Whether it is about shared mental states or about collective feelings and ideas, rituals can be taken to be essential means in the process of constituting the common ground on which a group recognizes and reaffirms itself.

The temporal horizon of this process may vary. This is where a crucial characteristic of ritual, namely repetitiveness, plays a fundamental role. Only by being repeated, ritual practices reaffirm the existence of common ground. In the case of groups formed through cooperation, ritual practices may justify legitimate praise and even attribute a transcendental origin to this process. It would be a mistake to think of such rituals as simply the means to sustain cooperation. Since cooperation is always more than a production-oriented set of practices, as has already been suggested, relevant rituals must be understood as implicitly linked to the development of relationships and of patterns of behavior.

Rituals of cooperation seem to have a firm grounding in the rural worlds. It is in conditions in which mutual help and coordinated work are made imperative that ritual practices are called upon to strengthen communitarian bonds and to sustain a feeling of common burdens and expectations. Cooperation among peasants, especially when they are not reduced to rural workers without any kind of attachment to land, often becomes the ground on which work is elevated to the status of communication and exchange with forces attributed to "nature" or to ancestors and deities. Cooperation, thus, is repeatedly affirmed as a shared tradition, as a set of values and rules that exceed mere practicality. In ritual conditions cooperation includes collaborators that are not human, or that are human in different ways than humans (Viveiros de Castro, 2014). Hunters collaborate in hunting but the quarry too is often considered as a participant in this process of mutual voluntary involvement. As Ingold suggests, Cree (who live in today's Canada), believe that the deer actually cooperates with the hunters by offering itself to them, connected as they are with bonds of kin (Ingold, 2002: 48–9).

When forced to migrate to big cities, rural populations carry with them beliefs and knowledges related to the efficacy of ritual acts that they are prone to apply in the setting of their new urban communities. Often in need of activating bonds of mutual help whether in order to construct homes in informal areas or to establish relations with informal or quasi formal networks of work in the street, they may call upon powers that ritual "magical efficacy" (to remember Bourdieu) will activate.

This is the case, for example, of the *Guelaguetza* rituals stemming from the Zapotec culture in the Oaxaca region of Mexico. Dating back to precolonial times, this series of ritual practices was initially a formal process of gift giving and receiving during a marriage ceremony. This was actually a form of building relations between households (the unit of Zapotec sociality) by developing reciprocal obligations. Interestingly, members of the elite would offer presents that were to demonstrate their power and wealth, whereas lay people would usually offer their work or the products of their work, mostly coming from land cultivation (Flores-Marcial, 2015: 96).

We know from social anthropological studies on various rural societies that the exchange of gifts is a process that creates obligations that are mutually binding (Mauss, 2002; Bourdieu, 1977). And it is also clear that the forming of those obligations is not to be reduced to an economic transaction that establishes debts. The alternating rhythms of giving and receiving mark important events in the society's calendar and are part of important ceremonies (as in the early Zapotecan ritual, marriage). Zapotec Guelaguetza was actually a way to resist colonial governance that imposed an economy of money with relevant obligations translated to taxation paid labor (Flores-Marcial, 2015: 110).

Exchanges forming networks of social bonds and celebrated in feasts that explicitly exalted the power of community included mutually supportive work, a kind of cooperation relationships based on strengthening community cohesion (Whitford, 2009).

The ritual characteristics of the Guelaguetza support and develop an ethically sanctioned tradition of cooperation, which should not be reduced to a legal framework meant to regulate a sharing economy. Festive conditions were, as it seems, an integral part of exchanges within this system of performances. Cooperation and offerings as well as communal work were symbolized and experienced as expressions of the community itself.

The adaptation of Guelaguetza rituals to the colonial period included integrating Christian religious references (offerings to a patron saint, relevant feasts organized during a saint's day, etc.) by keeping the ritual aspects of community empowerment. Preparing for the feast always meant different tasks for men and women, all of them directly involving offered work. It is important here to distinguish offered work from volunteer work. Volunteer offers usually refer to individual choices related to the engagement in a chosen "noble" scope. Offered work is of course the result of individuals engaging with a scope but this should not be distinguished from a deeply rooted feeling of obligation toward the community. Participation, thus, becomes a process of sustaining a collective identity by performing community tasks in common.

We have reasons to believe, as Hazel Marsh suggests, that Guelaguetza was transformed to an annual feast celebrating indigenous culture in Oaxaca by a smart politician seeking to attract the votes of indigenous people of this region (2021: 426).

The annual feast actually transformed the ritual as well as the commoning aspects of the Guelaguetza system to an advertised indigeneity that was reduced to a series of folkloric performances and to the marketing of Zapotec handcrafts. The feast, then, evolved to an important tourist attraction which, of course, attracted all kinds of relevant business initiatives: "In the hands of the state [Guelaguetza] came to refer to a commercialized festival of folkloric dances and gift showering" (Stephen, 2013: 66).

Guelaguetza feasts organized by Mexican immigrants in the United States met with a similar fate. Although for some immigrant families the ritual characteristics and the collaborative reciprocity still prevail (for example in marriage feasts or in patron saints' celebrations), the annual events are recognized institutionally (for example in Los Angeles and other cities) and are open to local enterprise activities.

One should not of course ignore efforts to recuperate the annual feast by the local communities of immigrants. The feeling of cultural pride that is so empowering for them in a society that often treats Mexicans as no-citizens or second-class citizens is very important. "In the United States, guelaguetza exchanges continue to fulfill many of the same functions as in Mexico: to help people host celebrations, or to provide aid in time of need. The exchanges create a network of voluntary household exchange and offer a measure of social security" (Flores-Marcial, 2015: 160). Communal work and an ethos of mutual support remain the symbolic nucleus of the process in such cases, even when reduced to a collective preparation for the annual event.

A very important turning point in Guelaguetza's recuperation by the people is marked by the organizing of the People's Guelaguetza in 2006 in Oaxaca. It was the year of the Oaxaca resurrection that resulted in the short-lived Oaxaca commune we have already encountered in this book. Reclaiming the indigenous culture from the state's folkloric appropriation as well as from the market's insatiable exploitation, mobilized Oaxacans made the feast again a set of powerful performances of self-management, mutuality, and indigenous culture (Figure 12).

Cooperation was, during 2006, raised to an alternative ethos of commoning, including rotation of duties in the maintenance of urban life's infrastructure and the active participation in assemblies and collaborative acts. It was this ethos that was meant to be transmitted by the People's Guelaguetza in a transformation of the ritual roots of the reciprocity system to symbolic performances of urban commoning and self-governance.

Since the year of the insurrection, 2006, the People's Guelaguetza has been organized by the Teachers' Union, the same union that ignited the insurrection by its struggle. The feast is explicitly self-organized, as opposed to the state-staged one, and it "declared opposition to neoliberal economic policies and in support of popular education and collective Indigenous rights" (Marsh, 2021: 428). The feast's motto is "Our culture is not for sale."

Figure 12 Graffiti in support of People's Guelaguetza. Oaxaca. 2007. Courtesy of Lynn Stephen.

It is important to observe that Guelaguetza tradition has become a contested terrain, and this shows the potentiality of cooperation rituals when transferred from a rural indigenous context to an urban one. In the city of Oaxaca as well as in the cities in which Zapotec Mexican immigrants live, potentialities of reinventing the commoning nucleus of this ritual depend upon its reconnection with collective communal work. In People's Guelaguetza, this kind of cooperation has its roots in struggle. It is by no chance that a union representing teachers has become the point of convergence of struggles to recuperate a cooperation ethos that combines indigenous traditions of community work with a culture of solidarity coming from the workers' movement.

Communal work is the collective work in which members of the community support a community project by offering their time and skills in many rural societies throughout the world. In many cases, rural populations that had to (or often merely forced to) migrate to cities, carried with them these traditions of collective work along with rituals and *cosmovisions* that firmly connected them to the life of the community. As we have seen in the case of Guelaguetza, this process includes adaptive practices and generates hybrid worlds of collective experiences, meanings, and ceremonial practices. What was termed as "indian territorialization" indicates "a process of appropriation/construction of indian territory in the city" (Robledo and Burguete Cal y Mayor, 2023: 85, author's translation).

This process generates new forms of cooperation as well as various kinds of rituals that support them. Especially in the case of Altos de Chiapas communities and those from the city of San Cristobal de las Casas, indigenous people continue to worship water (in springs, lakes, and rivers) as a crucial constituent element of their cosmovision and, at the same time, as a necessary source for the community's life. Protecting, taking care of water, and working to maintain its public use are parts of a shared culture that in some cases bridges indigenous traditions with current evangelical Christian beliefs. Committees formed by the leaders of the families have as their duty to both ensure the cleanliness of the water tanks as well as to perform rituals that promote the proliferation of water (for example, offering salt as a way of paying the "owner of water," the mythical creature Anjel) (Robledo and Burguete Cal y Mayor, 2023).

Water, considered as a common good that should be accessible to all, became the main focus of the Cochabamba struggle of 2000. This city of Bolivia became the center of a fierce confrontation between the city's communities and the central government that chose to concede the region's water resources to a multinational for forty years (Zibechi, 2009).

From 1990, the communities at the periphery of the city—comprising mainly immigrants coming from indigenous rural territories and former coal-miners who had to relocate—chose to work together in order to ensure necessary water resources for their neighborhoods. A huge effort of self-management and community work has miraculously produced a network for water distribution, community water tanks, and a set of organizational forms to maintain this shared infrastructure. Water was preserved as a common resource and was distributed to all those who worked together to make this possible. Indigenous traditions were very important for such a successful effort. As in the case of Mexican indigenous people, Bolivian indigenous populations, Aymara and Quechua, have enduring traditions of community solidarity work, "*ayni*," which was mobilized as part of a shared cosmovision. Added to this was a shared belief that considers water as sacred, "the blood of Pacha Mama [mother earth]'" (CENDA, 2022), which was performed in rituals meant to thank Mother Earth for providing to living beings the means to sustain themselves and to prosper.

The struggle against the privatization of water and against the appropriation of the work produced collectively by the communities of Cochabamba periphery was, thus, not only a clash with capitalist economic logic. It was also a struggle based on a different culture that respects nature and supports the rights of future generations.

The constitution of Bolivia protects the rights of indigenous communities but also declares the obligation to respect indigenous "*usos y costumbres*" knowledges and customs (articles 374, 375). This of course does not necessarily guarantee that the respect will be established in practice. The Indigenous Peoples Kyoto Water Declaration formed during the Third World Water Forum in Kyoto, Japan, in March 2003 also explicitly refers to what can be considered as the right of cultural self-determination: "Self-determination includes the practices of our cultural and spiritual relationship with water" (UNESCO, 2006: 177).

The ritual corroboration of cooperation supports a shared commoning ethos and translates within the symbolic world of the magic circle the wisdom of many indigenous people. Taking into consideration the needs of future generations as well as those of other living beings, cooperation rituals open fields of commoning that reconfigure the priorities of social life, especially those taken for granted by Western capitalist reason. As in the case of water-caring rituals, cooperation transcends the realm of productivist reasoning as well as the realm of human aggressive appropriation of natural resources. Societies or communities that include their cooperation habits in a predominant cosmovision based on conviviality, mutual help, and mutual respect practice commoning as a way of being in a world in which sharing is both a guiding principle and a source of meaning. A researcher suggests that we need to arrive at a cross-cultural definition to replace the term "water wars": "Integral water management and care" (Barrera Cordero, 2009: 99). In such a context, seemingly absurd practices (from the predominant Western point of view of course), as the Quechua "yaku-cambio," a ritual to attract rain (ibid.: 95), acquire the power to condense a shared wisdom that shows how important it is to reconsider water as commons. And this wisdom is urgently needed today, in a period of acute climate crisis. Amazingly, yaku-cambio, a combination of indigenous and Spanish words, can be translated as "transformation through the exchange of water" (ibid.).

In Popayan, Colombia, collective work aimed at building community infrastructures at an informal settlement of people displaced due to an ongoing civil war has also been connected to ritual activities. At the outskirts of the city, in the Estrella Roja settlement, comprising precarious shelters inhabited by people in struggle for descent housing, an emphasis on collective community work redefines cooperation. *Minga*, the word used by the Nasa indigenous people to signify collaboration for a community project, is also used to include assembly work, deliberation as a form of experience exchange,

Figure 13 A *minga* meeting at the *Estrela Roja* settlement of Popayan, Colombia. 2023. Author's photo.

and decision-making. The place for such meetings is protected by a large community-made shed and ceremonially activated by a construction on the ground comprising concentric cuts in the soil bearing a spiral arrangement of flower petals and lit candles. This is a ritual with which the deliberating community grounds itself on Mother Earth and has direct reference to a similar way in which the nearby urban garden is arranged (Figure 13).

For Nasa people, the spiral is a very important symbolic image indicating the connection of community with its territory through the action of weaving—weaving relations between people in the same way as weaving the famous "mochilas." Territory is understood both as Mother Earth and as a Great House, a collective hearth (Escobar, 2020). Again, commoning is developed as a form of sharing of work and duties while being obliged to respect nature.

The urban movement that has made this settlement possible (*Los Sin Techo*) has a strong focus on community building practices and supports cooperation both as a direct and efficient way to satisfy collective needs as well as a network of relations between people that is meant to create an emancipatory future of mutuality and equality.

Cooperation and Tracing

"The world is now urban not so much in terms of cities, suburbs or peripheries, not in terms of specific spatial designations or hybrids but in the *profusion of itineraries*, multiple times, disjoined places and ways of doing things" (Simone, 2020a: 1140, emphasis added). This approach to the urban, introduced by Simone, puts emphasis on extension and temporariness in an effort to understand the ways the current urban condition is lived by its residents, not simply by complying with urban normalization. Living life as an extensive set of potential itineraries is, according to Simone, a way to make use of opportunities especially for those who have to strive to become human in a world that denies their right to live or stigmatizes them as nonhumans. For Simone, struggling to be "non(urban) humans" (2020b) is already a framework of experiences that provides a possible life beyond the predominant traps of control and predetermination. As we have already seen, what he terms "generic blackness" (2016) hints at ways of being human (of being recognized as human), by departing from the dominant canons of urbanized humanity. We could say that such practices reinvent togetherness as an always changing, precarious, and temporary way of survival in spite of the continuing indifference of the state for the lives of those already expendable, beyond the normative definition of the human. For Simone, "momentary, sporadic and makeshift become the defining metaphors of many collective formations" (2022: 136).

In such an approach, the idea of tracing potentialities within the extensiveness of current urbanity can become a revealing indication of the importance of shared knowledges necessary for the literal or metaphoric navigation in the city. Cooperation may be understood in such a context as a shared diffuse knowledge of how to take advantage of a situation in the shifting ground of opportunities and hazards a lot of urbanites have to deal with every day.

To be able to recognize traces becomes vital if one tries to live within conditions of precarity. And this transfer of knowledges circulates in many different ways. It is not even a matter of learning a code to be able to decipher indications and follow relevant clues. Following traces, catching the glimpse of traces that may soon vanish in the huge conflicting cacophony or "voices" addressing "everybody" is a thing one learns while doing it. Through trial and error? By observing and imitating? A lot of combinations of urban inventiveness may develop such an ability to trace. All of them show that this kind of urban tracing is not to be reduced to the practice of finding one's way according to a predetermined itinerary but is actually about venturing toward the partially unknown by improvising an itinerary. Partially unknown? Indeed, because, as in hunting, everything may become temporarily familiar, so long as a partial knowledge is able to detect signs that may lead to a promising result.

The question is, how much of cooperation is employed in such an inventive creation of itineraries? As it appears, a lot. According to Ingold (2002), a kind of shared knowledge is developed when a novice is instructed to learn crucial ways to navigate himself or herself in a society's environment. The novice is guided to "attend" to "clues" rather than decipher signs by learning a code. "A clue is a landmark that condenses otherwise disparate strands of experience into a unifying operation which, in turn, opens up the world to perception of greater depth and clarity" (ibid.: 22). Tracing becomes an action that is collaborative because it is first of all connected to a transfer of knowledge that entails the development of a socially meaningful skill. At the same time, this kind of knowledge already includes the potentiality of inventiveness since it is a knowledge transmitted "within the context of a direct perpetual engagement with our environments. And we develop this capacity ... by having things shown to us" (ibid.: 21).

To show something to somebody means to engage in a relationship that is constructing an elementary form of cooperation. To direct perception toward an area that may become useful for someone is already an effort to contribute to someone's needs and aspirations. When W. Benjamin declares, "I needn't say anything. Merely show" (1999: 460), he directs our attention to the power of demonstration that does not base itself on the convincing power of the argument but on the revealing potentiality of guided perception. Perception, thus, will possibly be linked to generalizable patterns of action, exactly in the same way this happens in the case of a novice who is led to acquire a socially needed capacity.

Those expelled from the official city, those on the move toward the next opportunity to live a life worth living, need to be supported by networks of cooperation, solidarity, and mutual care. We do not have to think of these networks only as arrangements of empowerment and mutual support. Bonds are being made and remade and they are usually strengthened by shared tasks or shared exigencies. Cooperation, thus, becomes the very structure of everydayness without always ensuring, however, regular patterns of repetition.

We may possibly detect a kind of inventiveness that actually creates traces. That gives traces a value within cooperation and because of it—to show to those you work with a way out, a way to possible opportunities, or to more and diverse kinds of cooperation. Cooperation may thus be the very source of traces. And traces produced through cooperation may become diffuse calls, diffuse chances to further expand cooperation networks: as those, for example, who sustain newly arrived immigrants of refugees, who learn from those who have arrived earlier on how to find their way in a foreign, often hostile, big city. This is a kind of diffuse cooperation (although often quite explicitly organized by immigrant communities), which develops a shared knowledge not only of traces and possible itineraries but also of tracing practices in a city of potential itineraries.

W. Benjamin locates in the practice of two characteristic figures of modern urbanity a distinct developed skill to follow traces (1983). The detective and the flaneur in different but comparable ways have an acute inclination to observe and to connect traces. The detective being the hero of the urban literature par excellence, the crime, mystery, and noir novels, is more like an expert in deciphering the clues urban space and city life provide. The detective may deduce patterns of urban behavior as well as exceptions that mark events of deviation, of delinquency, of idiosyncratic acts, and so on. The flaneur is a detective who is not after solving mysteries or crime cases but after collecting experiences and the buried traces of a city's secrets. That is why he is immersed in the experiences of the city crowd, mesmerized by the urban phantasmagoria that he nevertheless observed with an entomologist's rigor.

Both figures represent the promises of modernity and their failure as dramatized in modern city life. However they hide from view the ways collective experiences of the city carry along the potentiality of urban tracing as a way to reinvent city life. Benjamin too referred to the groundbreaking events of the Paris Commune and the "disenchantment of the city" preformed in the struggle to reappropriate city center. The emphasis, however, on emblematic figures of exceptional types of urban individuals obscures the potentiality of collective and collaborative urban tracing.

In the figure of the archaeologist who cuts through the various layers of history while excavating the city, Benjamin sees represented the necessary faculty of any future agent of criticism, who may redeem modernity and liberate its promises (1983, 1999). Transferring this suggestion to collective action rather than to an emancipated individual, we may have something like a blueprint of the current criticisms of individualized urban tracing. Conformity is currently disguised behind a mask of individual choices that present the city as a network of potential itineraries, paths, and routes. Equipped with a personal digital tracer, a smartphone with its various applications, the contemporary urbanite may go "everywhere" as long as he or she follows the signs on the screen. No one may be deliberately or accidentally lost anymore. Furthermore, digital platforms combine tracing information with the provision of services: "algorithms ... have an in-bust teleological yearning towards a seamless hodology of the urban" (Brighenti and Pavoni, 2023: 52). Thus, in "user friendly atmospheres ... navigation may smoothly, efficiently and leisurely occur" (ibid.).

Benjamin's archeologist actually compares the findings of different layers while digging. Rather than navigating himself in the flat extensiveness of the city's present, he plunges himself in the city's depths. In a kind of allegory of revelatory tracing this practice may offer the ground for demythologizing current ubiquitous tracing possibilities.

Tracing acquires a temporal as well as a spatial dimension and this means that tracing may reinterpret the past, the present, as well as the future. If we add to this performance the necessary exchange of tracing findings within cooperation arrangements and the potentialities revealed in addressing others through the collective invention of traces, we have in crude form the outlines of a potentially emancipating urban tracing ethos.

Reclaiming the power of traces to indicate future potentialities may become the means to challenge both the illusion of time's continuity (that sees the present and the future in a linear relation of the past) as well as the illusion of progress (that sees a linear development toward a better future). Could this power be located in the capacity of those in struggle to actually invent traces?

In an effort to explore the power of such invented traces, let us follow the performances to trace production that developed during a recent urban uprising tin Athens. In those performances marking the city with emblematic stencil images collective actions toward the future.

On December 6, 2008, an incident took place in Exarchia, one of the central neighborhoods in Athens, which triggered an unprecedented series of dissident actions. A young schoolboy was murdered in cold blood by a policeman who "felt insulted" by the boy's attitude. What followed the murder of the boy was indeed amazing (Stavrides, 2010): Violent clashes with the police forces in huge demonstrations throughout the country, an immense number of school and university occupations, public building occupations that converted them to political centers and dissident culture laboratories (among them the occupied National Opera building and municipal buildings in many cities including Athens municipalities).

The December uprising used the city to express a shared spirit of anger as well as to develop a shared, albeit fragmentary and ambiguous, effort to develop forms of organization and life-in-common that opposed dominant values and dominant urban order. This is why the December stencil images, which appeared on the walls of Athens' neighborhoods and were reproduced through the social media, were not one more means to spread and disseminate the uprising's messages. These stencil images were actually stencil-acts, gestures that were both using and challenging the city. Calls to struggle and forms of struggle, those images were more like invented traces of an uprising in progress.

The most emblematic of such stencil-presences was, of course, the stencil image of the murdered boy himself. This was indeed an act of bringing to presence a murdered boy turned to a symbol. But it was not probably meant to represent or show how the boy actually looked like. The stencil art's characteristic minimalism helped in transforming the boy's photo to a generic image of Greek youth: "we are all Alexis," "we are everywhere in the city demanding to be seen" could have been the meaning of this stencil-act. One more example: A hooded ballerina stencil image attempted to transmit the dynamics of a coordinated expressive performance staged by hooded artists in ballerina style gestures in front of the occupied National Opera building. Equally interesting was the case of a stencil that appeared mostly near the trendy coffee shops of Kolonaki, a neighborhood of conservative upper middle class that nevertheless borders Exarchia. With a stylized image of a Molotov cocktail at its center, the stencil read "Relax you trendy guys and enjoy your drink. Your car is burning nearby." Stencil presence acquires here the performative character of a real threat: "You are not safe anywhere in the city, you, who are responsible for injustice and inequality."

Stencils are actually designed and executed in ways that make them repeatable, recurrent. So, they can somehow attempt to infiltrate the distracted person's perception and affect his or her unconscious memory. Reproducing a stencil image is an act that has to face ever-new contingencies, that has to be a distinct performance each time someone dares to, or someone insists on repeating a gesture in order to address others. And, as Andrea Mubi Brighenti insists, these acts of addressing others are not simply adding words or images to public space but actually shape public space (2013).

Those images, then, inculcated as they were on the city's body, marked presences that were demanding attention. Those stencils could not easily be overlooked. They were ridiculing, mocking, or praising actions and looks. Richard Sennett almost offered a definition of such acts when he described what he called the battle cry of graffiti in the context of early New York graffiti writing: "We exist and we are everywhere ... we write all over you" (Sennett, 1993: 207).

December stencils were vectors of engaged communication. They had a distinctive presence, since they were able to show, to mark, to address, and to indicate at the same time potential acts of collective anger and protest. What if December stencils were actually traces of a peculiar kind? What if they were meant to be not simply the remains of acts by those who acted to produce them, but also the indicative remains of acts toward which those schematic images actually gestured? What if those peculiar traces, those marks on the walls, were indeed calls to action by being remains and promises of acts at the same time—traces of potentially unexpected acts, traces of events that acquire their meaning as protest cries and as acts of delegitimization of existing authorities only insofar as they are repeatable.

December stencil-traces were the hieroglyphics of an uprising in progress. Dissident hieroglyphics. Acts of call in a code that had been developing during those days in and through expressive acts, in and through emblematic images that escaped the spectacularization of discontent.

Perhaps the most characteristic hieroglyphic of the December uprising—in its exceptional character and execution—is an image that survived many months after those days on the door of an unused building at one of the central streets in downtown Athens. It was made with white paint and it depicted in a very crude way the contour of a human figure with a raised hand, or more likely, with a raised fist. One could easily guess that this figure, hastily painted on a door in a city area under more or less heavy surveillance, was meant to recall those white line figures painted on the ground to mark the position of a corpse at a crime scene. Isn't the marking of the position and form of an absent dead body a kind of macabre stencil image? The body itself becomes the stencil's matrix. Death, a violent death always, motivates a delineation of the remains of life. A stencil that acquires the characteristics of a death mask is produced in the form of a trace, in the form of a marker of a violent event (Figure 14).

A trace that recalls a trace—what can be more definite as trace than the trace of death, the mark of a body on a site of death, on the place of a murder? Well beyond a realistic depiction, this schematic representation of a human body, an almost clumsy sketch of a standing figure, is an image that calls for action by being an invented trace. A trace that becomes the imprint of future actions because it recalls the imprint of a past action—a murder—that justifies, generates, inspires, motivates, shapes, or even expresses them.

Traces that address the future may reclaim the past and boldly question dominant narratives concerning collective memory. In Mexico, a movement that explicitly asks for justice and the punishment of those responsible for crimes of political and social violence has chosen to construct "anti-monuments." In those constructions a demand for "memory, truth and justice" is performed by establishing invented traces in Mexico City's prominent public spaces.

Symbolism is straightforward and both "anti-heroic" and "anti-glorious." In most of the cases, the figure of a number or a recognizable emblematic image (a dove, the sign of feminist movement) is materialized in the form of a prominent sculpture and a sign is added to state the relevant demand.

Cooperation as Commoning 141

Figure 14 December 2008 uprising in Athens: an invented trace. 2008. Author's photo.

In the case, for example, of the anti-monument for the forty-three students who disappeared in Ayotzinapa—a crime in which all indicators point to paramilitary and state terrorist action—a large sculpture of forty-three was erected on the main avenue in Mexico City with the writing, "Because alive they were taken, alive we want them" (Heinrich Böll Stiftung, 2020: 31–49). The anti-monument was established in a collective action that combined the characteristics of a demonstration and those of a commemoration ritual.

Such a collective performance is a trace making activity with the explicit aim to combine the actualization of a past event with a demand for the future. What distinguishes such gestures from the erection of monuments by official initiatives is that they come from an active collective that marks the city by its presence, especially by intervening in one of its most important public spaces. What the Athens December stencils did with a fugitive, almost guerrilla-like art, Mexican anti-monuments did with a bold public presence destined to remain as long as injustice remains.

It is not by chance that those gestures are using elementary, abstract forms of symbolism. It is as if those constructions try to retain the powerful ephemerality of a mark on a wall combined with a concrete presence of monumental dimensions. At the same time, these are sites of memory that cannot survive without the recurrent presence of people engaged and determined. Anti-monuments are the focus of care. Cooperation was not only a process related to the design and construction but remains as a process that keeps the monument alive. "Antimonuments are perlocutionary acts which realize a conative function in the process of communicative act. A reaction and an affective response are established … that put into question the dominant discourse" (Heinrich Böll Stiftung, 2020: 10).

Another case that shows the potentialities of urban tracing in acts of cooperation is the wave of public statue defacement that swept the world at the peak of the Black Lives Matter movement. In huge demonstrations that expressed an accumulated anger ignited by the brutal assassination of George Floyd by two policemen, statues symbolizing the commemoration of racism, slavery, and colonial invasions were overthrown, decapitated, or ridiculed through inventive interventions. The statue of a seventeenth-century slave trader was dumped by the protesting crowd into Bristol Harbor, England. In Antwerp, the statue of Leopold, the King of Belgium responsible for the massacres of people in Congo, was burned. In the United States, various statues depicting pro-slavery Confederate officials were also destroyed.

If Mexican anti-monuments were crafted traces of discontent and collective demands for justice, worldwide statue defacement performatively asked for the rewriting of history against the dominant myths of colonialism. Destroyed official memory constructions became sites of a trace war. Invented traces against official traces. Recuperated memories against imposed memories. Collective action against state-sanctioned "public" works.

During the major general strike of 2021 in Colombia, forms of public space reappropriation also gave prominence to the potentialities of collectively invented traces. Characteristic points of the urban tissue were renamed and recuperated in imaginative ways. Examples: the traffic bridge called Puente de los Mil Dias (Bridge of the Thousand Days) was renamed Puente de la Mil Luchas (Bridge of the Thousand Struggles), the Passage of Commerce was renamed Passage of Endurance, the Hill of the Cross was renamed Hill of Dignity, Siloe Roundabout was renamed Roundabout of Struggle, and so on.

In all those cases, coming from the city Cali (the third biggest city in Colombia and one of the centers of the 2021 insurrection), people did not limit themselves to marking the city spaces by attributing to them names connected with their struggle. Although in terms of cooperative tracing the acts of collective dissident renaming already exhibit the potentialities of invented traces, people also added temporary constructions to express the demands and values of their struggle.

Especially in Cali, a further step in recuperating the expressive potentialities of shared symbols was taken. The statue of the city's founder Sebastian de Belalcazar was toppled on April 28, 2021 by members of the Misak indigenous community. According to the decision made by the jury of Misak people in June 2020, the Spanish conquistador leader needs to be "rewritten in universal history as guilty of genocide" of the peoples who were part of the confederation of the valley of Pubenza. According to the decision, indigenous people "demand historical reparation in times of racism, discrimination, feminicide, corruption and assassination of social leaders." Interestingly after a long public debate about the statue's potential reerection, an agreement with the municipal authority was reached that dictated that the statue could be placed again on its base provided that a sign at its base would commemorate the heroic struggle of indigenous people against the brutal Spanish invaders. Indeed, this sign was placed at one side of the pedestal stating:

> We, the inhabitants of Cali, descendants and heirs of our indigenous ancestors, carve here, on this pedestal of the founder of Santiago de Cali, Sebastian Balcazar, our own voice, a voice of recognition and exaltation of the value and heroism that the indigenous peoples of the time offered with their blood, and we proclaim them as an example of love for the ancestral lands. It was they who resisted and died with honor, defending their land and their culture from the brutal Spanish conquest, which stripped them of their wealth and power and imposed Western culture … Municipality of Santiago de Cali … 2022.

Perhaps one of the most important acts of establishing new traces on the Cali's body during the 2021 uprising was the creation of the anti-monument

Resiste. It is an enormous construction depicting a hand holding a placard with the word "Resiste" and surrounded by images and faces of people in struggle. This monumental gesture of collective presence and determination was produced by collective work and was conceived by people who were in the barricades. Cooperation created a collective reference meant to celebrate the weeks of struggle and to support the collective memory that was shaped in those days in direct contrast to the vales of predominant individualism (Kavilando, 2021: 113–18).

This monumental trace not only marked the presence of the struggle but also aspired to project into the city's future the power of a struggle that had reignited the potentialities of cooperation and the collective ethos developed in urban communities.

The anti-monument *Resiste* was erected in a crucially emblematic area of the city: at the interstices between the "official" city and a vast area of informal housing mainly created by those who were forced to abandon their houses and villages due to the violence of the civil war, in a place renamed *Puerto Resistencia*, which became the epicenter of the insurrection, and in which community dynamics produced an immensely rich new urban collective infrastructure. A library, a women's meeting place, collective kitchens, workshop places, a community radio station, a collectively managed tailor shop and a barber shop comprised a miniature city of commoning in Puerto Resistencia. This miniature urban enclave continues to function as a meeting point for the *primera linea* activists and neighborhood people and as a node in an extensive network of community kitchens that support solidarity work in the vast poor urban neighborhoods around the monument. A small urban island squeezed between the two large highways that connect the city with its surrounds becomes itself an invented landmark of resistance. It is by no chance that in such an urban context the anti-monument *Resiste* found its place. The prevailing cooperation ethos had to find its expression in symbolic forms too. The potentiality of collectively invented traces was therefore the result of various forms and levels of cooperation (Figure 15).

Traces necessarily rehearse and reinterpret the past no matter how recent this past is. We may thus consider the production, the transmission, and the reading to those traces as performances of potentiality. What distinguishes this approach from the approach of the bourgeois guardians of the past is that such traces become promises instead of proofs. They become vectors pointing toward possible actions instead of documenting what has already reached its end as a past act. Could it be that traces may inventively call for a future that actually transcends the past?

Figure 15 Monumento de Resistencia in Cali, Colombia. 2023. Author's photo.

7

Contested Imaginaries of Potentiality

Shared Patterns of Imagination

E. Soja considers urban imaginaries as "the mental or cognitive mappings of urban reality and the interpretative grids through which we think about, experience, evaluate and decide to act in the places, spaces and communities in which we live" (Soja, 2000: 324).

It is interesting to observe in this definition the use of the descriptive term "mapping"—as if imaginaries are more or less constructed in ways that actually mirror practices of surveying space and spatial arrangements. The "interpretative grids," another obvious spatial metaphor projected on the workings of the urban imaginary, further seems to support a conviction that imagination when it comes to consider space is somehow constricted spatially.

It is possible however to consider urban imaginaries using the distinction Lefebvre proposes between representations of space and representational spaces. In this widely commented upon distinction, representations of space are, according to Lefebvre, "conceptualized" (1991: 38) and characterize "the dominant space in any society (or mode of production)" (ibid.: 39). "Representation spaces, on the other hand, need obey no rules of consistency or cohesiveness. Redolent with imaginary and symbolic elements, they have source in history—in the history of a people as well as in the history of each individual belonging to that people" (1991: 41).

In this distinction, the imaginary construction is directly related to relations of power. Dominant representations of space tend to become regulated, formalized, and stereotyped and thus acquire the status of reality: "scientists, planners, urbanists, technocratic subdividers and social engineers" construct them while attributing to them a certain certainty of knowledge. Representational spaces are spaces lived: People themselves construct imaginary and symbolic attributions to the spaces they live in, in the process of inhabiting them.

Although lived space is "passively experienced," "imagination seeks to change and appropriate" it (1991: 39). Rob Shields, who chooses to translate the term as "spaces of representation," suggests that it refers to "space *as it might be*, fully lived space" (Shields, 1996: 160 in Stanek, 2011: 129, italics in the original) and as L. Stanek remarks, the spaces of representation form the social imaginary" (ibid.). Christian Schmid also uses the term representation and believes that it concerns "the symbolic dimension of space" (2008: 37). And as he suggests, Lefebvre stresses the significance of symbols for humans in any given society: "[The symbol] constitutes the basis of social imaginary that is different from the individual imaginary" (ibid.: 36).

Is there a clash between representations of space and representational spaces? For Lefebvre, there seems to be a continuous rearrangement of their relations along with the other pole of his triad, "spatial practices." But this rearrangement is far more than a peaceful process of exchanges and shifts in roles according to historical contingencies. It is always a matter of power relations and spatially embedded social struggles.

The imaginary aspect, then, may be considered in light of Lefebvre's controversial triad as a contested terrain that is produced through historically specific confrontations between dominant and dominated approaches that attribute meaning to space. Specially sanctioned positions of meaning producers (priests, scientists, etc.) acquire different power in different societies. Contesting the power of those positions, challenging the keepers of positions, or creating different positions (even by dispersing their privileges throughout the social body) are ways in which imaginaries are being developed, destroyed, invented, and expressed.

Cornelius Castoriadis (1987) puts an emphasis on the role social creativity plays in shaping human history. Such creativity is in constant confrontation with the clearly constructed social condition, the "instituted society." And it produces radical novelty within the instituted society. Castoriadis does not see each society's history and history in general as a chain of causal relations that produce certain predictable and explainable changes within the limits imposed by "the instituted." In his view, history is the production of the new, the unexpected. And this is possible because all people possess the "capacity to make arise as an image something which does not exist and has never existed" (1987: 388 n.25).

Castoriadis names this capacity as the "radical imaginary" at work in the acts of transcending the limits of the instituted society. According to his view, this is actually the force that shapes society in and through history: "society is the work of the *instituting* imaginary" (1991: 145, italics in the original).

Of course this capacity does not project the nonexistent in total absence of already experienced images of the world (and images processed in various ways, including dreamwork as well as art work). Although Castoriadis's attempt to free sociological and political thought from historical determinism is understandable, his approach to radical novelty seems to lack the means to understand the ways people actually craft novelty and develop their capacity to "see" and target the nonexistent. Radical novelty arises not through a creative force that transcends the already instituted but by developing, while shaping them, the potentialities of the existent—not despite its socially instituted status but because of it. The "instituted" needs always to struggle to maintain itself since in hierarchical societies the many are kept under conditions that do not allow them to shape it according to their needs and aspirations. Radical imaginaries, if we choose to accept the term, develop in conditions of contestation and struggle: in efforts to go beyond the suffocating perimeter of dominant imaginaries that sustain and promote a certain recognized social "reality."

In an attempt to crudely sketch an inventory of current clashes around predominant urban imaginaries, we will have to return to the contemporary project of urban order: Urban imaginaries may be thought to stem from representations of space and representational spaces that get involved in the conceptualization of this order and in the processing of lived experiences related to this order.

Exploring the ways of challenging urban order will be the main scope of focusing on urban imaginaries. Who and how do they challenge such an order through their shared urban imaginaries? Is this about shared images and meanings that produce new approaches to lived realities or is it also about the capacity to develop new potential urban forms?

Shared imaginaries may construct and project visions of nonexistent, possible spaces. They thus challenge dominant representations of space by exploring (while performing them) the potentialities of the urban. Interestingly, such potentialities are not generated by the novelties of an alleged invention of a new urban. Although Lefebvre himself is more inclined to favor production as total creation, while downplaying to role of appropriation, urban imaginaries may open roads to change mainly by appropriating while transforming dominant representations. Imaginary constructions may thus employ collage patterns, bricolage-type inventiveness, and multilayered juxtapositions of figurative elements. Such constructions also share with dominant representations a crucial temporal element: in order to become embedded in ways of being in and through space, they need to be recurrent, they need to return again and again in the minds of people. Shared urban imaginaries only exist while being expressively performed again and again. They need to be expressed in order to survive.

So, urban imaginaries constitute a contested terrain. They are performed, expressed, and thus shared by being recurrently present in the acts and thoughts of those who share them. But they are not only ways to think of space or to project images of possible spaces. Here lies the nucleus of

Lefebvre's grand project that attempts to erect a theory of the production of space: we live in space and produce it in various ways that are socially prioritized and made meaningful, but, more than that, we develop socially inculcated ways to perceive, to imagine, to think, and to speak through space. Space is produced but it also produces conditions that shape the society that produces it. So, urban imaginaries also shape performances of the social, of the conditions that support and legitimize a certain social organization (or, better, a certain social order).

Let us then attempt to locate the areas of contestation shaped by patterns of urban imaginary constructions that explicitly focus on the potentialities of urban contemporary order.

Central to neoliberal ideology is the figure of the *sovereign individual*: always choosing to promote himself or herself, free but obliged to devise ways to advance, to succeed, to become victorious in every aspect of social antagonism. This view of the individual as a center of individualized tactics and strategies goes along with a value system that is actually used to measure the competencies and achievements of each and every one. Two scales of measurement are actually used: One measures individual ownership and the other the capacity to consume. The neoliberal individual is measured in both scales constantly. And those measurements are projected to each and everyone's self-esteem while directly or indirectly shaping each one's plans for the future.

Neoliberal ideology with its premises and with its persuasive power intervenes in the formation of individual fantasies, dreams, and aspirations and thus develops the conditions of personal imaginaries. Although such imaginaries are individually crafted, the basic characteristics remain the same for most as long as the dominant ideology controls the contour and the content of imaginary constructions. Shared imaginaries, thus, are patterns of imaginary constructions that oversee and control each individual imagination process by being repeatedly present and easily recognizable in interpersonal exchanges.

Since it is crucial for the neoliberal ideology to present the sovereign individual as always able to acquire a better place in the social ladder (the dream of social ascent), potentiality becomes a crucial factor both for the justification of this ideology as well as for the individual imaginaries that sustain it. It is however a specifically and artfully defined area of potentiality: the potentiality to become what within this systemic set of scopes and values is considered as a successful individual.

Individual creativity, as opposed to the collective creativity so far explored, is at the center of the dominant imaginary constructions in support of the successful sovereign individual. The idea of an emerging creative class introduced by the best-selling book of the economist Richard Florida has crucially contributed in providing the ground on which this imaginary became a real force to shape neoliberal urban policies. According to his definition, the members of this class "engage in work whose function is to 'create meaningful new forms'" (Florida, 2012: 38). Distinguishing between a "Super-Creative Core" and the "creative professionals" that belong to the Creative Class (always in capitals!), he locates three core values that characterize all of them: "individuality," "meritocracy," and "diversity and openness" (ibid.: 56–7). These values directly connect to a self-image of the successful creative individual: focused on developing one's capacities, demanding to be awarded for his or her accomplishments (no matter how unequal are the opportunities for many), and open to diversity more as a "lifestyle choice than a political trait" (Peck, 2005: 758). No matter how strongly Florida insists that "tapping and stoking the creative furnace inside every human being is the great challenge of our time" (Florida, 2005 as quoted in Peck, 2005: 757), the privileging of such individuals in city policies aimed at supporting the so-called creative economy directly becomes a "realpolitik of urban inequality" (Peck, 2005: 759). The "non-creative" ones are responsible for their fate, they don't understand how important it is to be creative and are stubbornly stuck in demands and struggles that belong to the past according to the guru of creativity. Peck is right to connect this logic to the perpetuation of the "extant 'order' of market oriented flexibility" (ibid.: 761). Creative economy policies and the idea that creativity may cause urban economic development are in essence a current form of neoliberal politics that uses creative production both as a propelling force of profit making and as a city-branding tool. And such politics enhances class divisions and corroborates the privileges of the few. The imaginary of creativity contributes in establishing the borders between a creative individualist elite (which may be creative in specific ways compatible with market-oriented scopes) and a majority left to play the role of consumers (or, even worse, totally excluded from the rights and opportunities connected to city life).

The mythologized potentiality that sustains the promises of individual success relies on two praised characteristics of social life: flexibility and affectivity. Both are supposed to ensure the most crucial characteristics of the sovereign individual that guarantee his or her power to be a subject: freedom and uniqueness. The individual becomes an autonomous subject (therefore responsible for successes and failures) only if he or she is considered free and distinct from every other person.

The mythological (fantasized as well as made meaningful in the context of dominant ideology) individual is supposed to be free because he or she is educated, tested, and called to action in conditions of flexibility: recognizing potentialities means in such a context being able to readjust, adapt, and invent so long as those maneuvers promise individual success. To be free means to be flexible.

On the other hand, to be unique, to be able to respond to real or fantasized challenges in ways that define you as a distinct subject, you need to be able to process your individual affects. Affects distinguish and personalize. To be unique means to be yourself, a self that is instituted by distinct and distinctive affects. It is the individual and individualizing responses that may present to the allegedly sovereign individual the potentialities of social life. All you have to do is feel the opportunities. And follow your "instinct" (a phrase that, surprisingly, although meant to indicate the very core of a subject's individuality actually uses a term—instinct—that refers to a common ground beyond the reach of individual tactics).

The Imaginary of Affect

Reasoning or critical processing of received stimuli is falsely presented as the opposite to affective responses. By demonizing criticism or by declaring the complexity of the existing systemic structure as beyond the reach of individual actors (Spencer, 2016), neoliberal ideology encourages individual subjects to "become themselves" by avoiding what may be considered as common to all. In such an almost perverted version of bourgeois individualism, which in the founding premises of liberal ideology was based in universal values and universal capacities (prominent among them being the capacity to reason, to think, and to criticize), affects are considered as personal links to the potentialities of social life while *Ratio* (rational thinking) is considered as a deindividualizing capacity.

There is a growing literature focused on understanding human behavior through the shaping of affects. Either stemming from feminist and queer activist sensibilities or from scientific findings and theorizations, this interest in affects and human affective responses has, as it seems, a performative influence on the discussion about the role of feelings, emotions, and affects in the experience and inhabiting of contemporary urban worlds. A mode of urban imaginary is crafted by the developing prioritization of feelings in the creation of relations with the urban environment (explicitly promoted by advertisements that emphasize a consumerist empathy with objects advertised). However, this imaginary becomes a contested terrain when new forms of deviant behavior and dissident acting are linked to a reappraisal of affects. In this reappraisal, affects are considered as the necessary means through which relations with the materiality of the lived world and with the presence of other humans may escape inculcated affective dispositions.

We have many clear indications that "affective response can be designed into spaces" (Thirft, 2004: 68) especially in our times in which knowledges and theories about the manipulation of senses and the production of organized sense-stimuli in and through space have greatly advanced (ibid.) Rancièrian diagnosis about the centrality of practices that guard the socially defined limits of the sensible may become a central hypothesis concerning the way "regimes of feeling" (ibid.) are advanced.

All relevant calls of architects, planners, and theorists to prioritize affect in response to space support, activate, or even help to produce an imaginary of affect that contributes to a potentialization of urban experience. Urban space is understood as a potential promoter of affects, as a generator of feelings that multiply the potentialities of individual responses. Such a form of potentialization, however, by indiscriminately valorizing affects sees no role in an engaged criticism of urban experience.

If we follow Douglas Spencer's (2016) main argument, we may link the emerging architecture of affect, and the imaginary that it helps to develop, to a neoliberal dismissal of social criticism in favor of a complete and positive acceptance of instituted reality.

"To keep perception trained on what is in front of it, untroubled by questions of meaning and interpretation" (Spencer, 2016: 159) seems to be the ultimate goal of such an imaginary of affect based on a false presupposition that senses may directly link us to the world. Along with this goes of course a peculiar cult of authenticity, already magisterially criticized by R. Sennett as the "tyranny of intimacy" (1986) a cult that in this case is predominantly focused on the idea of a self that is "true" because it links with the world without the intervention of reflective thinking or critical thinking in general. Curiously, such an individual is considered as freed from the social constrains of constructed meaning and, at the same time, as a "person," although personality gets shaped by a series of interlinks between the mental, the emotional and the perception-based responses to the world.

D. Spencer links such an overruling political project to an advancing "affective turn" in architectural theory and practice. Explicitly aiming at activating responses to affect, some of the contemporary star architects insist that the time of architecture considered as a language, or, predominantly as a vehicle of meaning (recognized individually or collectively) has passed. Along with this diagnosis that condemns an overanalysis of built environment in terms of meaning production and interpretation variations (including "deconstruction" tactics) comes a suspicion toward, if not a total dismissal of, criticism.

In line with theories that oppose affect to thinking and defend the power affective response allegedly has to bypass social control, architects propose a return to a supposed "immediacy of expression" (Spencer, 2016: 140). As Spencer shows, a paean to multiplicity and differentiation is connected to an emphasis of the individualizing, albeit pre-cognitive, influence of affect that may be triggered by the materiality and form of space. "As an affect can unfold into different affections or interpretations in different beings, it embeds a form with ability to be perceived in multiple ways," says Farshid Moussavi in her *The Function of Form* (quoted by Spencer, 2016: 142).

As many feminist and queer theory scholars show, it is necessary to start from a diagnosis of the predominant affective relations in order to challenge the dominant social hierarchies and instituted social order. The Argentinean anthropologist and feminist Rita Segato locates at the root of current capitalist-patriarchal social order a "pedagogy to cruelty" (Segato, 2016: 623), which is conditioning people "to the exercise of and indifference to cruelty" (ibid.: 622). Cruelty may become the all-encompassing affective response to human relations and may thus dominate an imaginary focused on affect. Enhanced by TV images, war news footage, experiences and stories of family, workplace, or sports fans violence, an imaginary of cruelty casts a dark shadow on urban experience by advancing to paroxysmal levels the proliferating tendencies of urban violence. This is an imaginary that creates urban dystopias, while at the same time "naturalizing" and "banalizing" violence to borrow Segato's adjectives.

Affective Solidarities

Aspirations for an emancipating society cannot be sustained by critical reasoning alone. Longing for a different future needs to connect with a critical recuperation of affective solidarities. Can people hope without feeling the joy this hope carries? Can people revolt without feeling the anger everyday injustices trigger?

Engaged affective orientation is the motivating force of an imaginary of affect: By putting an emphasis on relationality and reciprocity this kind of imaginary will host affective responses that, along with relevant practices, may possibly challenge the structure of capitalist sociality. Explicitly expressed in the affective regimes predominating the city, this model of social relations will be threatened not by simply attributing value to personal emotions but by the development of counter dominant affective sensibilities based on the reinvention of mutuality and equality.

As already mentioned, the neoliberal cult of individuality praises affective responses as genuine and authentic only to dismiss responses that are based on critical reflection and the problematization of dominant values. Narcissism and egoism are elevated to genuine expressions of a self that refuses to be submitted to reflexive criticism. And rational reasoning is taken to represent an almost totalitarian attempt to control behavior and to promote homogenization.

Neoliberal ideology actually reverses reality: homogenization is forced upon this society's members by exactly those mechanisms that are presented as the source and guarantee of diversity. Consumerist culture develops patterns of behavior (euphemistically elevated to everyone's chance to find a way to success) that shape life trajectories. The distinct rationality of capitalism is taken to be a set of natural laws: makes no sense to question such laws as it makes no sense to question the law of gravity. But to profit as much as you can from this condition, you need to be yourself. You need, they say, to trust your emotions and to follow your desires.

It is not enough to oppose this ideology by a reclaiming of rational thinking. It is not enough to explain and to interpret. We need to reclaim the power emotions have to shape and to sustain the sharing of liberating joy. As Rita Segato convincingly suggests, "compassion, empathy, local and community roots and all devotion to forms of the sacred capable of maintaining solid collective relationships operate as dysfunctional in relation to the historical project of capital" (2016: 621). Such affective approaches are opposed to the dominant "pedagogy of cruelty" (Segato's term) that banalizes violence and makes people unable to emotionally react to injustices inflicted upon the powerless. In place of an overemphasis on individual (albeit often pre-personal) liberation based on the total embracing of affective responses, affective solidarities may construct shared imaginaries of affect that support experiences of solidarity and mutual care.

Deviant imaginaries of affect may only arise through practices that expose people to different stimuli and often coordinate (not intentionally though) their responses by the improvising ad hoc orchestration of bodies. One possible source of such affective liberating coordination is the recuperation of the power rituals have to promote affective solidarity. Just think of an example related to Mexico's recent movement history: the ritualistic use of the *Virgen de las barricadas*. This was an emblematic image of Madonna raised to a symbolic manifestation of the struggle that took place in Oaxaca, Mexico, during the days of the Oaxaca Commune that was already discussed in this book.

Wearing a tear-gas mask and a dress adorned with flaming tires motifs, the Virgen de las Barricadas emblematizes a collective belief in a sacred presence that helps the people of Oaxaca in their struggle. A shared imaginary seems to have been developed by connecting a sacred image to the everyday experiences of the barricaded free city. Affective solidarity is at the base of such symbols that do not simply represent values or messages connected to the struggle but actually hint toward shared feelings and beliefs, shared emotions and appeals to mutual engagement, and humanized relations with figures that are usually considered to be of a transcendental nature. Same feelings and expectations also elevate the image of *Santo Niño de APPO* (Assamblea Popular de los Pueblos de Oaxaca) to an affective symbol. Baby Christ wearing a hat with a red star and depicted in a supermarket cart with stones and firecrackers (typical accessories of manifestations during those days) becomes a defender of the people and an affective reassurance of a just cause.

As Lauren Berlant suggests, "To cultivate new kinds of affective collective ground we have to embrace the sheer formalism of solidarity, the affective freedom to be different but mutual amid the risk-taking of changing structure through practice (Berlant and Greenwald, 2012: 87). What seems to be present in Oaxacan popular creations is the production of a common affective ground through the ritualistic use of transformed religious symbols. Imaginaries of affect are thus developed through the emergence of collective references that connect in practice shared beliefs, experiences, and emotions. Practices and words of solidarity that develop positive emotions of togetherness plant the seeds of a radical imaginary of affect. They thus "retrain affective practical being" (Berlant, 2016: 399).

The Imaginary of Flexibility

Incessantly we keep on hearing that we live in a globalized world. A world of multilayered connections, a world of flows and diverse trajectories. A world of unbelievable complexity but also of unbelievably many opportunities, they say. In this world a term, a mentality, and a catchword referring to every part of social life has emerged: flexibility. This word has arisen at the crossroads of erudite theoretical constructions and common stereotypical convictions that seem to support the same self-grounded image of liberty. What can be more descriptive of individual liberty than the freedom to change, to acquire new forms, and to accept ever-changing scopes and foci of acting? To be flexible is to be free.

Flexibility, however, is a quality that is mandatory for organisms or arrangements that have to face changes. Changes especially in the programming they do not participate—they only have to deal with them in the best way possible. Hidden in the "freedom of flexibility" lies the burden of adaptability. Is someone who always tries to adapt really free?

Flexibility is often attributed to a capacity directly connected to an organism's survival. Presuming that the problem of survival may be posed in terms of uneven confrontations between ontologically defined enemies, flexibility appears as the ingenuous manoeuvring of the weak in efforts to face the threats of the strong. This way of understanding nature and natural ecosystems is of course culturally biased. A different understanding of nature would put an emphasis on coexistence and complementarity, seeing flexibility from a different perspective. Using the same cultural frame to observe the "survival" of humans in a specific social context will necessarily include a view about society as the battleground of all against all. In terms of potentiality this view—Hobbesian in its genealogy—will see flexibility as one among the weapons to avoid defeat. Such a potentiality then is founded on the ambiguity, persistence, and continuous mutability of threats.

Based on the necessity of survival in a war-like social context, flexibility becomes ethically irrelevant: not a choice but a necessity. It may thus support acts of unlimited opportunism. Transferred to the constitution of a relevant imaginary, flexibility may acquire the form of a fantasized ability to overcome any kind of obstacle. A kind of perverse vision of freedom thus seems to sustain the imaginary of flexibility, if flexibility is equated to the capacity to survive, to become victorious in life considered as battle.

P. Virno insists that man is the animal that does not have the instinctual predetermination suitable to guide it in its efforts to survive. There is no predetermined appropriate milieu to which humans may best adapt. Humans will always invent the conditions of the struggle for their survival (2015). However, at the root of this seemingly ontological contingency lies the foundation of history as a multileveled construction of necessities. Humans, in their efforts to survive, construct both the temporal and the spatial relations of their survival acts. At the same time, aspects of human life that may be taken to depart from the necessities of "biological survival" directly shape the spatiotemporal conditions of survival, by introducing, depending on the spatialities of each society, different priorities and contrasting choices. In the context of each society, the inaugural indeterminacy of human milieu becomes a stake at issue in confrontations between antagonistic social agents. The problem of flexibility, thus, may be reformulated as the problem of socially embedded potentialities performed by different social groups within the society.

Departing from the model of society as a war of all against all may help us to understand flexibility as a constituent element of struggles within society rather than as an individual capacity to be developed by society's members. Neoliberal reason, however, has ingenuously crafted a third option for the imaginary of flexibility: flexibility as a personal guarantee for achievements in a world of inherent unpredictability and of complexity impossible for individuals to make sense of.

Neoliberal rhetoric not only praises liberty but also creates an image of liberty by locating it at the heart of the market: to be free is to be a consumer. However, the only possible source of freedom, albeit an idealized one, is to be a producer, a producer according to your own needs and aspirations. Consumer flexibility is one more form of adaptability. Behind the false appearance of individual choice is a constructed grid of behavior patterns, profit-oriented production priorities, and calculated innovations opening new fields of profit making. The consumer-self reflects the entrepreneur-self. Both need to be flexible, both need to be able to follow the opportunities presented by the market.

Adaptability, some may object, is a kind of wisdom that limits individual freedom on certain aspects only to keep it as a guiding principle for the organization of society in general. We know that neoliberal ideology's main enemy target has always been planning: to plan is to restrict liberty—see what kind of totalitarianisms have emerged in countries of planned economy, neoliberals say.

As it appears, neoliberal theorists have explicitly equated planning with the destruction of freedom. "Planning leads to dictatorship because dictatorship is the most effective instrument of coercion and the enforcement of ideals" writes Hayek (in Spencer, 2016: 18). In such a denial of planning, adaptability becomes the supreme capacity that will give people the means to connect to changes in the future without attempting to either control or understand them. The paradox of the neoliberal promise of freedom, which is to be exercised according to the self-regulating potentialities of the market (and thus not really freedom), matches the paradox of neoliberalism's sovereign individual—flexible, therefore, not really sovereign.

Under these ideological circumstances, the imaginary of flexibility colonizes every aspect of urban life. Transformed from a threat that is always present in most people's lives (epitomized in work precariousness and conditions of unpredictability that indeed make it difficult for them to make plans for a decent life in the future), flexibility becomes a virtue. Embrace with the potentialities of urban life if you want to take advantage of opportunities to live better, they say.

Opportunism and cynicism are for P. Virno the principal "emotional tonalities of the multitude" (Virno, 2004: 86). He suggests that hidden within the practices of opportunist and cynical agents lie the possibilities of exodus (2004: 86–7). Losing any illusionary attachment to myths that present a peaceful search for opportunities and realizing that to "win" you need to fight using all available means, such figures actually free themselves from the false promises of dominant ideology. In the malign imaginary of such unrestricted personal egoism, we, however, find again a Hobbesian image of society. If the awareness of the fact that laws and habits inculcated rules does not lead to the development of shared imaginaries of mutual flexibility, a precapitalist or postcapitalist society of cruelty will emerge—which of course does not mean that capitalist societies do not nourish forms of utmost cruelty.

Flexibility as Solidarity

There is however a different value system that may challenge the dogma of adaptability through flexibility. This cosmovision is based on relations of complementarity and mutuality. Obviously, it can only flourish in social contexts in which the collective rather than the individual becomes the starting point for the problematization of adaptability.

In Ano Meria of Folegandros, a village community in a Greek island, people used to share a particular kind of practical wisdom that has permeated many aspects of communal life. Let us see how such wisdom has created a shared imaginary of flexibility that departs from neoliberal individualism.

This is a very windy village. So, protecting houses and cultivated land from menacing winds is a primal issue for inhabiting the island. But people in Ano Meria do not confront the wind's force by erecting strong protective barriers. After all, secondary wind whirlpools created behind protective walls in the small cultivated fields would unavoidably destroy crops. So, their tactic is more flexible: they devise ways to moderate the wind's blows by employing semipermeable barriers (comprising used fishing nets, consecutive low walls, plants that may lower down wind's velocity by partially resisting the blows, and so on). The same practical wisdom of flexibility is applied in the building of walls (to fence areas for cultivation by creating small plateaus or to build small stables and rural houses). Since most of the stones available are not of a quality good enough to shape them with the help of appropriate tools, Ano Meria's masons learn to carefully hit the stones with a small hammer to only slightly shape their contours in order to use them. Hitting too hard will simply result in the stone crumbling to pieces. Flexibility then ensures better results than a straightforward attack.

People in Ano Meria seem to have integrated this knowledge to a kind of shared imaginary at work in everyday social encounters. The same flexibility is expressed in jokes: Instead of outwardly expressing discontent or hostility they learn to treat relationships of disagreement or trust-crisis with jokes that implicitly show a kind of criticism while at the same time creating bridges between opposing views or acts. To see their community through the lens of everyday moderation is to craft a shared imaginary of flexibility that is essentially a shared imaginary of belonging to community.

R. Segato refers to "the mode of existence of the village world" to characterize "societies that are still governed by communitarian and collectivist models of coexistence" (2016: 615). In this world a different way of defining the public and the private develops, which may trigger interesting hypotheses concerning the potentialities of flexibility. "Domestic life is not intimate or private at all" (ibid.: 618). And "public space, inhabited by men and their tasks ... does not encompass or subsume domestic space, inhabited by women and families and their many types of tasks and shared activities" (ibid.: 616). From such a dual world of "low intensity patriarchy" in which man is not elevated to the universality of the human-One, we pass under capitalist colonial modernity to the "high-intensity modern-colonial patriarchy of universal domain" (ibid.: 619).

Corresponding imaginaries thus seem to change from a focus on a flexible definition of the public realm that traverses domestic and public space in different ways to an aggressively defined public realm by the capitalist colonial state. Complementarity permeates the village world imaginary, and flexibility is experienced in negotiations within a world of irreducible plurality of community roles. Precariousness and anxiety permeate the urban colonial world that sees flexibility both as a disease and as a promise for cure. The way gender relations are experienced, performed, and embedded in shared imaginaries becomes crucially important in the development of flexibility's contested appraisals and imaginary projections.

What may be the qualities of an emerging "we" that will make it capable of devising relations with itself and its possible "outsides" in order to adapt to a world of multiple forces and potentialities? Depending on the ways this kind of "we" understands its outside, we can even question the very presupposition that adaptation always has to do with actions that refer to a clearly distinct outside. We can even question the very premises on which adaptation appears to be the only possible course of action for individuals as well as for groups and societies. What if there is actually not an outside but only different tropes of potential cooperation and emerging synergies between different potential agents? What if the firmly established dichotomies of Western thought, namely individual versus society, culture versus nature, and inside versus outside may be thought either in terms of mutual definition or in terms of complementarity? What if those dichotomies can be replaced by flows of exchange that incessantly reconfigure the limits, if any, between the dichotomy's poles?

Communities that were often presented as monolithic, as not changing, as not flexible at all, communities constituted by members who allegedly simply follow established patterns of action, may teach us a lot. There is more change in their version of adaptation. There is more wisdom in their ways of problematizing flexibility: not as an individual capacity that may become the stage of an individual "success" or of an individual "failure" (always measured by comparing individual gains and losses) but as a shared capacity that aims at producing, sustaining, and guarding the common. And the common is not simply an agglomeration of common goods to be shared but a horizon of understanding and feeling that creates an always-in-the-making common ground. Flexibility in this context refers to the wisdom of endless negotiations that develop in conditions of mutual trust meant to sustain an inclusive common world—a common world that may include many different worlds.

Maybe in this lesson to be learned from indigenous communities that struggle against neoliberalism's enclosure we may locate a way out of a nightmare that keeps on developing in many parts of the capitalist world. People terrified by the dangers and precarity of neoliberal flexibility seek refuge in the false promises for a "sedentary" safety. A reemergent wave of particularisms, nationalisms, and racisms promises a relief from the burdens of flexibility and a truly monolithic adherence to essentialized identities. Could this be a mutation of neoliberalism with its promise of conditional freedom (as long as the market roles are left to regulate society's organization)? Could this be the true face of a system based on antagonism rather than on cooperation? Or maybe it is a proof that on the flip side of capitalist free market is the violence of unlimited individualism?

This is the time to reclaim the wisdom of flexibility as a means to constitute an inclusive and open-to-newcomers "we." Otherwise, in the current period of global crisis, augmented by the recent Covid-19 pandemic, people will be directed to choose between two equally false promises: the promise of freedom understood as individual flexibility or the promise of safety understood as self-enclosure. Only solidarity, respect, and trust may open a way out of these equally destructive options.

8

Conclusion

The central scope of this book is to locate in the contemporary urban condition forces that may sustain the process of social emancipation. Instead of seeing contemporary cities as structured worlds that enforce stable geometries of power, an attempt is being made to explore the dynamics of spatial ordering. It is due to such dynamics that dominant urban behavior patterns are both sustained as well as challenged.

Considered at an abstract level, space is pure relationality. Distance and proximity regulate this relationality and make positions in space comparable. If, however, we attribute to this relationality meanings that have to do with people occupying and experiencing space, relationality becomes a process: To be near to someone is a performance. It employs spatial relationality the moment it makes it socially significant. The overall social engineering of spatial relationality is actually based on the crafting, sustaining, repairing, extending, and so on of a force field of power relations. Urban space, thus, is not only the expression of the society that inhabits it but, more importantly, a constituent element, a shaping factor of the kind of social organization that characterizes this society.

The dynamics of urban ordering is the result of the stabilities and instabilities, the continuities and discontinuities, the functioning and mutations of this force field. In contemporary urban worlds, this force field is shaped by the core mechanisms of capitalist reproduction, namely the exploitation of labor and the domination of economic and political elites based on gender, race, and culture discriminating suppression. Directly connected to the functioning of the urban force field is the attribution of value to urban space according to the immanent capitalist market logic that transforms everything (including human relations) to merchandise. More specifically, city space in all its possible levels of performed relationality (center–periphery relations, domestic vs. public space, resource connected spaces that become targets of urban extractivism, etc.) becomes entangled in market relations in the form of commodity.

Dominant processes of space valorization as well as dominant forms of social organization (that eventually are meant to shape society's members) have to sustain the dynamics of the force field in service of the perpetuation of the system's defining characteristics. Social antagonism, however, is always a source of instability. Although antagonistic forces are necessary to sustain the field's dynamics, their balance in favor of a stable functioning of the field is not guaranteed.

Included in the main argument of this book is the suggestion that the excluded and exploited, who constitute a huge part of contemporary urban populations, implicitly or explicitly challenge the stability of urban order not only by revolting against injustice, but also by developing forms of everyday mutual help, cooperation, and solidarity. In direct confrontation with a modernist imaginary that sees a future society as produced primarily through total innovation, this argument is developed along the idea that everyday acts of resistance and survival may shape patterns of a different kind of social organization. A unifying characteristic of such everyday practices is the reclaiming of community relations and the development of shared values that depart from neoliberal individualist ethos. Commoning is the term that may encompass such practices along with the emerging value system and the social relations that sustain them.

Commoning, and especially urban commoning that includes practices of commoning city space, is a force that explicitly affects the imposed balance of the urban force field. Commoning performances are developed under the predominance of capitalist command but may escape it as long as people struggle to liberate their labor or life conditions from direct exploitation. We have seen how cooperation may develop beyond, in spite of and sometimes in direct clash with, capitalist command. Commoning performances may also emerge as the reinventions of community bonds and relevant cultural accomplishments as in the cases explored that show how an understanding of "we" or togetherness may be transferred from rural contexts to the experience of urban neighborhoods. And some commoning performances may arise in situations that demand new forms of exchange, control, and belonging as for example in the context of information-sharing technologies and ubiquitous connectivity.

Commoning, thus, is a condition of social dynamism, a set of relations that are at the same time economic, social, and affective. These relations are actually performed, not only in acts but also in reflexive and imaginary treatments of shared realities by the subjects that share them. It is because commoning is performed and performative that commoning takes the form of recurrent practices: Here lies an important point in the description of urban potentiality. There is the option of considering the potential as the source (and guarantee) of novelty. What may emerge as new is being presented in this case as singular, as not reducible to the existent, as not recognizable, but approached as a surprise. What is being suggested in this book, however, is that potentiality is performed and can only be traced in its performances. Potentiality is the dynamism of urban performances that depart from capitalist preconditions and command and, thus, expands, rearranges, and crafts the limits of reality, or, in Rancièrean terms, the "order of the sensible," understood as the socially crafted reality.

Performances never exhaust the potentialities; they actually extend them, develop them, if not outwardly invent them. In the quest for developing the potentiality of social emancipation, it is important to look for new patterns of repeatability rather than for singular events that will epitomize the "new." This is not however to repeat in a different way the mantra of social-democratic promises of a gradual "betterment" of society. Ruptures are part of the transformative momentum of new recurrent practices. What could introduce more deep ruptures in social transformation than the development of new habits, new rituals, and new tracing capacities?

The three modes of recurrent practices that are being explored in this book indeed seem to show in an explicit way that potentialization is not a purely temporal process (something that happens after a certain possibility becomes actualized) but, equally, a spatial process. Habits institute places. And place making may become the breeding ground of mutuality and solidarity as long as it sustains commoning habits. Rituals activate space as the stage of potential relations between humans and between humans and no-humans. In their magic circle, rituals extend and potentially transform shared social worlds. And tracing, the capacity to read and invent traces, makes space a means to indicate possibilities of action and shared emotions (feelings, affects, sensations).

An effort is being made to locate the emergence of urban habits, rituals, and tracing practices in processes that reinvent urban communities (while empowering them with emancipatory potentialities) as well as in processes that reclaim the creative liberating power of cooperation. Examples analyzed may surely proliferate as long as a sensitive approach to the sometimes ignored dynamics of the mundane and the everyday is carefully followed. In all the examples, the choice made to observe a specific part of a complicated process should not however be used to reduce actual performances to bounded types of action.

Refugee settlements indeed produce interesting indications of nondominant tracing practices in the reinvention of communities of people uprooted. But at the same time new habits are being developed and shared, rituals become areas of exchanges and hybridizations. Cooperation characterizes the Guelaguetza rituals performed in Mexico as well as in United States but such forms of communal cooperation at the same time support and express habits that reinvent communities (as in the case of communities of struggle during the days of Oaxaca Commune).

The attribution of the examples used for distinct categories of repeated performances can thus be considered only as indicative. Potentialities emerge often in the cross-fertilization of habits, rituals, and tracing practices.

Through the performance of habits, of rituals, and of tracing, space is produced and reinvented. Interestingly, those same modalities of potentiality performances may sustain and extend the dominant patterns of being in society as well as defy and transform them. Here lies perhaps an important stake for the struggles to establish equality, justice, solidarity, and mutual care. How can people develop such performances in ways that do not repeat the already existing urban and social order in their recurrent appearance? The answer seems to be in the direction of pursuing the potentiality of commoning as an emerging urban condition, a counter-dominant ethos, and a support of shared imaginaries. Does this mean that this is a clearly demarcated road to follow? Not at all. All we have is criteria developed through practice that may show us whether what is being experienced and imagined may indeed be repeated with emancipatory results. Because emancipation will not "arrive" as if it is a long-awaited messianic apocalypse. It will be built by crafting a world in which recurrent performances will not be the Procrustean bed of social homogenization or uniformity but the fertile ground of plurality created within and because of relations of mutual care.

Singularities, thus, will develop not in spite of shared performances but because of the richness that those performances will host. Let us remember Lefebvre's aphorism on his last work on rhythm analysis. A machine sound is pure repeatability. A clear case of normalizing rhythmicality. But the dawn? We all recognize it, we all have experienced it again and again. But how different each time it was! "The dawn is always new" (Lefebvre 2004: 90). Social emancipation will develop its own sunrises and sunsets perhaps not by an "electromagnetic victory over the sun" that El Lissitzky heroically proclaimed, but in reclaiming the sun's beauty and energy for all.

Opening: Geometries of the Future

In his *Pedagogical Sketchbook*, the painter Paul Klee observes the production of lines in a drawing in ways that may suggest a rethinking of the future as performed potentiality. Lines according to his approach are produced from the process of drawing and, we might add, retain the qualities and the potentialities of this process.

The pendulum creates a line that depicts the dynamics of equilibrium: back and forth, movement and counter-movement, forever. Or, at least, until "friction" will result in a final stasis after all the kinetic energy is consumed. Then, there is the motion that creates the circle. No starting point, no end. A motion that may start from any point. A line that circumscribes but encloses too. A world enclosed into itself. A totality that may even admire itself for its perfection.

What about the spiral? By changing the radius of the circle as we move in the direction of drawing it, the spiral starts to emerge. The larger the radius grows, the more we distance ourselves from the center. But its force of attraction never ceases to exist. The motion that creates the spiral has the potentiality to escape the center exactly because it relies on the constant development of a calculated (and, thus, calculating) distance.

We may move in the direction of the future in ways similar to the three patterns of line drawing described by Klee. Pendulum-like motion traps our efforts in a recurrence that is bound to finally lose its momentum. A genuine attempt to release ourselves from the dominating gravity is present in our pendulum-like movements. And we should never underestimate hopes and aspirations linked to those although the efforts might prove futile. Maybe sometimes our hopes for a different future get the power to defy gravity (even for a short time) like when we used to think that we were able to fly the moment that our childhood's swings seemed to reach for the sky.

Drawing a circle is a dream of transcendence, a dream of establishing a word totally new, separated from a before and an after. Motion erases itself in this perfect creation. Where did we start? Could every point be at the same time a reached end and a forgotten beginning? And what about the center? Is every point eternally bound to a relation with this center?

In Jean Pierre Vernant's accounts of the ancient democracy (2006), the circle represents the ideal of total equality. The center is there to be occupied by each speaker in a row, who, after delivering a speech, will eventually retreat to the periphery, as all the others. There is a crucial, painfully present, possibility however. The moment the center becomes more permanently occupied by someone (a concertized point of gravity), the circle reverts to the opposite of democracy: to a tyranny. So, the circle as future imagined and drawn is a promise and a nightmare at the same time. The promise itself is also questionable. Drawing a line enclosed to itself is suggesting that any future is already finished. A circular motion is a motion that will repeat itself. And as in the case of the pendulum, friction (the materiality of a world full of obstacles) will eventually lead to stasis. The difference from the pendulum line is that the circle will remain as the mark of a movement that aspired to enclose a future.

The spiral seems to retain the dynamics of future-making. Distancing itself from the center that has been the necessary starting point of its creation— the spiral line always moves forward. But it is not really a careless random movement. There is a pattern in this movement (a calculated distance from the center, a radius), a pattern that is however changing. A form in the making? A form to be redrawn by consecutive adjustments? A developing distancing that, nevertheless, does not forget that there is a center to confront, a point of reference to take into consideration? As Klee remarks, reversing the direction of the spiral movement will result in being gradually trapped in a center. An absorbing, hidden center. As the one to which a snail retreats. The spiral, however, produced from the center to its outside is always a flight to liberation. Or the always risky attempt of the snail to reach the world outside.

No need to reduce the hope for a different, just, and emancipated world to a defining schema. Could we however learn from an artist's thoughts on drawing something that will help us reflect upon the potentialities of future-building? Could we perhaps see ourselves as spiral drawing movements that neither advance toward a predetermined future nor are hopelessly trapped in the pendulum of successes and failures but actually always move in the direction of struggle by learning from our past? We may return but never exactly to the point we started from. Just near to it. We become, thus, able to reconsider its potentialities. Every struggle develops an always expanding distance from a vortex-like center that seeks to engulf all those popular dreams for collective emancipation. This is how we make the road to liberation by actually walking on it. After all, even snails enjoy the freedom of a rainy day! Imagine what this would mean for their lives if they could extend their spiral-like shell to meet the spirals of their snail comrades!

References

Abidor, M. (2015). *Voices of the Paris Commune*. Oakland: PM Press.
Abreek-Zubiedat, F. (2022). In the Name of Belonging Developing Sheikh Radwan for the Refugees in Gaza City, 1967–1982. In L. Beeckmans, A. Gola, Ash Singh, and H. Heynen (eds.), *Making Home(s) in Displacement Critical Reflections on a Spatial Practice*. Leuven: Leuven University Press, 117–38.
Acosta, A. (2013). Extractivism and Neoextractism: Two Sides of the Same Curse. In *Beyond Development: Alternative Visions from Latin America*. Permanent Working Group on Alternatives to Development (eds.). Quito: Fundación Rosa Luxemburg, 61–86.
Agamben, G. (1993). *The Coming Community*. Minneapolis: University of Minnesota Press.
Agamben, G. (1998). *Homo Sacer. Sovereign Power and Bare Life*. Stanford: Stanford University Press.
Agamben, G. (1999). *Potentialities*. Stanford: Stanford University Press.
Agamben, G. (2000). *Means without End. Notes on Politics*. Minneapolis: University of Minnesota Press.
Agamben, G. (2005). *State of Exception*. Chicago: University of Chicago Press.
Agamben, G. (2014). What Is Destituent Power? *Environment and Planning D: Society and Space*, 32: 65–74.
Agamben, G. (2016). *The Use of Bodies*. Stanford: Stanford University Press.
Agamben, G. (2019). *Creation and Anarchy*. Stanford: Stanford University Press.
Ahmed, S. (1999). Home and Away. Narratives of Migration and Enstrangement. *International Journal of Cultural Studies*, 2(3): 329–47.
Arendt, H. (1958). *The Human Condition*. Chicago: University of Chicago Press.
Avermaete, T. (2013). A Thousand Youth Clubs: Architecture, Mass Leisure and the Rejuvenation of Post-War France. *The Journal of Architecture*, 18(5): 632–46.
Bachelard, G. (1994). *The Poetics of Space*. Boston: Beacon Press.
Bachelard, G. (2013). *The Intuition of the Instant*. Evanston, IL: Northwestern University Press.
Badiou, A. (2001). *Ethics An Essay on the Understanding of Evil*. London: Verso.
Badiou, A. (2004a). *Infinite Thought*. London: Continuum.
Badiou, A. (2004b). Afterword: Some Replies to a Demanding Friend. In P. Hallward (ed.), *Think Again. Alain Badiou and the Future of Philosophy*. London: Continuum, 232–7.
Badiou, A. (2005). *Being and Event*. London: Continuum.
Badiou, A. (2009). *Logics of Worlds. Being and Event, 2*. London: Continuum.
Badiou, A. (2010). The Idea of Communism. In C. Douzinas and S. Žižek (eds.), *The Idea of Communism*. London: Verso, 1–19.

Barrera Cordero, J. (2009). La guerra del agua en Cochabamba: un caso de palabras que hablan mal. *Investigación Ambiental*, 1(1): 91–100.

Baschet, J. (2018). *Rebeldía, resistencia y autonomía!: la experiencia Zapatista*. Mexico: Ediciones Eón.

Batista, E. (2017). *Dissenting Words. Interviews with Jacques Rancière*. London: Bloomsbury Publishing.

Bauman, Z. (1998). *Globalization. The Human Consequences*. Cambridge: Polity Press.

Bauman, Z. (2000). *Liquid Modernity*. Cambridge: Polity Press.

Beecher, J. (2012). Women's Rights and Women's Liberation in Charles Fourier's Early Writings. In M. A. Ramiro Avilés and J. C. Davis (eds.), *Utopian Moments: Reading Utopian Texts*. London: Bloomsbury Academic, 92–8.

Bell, C. (1992). *Ritual Theory, Ritual Practice*. New York: Oxford University Press.

Bell, C. (1997). *Ritual Perspectives and Dimensions*. New York: Oxford University Press.

Benjamin W. (1983). *Charles Baudelaire: A Lyric Poet in the Era of High Capitalism*. London: Verso.

Benjamin, W. (1992). Theses on the Philosophy of History. In H. Arendt (ed.), *Illuminations*. London: Fontana Press.

Benjamin, W. (1998). *Understanding Brecht*. London: Verso.

Benjamin, W. (1999). *The Arcades Project*. Cambridge, MA: Belknap Press.

Benjamin, W. (2006). What Is the Epic Theater (II). In M. W. Jennings, M. Bullock, and G. Smith (eds.), *Selected Writings Vol. 4 1938–1940*. Cambridge, MA: The Belknap Press, 302–9.

Berardi, F. (2019). *Futurability. The Age of Impotence and the Horizon of Possibility*. London: Verso.

Bergson, H. (1977). *The Two Sources of Morality and Religion*. Notre Dame, IN: University of Notre Dame Press.

Bergson, H. (1988). *Matter and Memory*. New York: Zone Books.

Berlant, L. (2016). The Commons: Infrastructures for Troubling Times. *Environment and Planning D: Society and Space*, 34(3): 393–419.

Berlant, L., and Greenwald, J. (2012). Affect in the End Times: A Conversation with Lauren Berlant. *Qui Parle*, 20(2): 71–89.

Berman, M. (1982). *All That Is Solid Melts into Air. The Experience of Modernity*. London: Verso.

Bishop, Cl. (2004). Antagonism and Relational Aesthetics. *October*, 110: 51–79.

Boltanski, L. (2011). *On Critique. A Sociology of Emancipation*. Cambridge: Polity Press.

Bourdieu, P. (1977). *Outline of a Theory of Practice*. Cambridge: Cambridge University Press.

Bourdieu, P. (1991). *Language and Symbolic Power*. Cambridge: Polity Press.

Bourdieu, P. (1992). *The Logic of Practice*. Cambridge: Polity Press.

Bourdieu, P. (2000). *Pascalian Meditations*. Cambridge: Polity Press.

Bourdieu, P., and Wacquant, L. (1992). *An Invitation to Reflexive Sociology*. Cambridge: Polity Press.

Bourriaud, N. (2002). *Relational aesthetics*. Dijon: Presses du Réel.

Bremner, L. (2005). Border/Skin. In M. Sorkin (ed.), *Against the Wall*. New York: The New Press, 122–37.

Brighenti, Andrea Mubi (2013). A Territoriology of Graffiti Writing. In Cl. Musso and F. Naldi (eds.), *Frontier: The Line of Style*. Bologna: Damiani, 51–5.

Brighenti, M. A., and Pavoni, A. (2023). On Urban Trajectology: Algorithmic Mobilities and Atmocultural Navigation. *Distinktion. Scandinavian Journal of Social Theory*, 24(1): 40–63.

Brown, O. (2020). Habit as Resistance: Bergson's Philosophy of Second Nature. *European Journal of Philosophy* 28 (2):394–409

Buck-Morss, S. (2009). *Hegel, Haiti and Universal History*. Pittsburgh: University of Pittsburgh Press.

Butler, J. (1993). *Bodies That Matter. On the Discursive Limits of "Sex."* New York: Routledge.

Butler, J. (1997). *A Politics of the Performative*. New York: Routledge

Butler, J. (1999). *Gender Trouble. Feminism and the Subversion of Identity*. New York: Routledge.

Casey, E. (1997). *The Fate of Place. A Philosophical History*. Berkeley: University of California Press.

Castoriadis, C. (1987). *The Imaginary Institution of Society*. Cambridge: Polity Press.

Castoriadis, C. (1991). Power, Politics, Autonomy. In D. A. Curtis (ed.), *C. Castoriadis, Philosophy, Politics Autonomy*. Oxford: Oxford University Press, 143–74.

CECOSESOLA (2007). *Construyendo aquí y ahora el Mundo que Queremos*. Barquisimeto: Central Cooperativa de Servicios Sociales Lara.

CECOSESOLA (2010). Towards a Collective Mind? Transforming Meetings into Get-togethers; https://CECOSESOLA.org/wp-content/uploads/2020/06/Collective-mind.pdf (accessed May 21, 2022).

CENDA (2022) Laguna Larati: Gobernanza del agua, usos y costumbres. Available at https://www.cenda.org/secciones/agua-y-mineria/item/917-laguna-larati-gobernanza-del-agua-usos-y-costumbres.

Childe, V. G. (1936). *Man Makes Himself*. London: Watts & Company.

Colectivo Situaciones (2002). *19 & 20: Notes for a New Social Protagonism*. New York: Common Notions et al.

Constantinou, M., and Madarasz, N. (2009). Being and Spatialization: An Interview with Alain Badiou. *Environment and Planning D: Society and Space*, 27: 783–95.

Darot, P., and Laval, Chr. (2019). *Common. On Revolution in the 21st Century*. London: Bloomsbury Academic.

Deleuze, G., and Guattari, F. (2004). *A Thousand Plateaus*. London: Continuum.
Della Costa, Fr. (2023). Ritual as Metaphor. *Anthropological Theory*, 23(1): 3–32
Descola, Ph. (2013). *Beyond Nature and Culture*. Chicago: University of Chicago Press.
Dikec, M. (2015). *Space Politics and Aesthetics*. Edinburgh: Edinburgh University Press.
Dilingham, A. S. (2021). *Oaxaca Resurgent. Indigeneity, Development, and Inequality in Twentieth-Century Mexico*. Stanford: Stanford University Press.
Durkheim, E. (2001 [1912]). *The Elementary Forms of Religious Life*. Oxford: Oxford University Press.
Escobar, A. (2017). *Designs for the Pluriverse. Radical Interdependence, Autonomy, and the Making of World*. Durham: Duke University Press.
Escobar, A. (2020). *Pluriversal Politics*. Durham: Duke University Press.
Esposito, R. (2006). An Interview with T. Campbell. *Diacritics*, 36(2): 49–56.
Esposito, R. (2010). *Communitas. The Origin and Destiny of Community*. Stanford: Stanford University Press.
Esposito, R. (2013). Community, Immunity, Biopolitics. *Angelaki*, 8(3): 83–90.
Esteva, G. (2010). The Oaxaca Commune and Mexico's Coming Insurrection. *Antipode*, 42(4): 978–93.
Esteva, G. (2015a). The Hour of Autonomy. *Latin American and Caribbean Ethnic Studies*, 10(1): 134–45.
Esteva, G. (2015b). Enclosing the Enclosers: Autonomous Experiences from the Grassroots—beyond Development, Globalization and Postmodernity. In F. Luisetti, J. Pickles, and W. Kaiser (eds.), *The Anomie of the Earth. Philosophy, Politics, and Autonomy in Europe and the Americas*. Durham: Duke University Press.
Esteva, G., Babones, S., and Babcicky, Ph. (2013). *The Future of Development: A Radical Manifesto*. Bristol: Bristol University Press.
Feldman, I. (2006). Home as a Refrain: Remembering and Living Displacement in Gaza. *History and Memory*, 18(2): 10–47.
Ferro, S. (2016). Dessin/Chantier. An Introduction. In Katie L. Thomas, Tilo Amhoft, and Nick Beech (eds.), *Industries of Architecture*. New York: Routledge, 95–105.
Flores-Marcial, X. M. (2015). A History of Guelaguetza in Zapotec Communities of the Central Valleys of Oaxaca, 16th Century to the Present. Permalink; https://escholarship.org/uc/item/7tv1p1rr (accessed December 26, 2023).
Florida, R. (2005). *Cities and the Creative Class*. New York: Routledge.
Florida, R. (2012). *The Rise of the Creative Class, Revisited*. New York: Basic Books.
Flynn, A. (2013). Mistica, Myself and I: Beyond Cultural Politics in Brazil's Landless Workers' Movement. *Critique of Anthropology*, 33(2): 168–92.

Flynn, A. (2016). Subjectivity and the Obliteration of Meaning: Contemporary Art, Activism, Social Movement Politics. *Cadernos de Arte e Antropologia*, 5(1): 59–77.
Foucault, M. (1978). *The History of Sexuality. Volume 1: An Introduction.* New York: Pantheon Books.
Foucault, M. (1983). The Subject and Power. In H. Dreyfus and P. Rabinow (eds.), *Michel Foucault: Beyond Structuralism and Hermeneutics*. Chicago: University of Chicago Press, 208–26.
Foucault, M. (2007). The Meshes of Power. In J. Crampton and S. Elden (eds.), *Space, Knowledge and Power. Foucault and Geography*. Aldershot: Ashgate, 153–62.
Foucault, M. (2008a). *The Birth of Biopolitics. Lectures at the Collège de France 1978–1979*. Edited by Michel Senellart. Basingstoke: Palgrave Macmillan.
Foucault, M. (2008b). Of Other Spaces. In L. De Cauter and M. Dehaene (eds.), *Heterotopias and the City: Public Space in Postcivil Society*. London: Routledge, 13–30.
Foucault, M. (2009). *Security, Territory, Population. Lectures at the Collège de France 1977–1978*. Basingstoke: Palgrave Macmillan.
Fourier, Ch. (1996). *The Theory of the Four Movements*. Cambridge: Cambridge University Press.
Gatt, C., and Ingold, T. (2013). From Description to Correspondence: Anthropology in Real Time. In W. Gunn, T. Otto, and R. Ch. Smith (eds.), *Design Anthropology. Theory and Practice*. London: Routledge, 139–58.
Godelier, M. (2011). *The Mental and the Material*. London: Verso.
Gosseye, J., and Heynen, H. (2013). Architecture for Leisure in Post-War Europe, 1945–1989: Between Experimentation, Liberation and Patronisation. *The Journal of Architecture*, 18(5): 623–31.
Graeber, D. (2004). *Fragments of an Anarchist Anthropology*. Chicago: Prickly Paradigm Press.
Graeber, D. (2007). *Possibilities. Essays on Hierarchy, Rebellion and Desire*. Oakland: AK Press.
Grosz, E. (2013). Habit Today: Ravaisson, Bergson, Deleuze and Us. *Body and Society*, 19(2&3): 217–39.
Gudynas, E. (2013). Transitions to Post-Extractivism: Directions, Options, Areas of Action. In Permanent Working Group on Alternatives to Development (eds.), *Beyond Development. Alternative Visions from Latin America*. Quito: Fundación Rosa Luxemburg, 165–88.
Han, Byung-Chul (2020). *The Disappearance of Rituals*. Cambridge: Polity.
Hammond, J. L. (2014). Mística, Meaning and Popular Education in the Brazilian Landless Workers Movement. *Interface*, 6(1): 372–91.
Hardt, M., and Negri, A. (2005). *Multitude. War and Democracy in the Age of Empire*. London: Hamish Hamilton.

Hardt, M., and Negri, A. (2009). *Commonwealth*. Cambridge, MA: Harvard University Press.
Harvey, D. (2003). *Paris, Capital of Modernity*. New York: Routledge.
Hastrup, Kirsten (2004). *Action: Anthropology in the Company of Shakespeare*. Copenhagen: Museum Tusculanum Press.
Heinrich Böll Stiftung (2020). Anti Monumentos. Memoria, Verdad y Justicia. Mexico DF: Heinrich-Böll-Stiftung; https://mx.boell.org/es/2020/11/30/antimonumentos (accessed December 26, 2023).
Heynen, D. (1982). *The Grand Domestic Revolution*. Cambridge, MA: MIT Press.
Hewlett, N. (2007). *Badiou, Balibar, Ranciere: Re-thinking Emancipation*. London: Continuum.
Howard, E. (1902). *Garden Cities of To-morrow*. London: Swan Sonnenschein.
Ingold, T. (2002). *The Perception of the Environment: Essays on Livelihood, Dwelling and Skill*. New York: Routledge.
Ingold, T. (2011). *Being Alive. Essays on Movement, Knowledge and Description*. London: Routledge.
Ingold, T., and Hallam, E. (2007). Creativity and Cultural Improvisation: An Introduction. In T. Ingold and E. Hallam (eds.), *Creativity and Cultural Improvisation*. Oxford: Berg, 1–24.
Issa, D. (2007). Praxis of Empowerment: Mística and Mobilization in Brazil's Landless Rural Workers' Movement. *Latin American Perspectives*, 34(2): 124–38.
Kanavaris, N. (2022). Refugee Housing Squats as Shared Heterotopias. The Case of City Plaza Athens Squat. In S. Stavrides and P. Travlou (eds.), *Housing as Commons. Housing Alternatives as Response to the Current Urban Crisis*. London: Bloomsbury, 162–90.
Kapferer, B. (2002). *Beyond Rationalism: Rethinking Magic, Witchcraft and Sorcery*. New York: Bergham Books.
Kapferer, B. (2010). Beyond Ritual as Performance. Towards Ritual as Dynamics and Virtuality. *Paragrama*, 19(2): 231–49.
Katrini, E. (2020). Spatial Manifestations of Collective Refugee Housing—The Case of City Plaza. *Radical Housing Journal*, 2(1): 29–53.
Katz, Ir. (2022). Bare Shelter. The Layered Spatial Politics of Inhabiting Displacement. In L. Beeckmans, A. Gola, Ash. Singh, and H. Heynen (eds.), *Making Home(s) in Displacement: Critical Reflections on a Spatial Practice*. Leuven: Leuven University Press, 155–72.
Kavilando Grupo de Investigación y Editorial (2021). *Colombia: entre la rebeldía y la esperanza. Reflexiones en torno a la Movilización Social 28 de abril de 2021*. Kavilando: Medellín–Colombia.
Klee, P. (1968). *Pedagogical Sketchbook*. London: Faber and Faber.
Kunst, B. (2015). *Artist at Work, Proximity of Art and Capitalism*. Winchester: Zero Books.

Lafazani, O. (2017). Intervention—"1.5 Year City Plaza: A Project on the Antipodes of Bordering and Control Policies"; https://antipodeonline.org/2017/11/13/intervention-city-plaza (accessed January 17, 2023).
Lane, J. (2007). Rehearsing Revolution in Peru. *Georgetown Journal of International Affairs*, 8(1): 79–85; http://www.jstor.org/stable/43134149 (accessed February 19, 2023).
Lazzarato, M. (2012). *The Making of the Indebted Man. An Essay on Neoliberal Condition*. Los Angeles: Semiotext(e).
Lefebvre, H. (1969). *The Explosion. Marxism and the French Revolution*. New York: Modern Reader Paperbacks.
Lefebvre, H. (1971). *Everyday Life in the Modern World*. New York: Harper&Row.
Lefebvre, H. (1987). Everyday and Everydayness. *Yale French Studies*, 73: 7–11.
Lefebvre, H. (1991). *The Production of Space*. Oxford: Blackwell.
Lefebvre, H. (1996). The Right to the City. In E. Kofman and E. Lebas (eds.), *Writings on Cities*. Oxford: Blackwell, 63–181.
Lefebvre, H. (2003). *The Urban Revolution*. Minneapolis: University of Minnesota Press.
Lefebvre, H. (2004). *Rhythmanalysis. Space, Time and Everyday Life*. London: Continuum.
Lefebvre, H. (2016). *Metaphilosophy*. London: Verso.
Lemke, T. (2011). *Biopolitics: An Advanced Introduction*. New York: New York University Press.
Levi Strauss, Cl. (1966). *The Savage Mind*. Chicago: University of Chicago Press.
Mariani, A. (1988). *Façades. Maisons Populaires du Nordeste*. Rio de Janeiro: Editora Nova Fronteira.
Marsh, H. (2021). "Our Culture's Not for Sale!": Music and the Asamblea Popular de los Pueblos de Oaxaca in Mexico. *Bulletin of Latin American Research*, 40(3): 416–31.
Marx, K. (1973). *Grundrisse Foundations of the Critique of Political Economy (Rough Draft)*; https://www.marxists.org/archive/marx/works/1857/grundrisse/index.htm (accessed December 26, 2023).
Marx, K. (1990). *Capital. Volume I*. London: Penguin Classics.
Maturana, H., and Varela, F. (1980). *Autopoiesis and Cognition: The Realization of the Living*. Boston: D. Reidel.
Maturana, H., and Varela, F. (1987). *The Tree of Knowledge. The Biological Roots of Human Understanding*. Berkeley: Shambhala.
Mauss, M. (2001). *A General Theory of Magic*. London: Routledge.
Mauss, M. (2002). *The Gift*. London: Routledge.
Maxim, J. (2015). Enchanting Views. The Politics of Seduction in Early Romanian Socialist Resorts. In A. Serban, K. Dimou, and S. Istudor (eds.), *Enchanting Views. Romanian Black Sea Tourism Planning and Architecture of the 1960s and 70s*. Bucharest: Asociatia pepluspatu.

Mills, C. (2008). Playing with Law: Agamben and Derrida on Postjuridical Justice. *South Atlantic Quarterly*, 107(1): 15–36.
Mrduljaš, M. (2018). Toward an Affordable Arcadia: The Evolution of Hotel Typologies in Yugoslavia, 1960–1974. In M. Stierli and V. Kulić (eds.), *Toward a Concrete Utopia: Architecture in Yugoslavia, 1948–1980*. New York: Museum of Modern Art, 78–83.
Nancy, J. L. (1991). *The Inoperative Community*. Minneapolis: University of Minnesota Press.
Nancy, J. L. (2000). *Being Singular Plural*. Stanford: Stanford University Press.
Negri, A. (2008). Sovereignty: That Divine Ministry of the Affairs of Earthly Life. *Journal for Cultural and Religious Theory*, 99(1): 96–100.
Nasioka, K. (2017). *Ciudades en Insurrección. Oaxaca 2006/Atenas 2008*. Guadalajara: Cátedra Jorge Alonso.
Peck, J. (2005). Struggling with the Creative Class. *International Journal of Urban and Regional Research*, 29 (4): 740–70.
Peller, B. (2016). Self-Reproduction and the Oaxaca Commune. *Roar*, 1: 71–7.
Prada, R. (2013). Buen Vivir as a Model for State and Economy. In Permanent Working Group on Alternatives to Development (eds.), *Beyond Development. Alternative Visions from Latin America*. Quito: Fundación Rosa Luxemburg, 145–58.
Rancière, J. (2006). *The Politics of Aesthetics*. London: Continuum.
Rancière, J. (2009). *The Emancipated Spectator*. London: Verso.
Rancière, J. (2010). *Dissensus: On Politics and Aesthetics*. London: Continuum.
Robledo, G., and Burguete Cal y Mayor, A. (2023). Rituales al agua en San Cristóbal: nuevas formas de territorialización india. *Iztapalapa Revista*, 44(94): 83–108.
Ross, Chr. (2008). *The Emergence of Social Space. Rimbaud and the Paris Commune*. London: Verso.
Ross, Chr. (2015). *Communal Luxury. The Political Imaginary of the Paris Commune*. London: Verso.
Rossi, A. (1982). *The Architecture of the City*. Cambridge, MA: MIT Press.
Rossi, U., and Tola, M. (2019). The Common. *Keywords in Radical Geography: Antipode*, 50: 259–63.
Sahlins, M. (2008). *The Western Illusion of Human Nature*. Chicago: Prickly Paradigm Press.
Santos, B. de Sousa, and Meneses, M. P. (2020). *Knowledges Born in Struggle. Constructing Epistemologies of the Global South*. New York: Routledge.
Schechner, R. (1985). *Between Theater and Anthropology*. Philadelphia: University of Pennsylvania Press.
Schmid, Chr. (2008). Henri Lefebvre's Theory of the Production of Space: Towards a Three-Dimensional Dialectic. In K. Goonewardena, S. Kipfer, R. Milgrom, and Chr. Schmid (eds.), *Space, Difference, Everyday Life. Reading Henri Lefebvre*. New York: Routledge, 27–45.

Segato, R. (2016). Patriarchy from Margin to Center: Discipline, Territoriality, and Cruelty in the Apocalyptic Phase of Capital. *The South Atlantic Quarterly*, 115(3): 615–24.

Seligman, A., Weller, R., Puett, M., and Simon, B. (2008). *Ritual and Its Consequences: An Essay on the Limits of Sincerity*. New York: Oxford University Press.

Sennett, R. (1986). *The Fall of Public Man*. London: Faber and Faber.

Sennett, R. (1993). *The Conscience of the Eye*. London: Faber and Faber.

Sennett, R. (2012). *Together. The Rituals, Pleasures and Politics of Cooperation*. New Haven: Yale University Press.

Sennett, R. (2019). *Building and Dwelling. Ethics for the City*. London: Penguin Books.

Simone, A. (2016). Urbanity and Generic Blackness. *Theory, Culture & Society*, 33(7–8): 183–203.

Simone, A. (2020a). To Extend: Temporariness in a World of Itineraries. *Urban Studies*, 57(6): 1127–42; https://doi.org/10.1177/0042098020905442.

Simone, A. (2020b). (Non)Urban Humans: Questions for a Research Agenda (the Work the Urban Could Do). *International Journal of Urban and Regional Research*, 44(4): 755–67.

Simone, A. (2022). *The Surrounds: Urban Life within and beyond Capture*. Durham: Duke University Press.

Soja, Ed. (2000). *Postmetropolis: Critical Studies of Cities and Regions*. Malden: Blackwell Publishing.

Spencer, D. (2016). *The Architecture of Neoliberalism: How Contemporary Architecture Became an Instrument of Control and Compliance*. London: Bloomsbury.

Stanek, L. (2011). *Henri Lefebvre on Space. Architecture, Urban Research, and the Production of Theory*. Minneapolis: University of Minnesota Press.

Stavrides, S. (2010). The December 2008 Youth Uprising in Athens: Spatial Justice in an Emergent "City Of Thresholds." *Spatial Justice*, 2; http://www.jssj.org/archives/02/media/public_space_vo2.pdf (accessed December 26, 2023).

Stavrides, S. (2016). *Common Space: The City as Commons*. London: Zed Books.

Stavrides, S. (2019). *Common Spaces of Urban Emancipation*. Manchester: Manchester University Press.

Stavrides, S. (Forthcoming). Introduction to Urban Commons and Social Participation. In N. Bobic and F. Haghighi (eds.), *The Routledge Handbook of Architecture, Urban Space and Politics, Vol II: Ecology, Social Participation & Marginalities*. New York: Routledge.

Stavrides, S., and Travlou, P. (eds.) (2022). *Housing as Commons*. London: Bloomsbury.

Stephen, L. (2013). *We Are the Face of Oaxaca: Testimony and Social Movements*. Durham and London: Duke University Press.

Strathern, M. (2005). Imagined Collectivities and Multiple Authorship. In Rishab Aiyer Ghosh (ed.), *Collaborative Ownership and the Digital Economy*. Cambridge, MA: MIT Press, 13–28.
Tanović, I., and Mraović, B. (2018). The Contradictions of the Break-Up. The Working People, Organized Holidays and Indivisible Remains. In V. Knežević and M. Miletić (eds.), *We Have Built Cities for You. On the Contradictions of Yugoslav Socialism*. Belgrade: Center CZKD – Center for Cultural Decontamination.
Thirft, N. (2004). Intensities of Feeling: Towards a Spatial Politics of Affect. *Geografiska Annaler. Series B, Human Geography*, 86(1): 57–78.
Turner, V. (1977). *The Ritual Process*. Ithaca: Cornell University Press.
Turner, V. (1982). *From Ritual to Theatre*. New York: PAJ Publications.
UNESCO (2006). *Water and Indigenous Peoples*. R. Boelens, M. Chiba, and D. Nakashima (eds.), Knowledges of Nature 2, Paris: UNESCO.
Varela, F. (1997). Patterns of Life: Intertwining Identity and Cognition. *Brain and Cognition*, 34: 72–87.
Vercellone, C. (2007). From Formal Subsumption to General Intellect: Elements for a Marxist Reading of the Thesis of Cognitive Capitalism. *Historical Materialism*, 15: 13–36.
Vernant, J. P. (2006). *Myth and Thought among the Greeks*. New York: Zone Books.
Vich, V. (2004). Desobediencia Simbólica:Performance, Participación y Política al Final de la Dictadura Fujimorista. In Alejandro Grimson (ed.), *La cultura en las Crisis Latinoamericanas*. Buenos Aires: Clacso. 63–80; http://biblioteca.clacso.edu.ar/clacso/gt/20100918085432/4vich.pdf (accessed February 19, 2023).
Virno, P. (2004). *A Grammar of the Multitude*. New York: Semiotext[e].
Virno, P. (2008). *Multitude. Between Innovation and Negation*. Los Angeles: Semiotext[e].
Virno, P. (2015). *Déjà vu and the End of History*. London: Verso.
Viveiros de Castro, Ed. (2007). Metaphysics as Mythophysics. Or, Why I Have always Been an Anthropologist. In P. Charbonnier, G. Salmon, and P. Skafish (eds.), *Comparative Metaphysics*. London: Rowman &Littlefield, 249–73.
Viveiros de Castro (ed.) (2014). *Cannibal Metaphysics*. Minneapolis: Univocal.
Wacquant, L. (2012). Three Steps to a Historical Anthropology of Actually Existing Neoliberalism. *Social Anthropology*, 20(1): 66–79.
Weber, S. (2008). *Benjamin's Abilities*. Cambridge, MA: Harvard University Press.
Whitford, M. (2009). Oaxaca's Indigenous Guelaguetza Festival: Not All That Glistens Is Gold. *Event Management*, 12: 1–17.

Winnicott, D. (1989). The Fate of the Transitional Object. In C. Winnicott, R. Shepherd, and M. Davis (eds.), *Psycho-analytic Explorations*. Cambridge, MA: Harvard University Press, 53–8.

Zibechi, R. (2009). *Cochabamba. De la guerra a la gestión del agua*; https://www.cetri.be/Cochabamba-De-la-guerra-a-la?lang=fr (accessed December 20, 2023).

Index

affect 17, 102, 152–6, 165, 170, 178
affective 105–6, 116, 142, 152–6, 164
Agamben, G. 6–8, 11, 19, 34, 76–7, 86, 107
Ahmed, S. 105
alternative 8, 18, 53, 55, 58, 69, 71, 89, 93–5, 100, 119–20, 130
Ano Meria (Folegandros, Greece) 159
anthropology 18, 44, 68
anti-monument 141–4
appropriation 5, 8, 41, 49, 63, 65, 68, 71, 80, 85, 88, 107, 117–18, 123–4, 130, 132–3, 142, 149
architect 56, 103, 153–4
architecture 25, 27, 56, 102, 124, 153
Arendt, H. 83–5, 107
Aristotle 6
art xi, 7–8, 14, 38, 63, 71, 74–8, 88, 92, 123–6, 139, 142, 148
Art Deco 124–5
artistic practice 7–8, 75, 90, 99, 125
autonomy 46, 54, 71–4, 76–8, 80, 83–5, 92–3, 118
autopoiesis 71–2

Bachelard, G. 36–7, 43–4, 90
Badiou, A. 9–11
Barquisimeto 119–21
Bell, C. 46, 53
Benjamin, W. 4–5, 16, 58–9, 65–6, 80, 136–8
Berardi, F. 60, 88–9, 117
Bergson, H. 35–8
biopolitics 7, 28–30
Black Lives Matter movement 66, 142
Blackness 68–9, 135
Boltanski, L. 46, 48, 50, 59
Bourdieu, P. 38, 42, 45–7, 128–9

Buen Vivir 73, 81–2, 84
Buenos Aires x, 66, 85, 111
Butler, J. 39–41

Cali (Colombia) x, 66, 143, 145
capitalism 9, 14, 17, 21, 30, 67, 71, 82, 88–9, 115, 119, 155
capitalist, command 9, 16–7, 51, 80, 119, 123, 164
  ethos 1, 12, 120
care 9, 61, 69, 80–1, 83, 91, 93–5, 118, 122–3, 127, 132–3, 136, 142, 155, 166
carnival 8, 99
  Exarchia 100–1
  Metaxourgeio 100
  Naples 102
Castoriadis, C. 73, 148
CECOSESOLA x, 119–22, 126–7
Chiapas 132
citability 5–6
city 1–2, 5, 12, 16, 21–4, 28, 30–1, 38, 65–69, 79, 87, 91–95, 102–4, 107, 111, 115, 119–20, 126, 131–33, 135–44, 151, 154, 156, 163–4
  garden 24, 79
  smart 61
  socialist 25
City Plaza (occupied hotel in Athens) 107–110
Club Méd 25
Cochabamba 132
common(s) viii, x–xi, 1–2, 13–14, 17, 24, 29, 34–6, 44, 46, 53, 61, 66, 68, 71, 73–4, 76–8, 81, 83–7, 92, 95, 100, 102–5, 108, 119–20, 126–9, 132–3, 138, 152, 156, 161
commoning viii, x, 1, 17, 44, 51, 65–6, 71, 73, 77, 81–2, 84–86, 102–4,

110, 115, 120–2, 129–31, 133–4, 144, 164–6
Commune, Oaxaca 92, 94, 130, 155, 165
Paris 91–2, 94, 125, 137
community vii, viii, 1, 11, 27, 36, 45, 47–8, 51, 53, 69, 71–4, 77–8, 80–1, 83–7, 90–5, 98–107, 109, 111, 120, 122–3, 127, 129, 131–4, 143, 155, 159–60, 164
connectivity vii, 59–61, 88, 164
contingency 9–12, 14–15, 21, 37, 41, 66, 76, 85, 157
cooperation viii, 1, 16–17, 24, 44, 51, 61, 65–6, 78, 80–4, 102, 115–23, 126–38, 142, 144, 160–1, 164–5
cooperative 1, 119–23, 127, 143
creativity vii, xi, 9, 11–4, 41, 47, 52–4, 64–6, 71, 74–6, 78, 84, 86–7, 98–9, 117, 123–4, 126, 148, 150–1
crisis 41, 48, 55, 87, 107, 120, 133, 159, 161
cultural x-xi, 7–8, 17, 51, 53–4, 65, 71, 76, 85, 96, 98, 102, 108, 115, 117, 123, 126, 130, 133, 157, 164
culture(s) x, 5, 13–15, 18–19, 22–3, 25–6, 40, 47, 64–5, 68–9, 71, 73, 81, 84, 90, 92, 100, 104, 108, 110, 117, 121–3, 126–33, 138, 143, 155, 160, 163

Dardot, P. and Laval Chr. 119, 123
December uprising (2008 Athens) 138, 140
decoration 123–4
Deleuze, G. 19, 34, 106
Descola, Ph. 22
disciplinary power 27–8
displaced x, 106–7, 133
disposition(s) 38, 43–4, 90, 153
Diyarbakir 103
domestication xi, 21–2, 24–6, 33
domination 29–30, 53, 55, 87, 118, 163
duration 34, 36–7

emancipated 8, 15–16, 18, 75, 123, 127, 137, 168
emancipation 8–9, 11–12, 14–16, 33, 41, 67, 72–3, 75, 77, 83, 111, 119, 163, 165–6, 168
emancipatory vii, 1, 6, 8–9, 11, 14, 18–9, 66, 76, 78, 80, 86–7, 97–8, 119, 121, 134, 165–6
environment 5, 17, 26, 31, 43, 46, 53, 57, 67, 72, 78, 84, 87, 90–1, 95, 102, 104, 136, 152–3
Escobar, A. 3, 79–80, 85, 95, 134
Esposito, R. 73–4
Esteva, G. 74, 76–8, 85, 93
ethos, 24, 34, 65, 68–9, 81–2, 97, 122, 124, 126, 130–1, 138, 144, 166
capitalist 1, 12, 120
commoning 133
cooperation 131, 144
egalitarian 55
extractivist 14, 79, 82
individualist 86, 164
modernist 90
neoliberal 78
socialist 119
urban 68
event(s) vii, 9–11, 18, 30–1, 35–7, 43, 45, 48, 55, 88, 93, 99, 103, 109, 129–30, 137, 140, 142, 165
evental site 10–11
everyday 12–15, 21, 25, 41–2, 45, 48, 50–2, 59, 61, 65, 77, 87, 90–5, 98, 110, 122–3, 154–5, 159–60, 164–5
everydayness x, xi, 5, 12, 14–15, 25–6, 48, 59, 67, 69, 93–4, 107, 119, 121, 136
expressive 3, 34, 39, 96, 124, 139–40, 143

feast 8, 14, 99–100, 129–30
feminist 39, 140, 152, 154
Ferro, S. 124, 126
flexibility, viii, 151–2, 156–61

Florida, R. 151
Flynn, A. 97–8
Foucault, M. 19, 27–31, 53
Fourier, Ch. 90–1, 127
Fujimori (former Peru president) 99

gender x, 8, 12, 39–42, 94, 160, 163
gesture(s) 1, 4–5, 16, 34, 40, 44, 53,
    58, 60–1, 65, 94, 99, 108–10, 112,
    124, 138–9, 142, 144
Godelier, M. 29
government 27–30, 76, 80–2, 92, 99,
    119, 122, 132
Graeber, D. 54–5
Graffiti xii, 139
Grosz, E. 35, 42
Guatari, F. 19, 34, 106
Guelaguetza 128–31, 165

habit vii-viii, 1–2, 6–9, 14, 16, 18,
    33–9, 41–4, 46–7, 49, 51, 55, 63,
    65, 78, 85–94, 108, 110, 119, 123,
    133, 159, 165–6
habitus 38–9, 42, 47, 49, 87
Hammond, J. 95–6
Han, B.-Ch. 47
Hardt, M. 30, 79, 118
Harvey, D. 92
hegemonic 29, 33, 53, 80
house(s) 1, 24, 27, 42–4, 57–8, 61,
    80, 93–4, 107, 123–4, 126, 134,
    144, 159

identity 5–6, 9, 39, 43, 48, 50, 55, 60,
    72–3, 76, 83, 85–6, 89, 95–6, 105,
    108, 124, 129
image(s) 4–5, 26, 35, 43, 55, 63–4,
    75, 82–3, 98, 111–12, 123–4,
    134, 138–40, 144, 148–9, 151,
    154–6, 158–9
imaginary viii, 1, 23, 59, 74, 80, 90, 92,
    106, 124, 147–60, 164
imagination viii, 43, 55–6, 147, 150
imitation 11, 13–15, 29, 86, 124

immigrants 105, 130–2, 137
immunitary 73–4, 78
immunity 74
immunization 73–4
Ingold, T. 57, 64–5, 68, 128, 136
innovative 15, 41, 64
inoperative 8
intellectual labor 117
interpretation 5–6, 48, 53, 58, 123–4,
    153–4
inventiveness vii, 42, 44, 60, 63–5, 69,
    71, 74, 123, 135–6, 149
Issa, D. 95–7
Istanbul 27, 103

Kanavaris, N. 109–10
Kapferer, B. 48–9, 52
Katrini, E. 108–9

Lefebvre, H. vii, 12–15, 42, 57, 66, 69,
    87–8, 147–9, 166
liberalism 28–9
liberation 14, 26, 51, 83, 89, 97, 107,
    111, 122, 133, 155, 168
liminal 50–1

magic circle vii, 18, 44–9, 52–5, 63, 95,
    98–9, 133, 165
Marx, K. 11, 115–17
materiality 76, 85, 89, 153–4, 168
Maturana, H. 72
Mauss, M. 45, 47, 119, 129
mentality 27, 58, 156
metropolis 2–3, 16, 18, 33, 44, 67, 77
migration 105
mimesis vii, 12–14
Minga 10, 133
Mística 95–8
modernity vii, 7, 59, 68, 71, 78, 80,
    137, 160
modernization 59, 78, 80, 124
Montevideo 10, 111
Morris, W. 92, 125–6
Mothers (of the Plaza de Mayo) 111

MST (Movimento dos Trabahadores Rurais Sem Terra) 95–8
mythological 27, 151

Nancy, J. L. 83–5
Nasioka, K. 93–4
naturalize 29, 42, 87
nature 2, 8, 10, 12, 14, 19, 22–7, 36, 38, 50, 52, 64, 67–8, 79, 81, 83–4, 89, 97, 118, 120, 128, 133–4, 156–7, 160
Negri, A. 30, 79, 118
neoliberal 17, 47, 65, 67, 69, 78, 92–3, 102, 130, 150–5, 157–9, 161, 164
nbeoliberalism 47, 158, 161
normalization vii, 21, 27–31, 33, 69, 135

Pacha Mama (Mother Earth) 95, 132, 134
Palestinians 106
participation 4, 63, 81, 93, 96, 98, 100, 112, 120–2, 129–30
performance(s) vii, 1, 3, 6, 9, 13, 16–18, 33–5, 37, 39–42, 44–47, 49–51, 54–5, 59, 63, 65–6, 85–7, 89–90, 96–9, 102–3, 111–12, 116, 118, 129–30, 138–9, 142, 144, 150, 163–6
performative 4, 16, 39–40, 55, 82, 85, 97–8, 139, 152, 164
perspectivism 68
place vii, 3–4, 6, 15, 18, 21, 26–7, 35, 41–5, 47, 49, 55–7, 68, 72, 77, 84, 86–7, 89–90, 99–100, 102–3, 105–6, 109–10, 112, 124–5, 134–5, 138, 140, 144, 147, 150, 155, 165
poetic(s) 8, 12, 14, 43, 74, 126
Popayan 133
possibility 6, 9–10, 12, 14, 19, 34, 36, 39–41, 47, 49, 52–3, 74, 76, 90, 95, 117, 165, 168

possible x–xi, 3, 6–14, 18, 25, 29–30, 37–8, 40–1, 49, 52–3, 55, 58, 63, 66, 71, 72–6, 78, 80, 82–3, 85, 87, 90, 98, 100, 102, 105, 116, 118–20, 122, 127, 132, 134–7, 144, 147–9, 155–6, 158, 160, 163
potentiality vii–viii, 1–11, 16–19, 22, 36, 39–41, 47, 49–50, 52–4, 56–8, 60, 63, 65–6, 68, 77, 84, 87, 95, 115–16, 120, 131, 136–7, 144, 147, 150–1, 157, 164–7
Praxis 10–15, 34, 54

Rancière, J. 3, 10, 50, 67, 75–7, 165
rationality 15, 25, 29, 155
refugees 1, 105, 107–8, 137
reinvention viii, 16, 51, 66, 71, 80–1, 84–5, 92, 95, 99, 104, 154, 164–5
repeatability vii, 1, 18, 33, 36, 38, 40, 44, 53, 60, 63, 87, 89, 165–6
repetition 5–6, 13–15, 34–42, 44, 54, 57–8, 86, 136
repetitive 1, 12–14, 39, 46, 87, 106, 123
resistance(s) x, 8–9, 12, 18, 30, 40, 53, 69, 80, 84, 107, 112–13, 144, 164
revolutionary 15, 55, 99
rhythm(s) 15, 33, 37, 129, 166
rhythmicality vii, 12, 14–15, 33–4, 42, 79, 104, 107, 166
ritual vii–viii, 1, 8, 13–15, 18, 33, 44–55, 58, 63, 65, 71, 81, 87, 94–100, 102–3, 111, 117, 126–34, 142, 155, 165–6
Ross, K. 92, 94, 125

Sahlins, M. 22–3, 67
security 27–31, 106–7, 130
Segato, R. 154–5, 160
self-managed 94, 102, 107, 120, 122
Sennett, R. 126–7, 139, 153
shelter 94, 107, 133
Simone, A. 68–9, 135

solidarity viii, x, 1, 16–17, 44, 59, 61, 65, 71, 81, 83, 92, 94, 102–3, 107–8, 119–20, 123, 127, 131–2, 136, 144, 155–6, 159, 161, 164–6
sovereign 23, 31, 77
  individual 150–2, 158
  power 27–8, 30–1, 115
spatiality 3, 18, 30–1, 47, 49, 54, 109
Spencer, D. 152–4, 158
Stanek, L. 25, 148
stencil 112–13, 138–40, 142
Strathern, M. 117
symbolism 124, 140, 142

taxonomy 39
tender 71, 81
territory 22, 26, 30, 40, 58, 68, 71, 80–1, 94–5, 104, 106, 132, 134
trace vii-viii, xii, 1, 3, 11–12, 23–4, 31, 56–9, 63, 66, 71, 91, 93, 94, 104, 106–13, 135–40, 142–44, 165

tradition vii, 1, 4, 66, 76, 78, 80–1, 83, 95, 124, 128–9, 131–2
trajectory 18, 60, 66, 107, 111
Traverso, F. 112
Turner, V. 49–51, 53–4

urban order vii, 2, 16, 18, 21–4, 27, 33, 49–50, 63, 66, 68, 87, 89, 138, 149, 164
utopia 2, 24, 79, 93, 97–8, 127

Varela, F. 72–3
Vercellone, C. 116
Virno, P. 19, 41, 79, 157–8
Viveiros de Castro, E. 68, 128

Zapatista(s) x, 67, 80
Zapotec, 128–9, 131
Zibechi, R. x, 132